SECRETS TO SUCCESS

INSPIRING STORIES FROM LEADING ENTREPRENEURS

SEAN GALLAGHER

MERCIER PRESS
IRISH PUBLISHER – IRISH STORY

MERCIER PRESS
Cork
www.mercierpress.ie

ISBN: 978 1 78117 525 5

10 9 8 7 6 5 4 3 2 1

A CIP record for this title is available from the British Library

Printed and bound in the EU.

TESTIMONIALS

'*Secrets to Success* contains invaluable lessons about what it takes to become successful. Whether you are an existing business owner or an aspiring entrepreneur, be prepared to be both informed and inspired.'

Jack Canfield, *New York Times* best-selling author of *Chicken Soup for the Soul*® and *The Success Principles,* star of *The Secret* and America's #1 Success Coach

'The stories featured in Sean Gallagher's *Secrets to Success* are inspiring and uplifting, and prove yet again how important confidence and determination are in achieving success.'

Senator Feargal Quinn, founder of Superquinn

'Sean Gallagher's *Secrets to Success* is a wonderful book on success and achievement. Full of practical and proven strategies, it will help you accomplish your goals faster than you ever thought possible.'

Brian Tracy, international speaker, *New York Times* best-selling author of *Eat That Frog, The Psychology of Selling* and *Maximum Achievement*

'Every success has a mother. For some it is the raw need to survive, for others it is an uncontrollable desire to achieve. In Sean's book he captures the soul of the entrepreneur across the widest spectrum of individuals and their vastly different circumstances and motivations.'

Gene Murtagh, CEO, Kingspan

'There are many predicable evolutions in the journey from starting a business with a handful of employees to scaling it to something significant that has a chance of putting a dent in the universe or at least dominating its industry. Those who achieve such levels of growth understand the key fundamentals of leading people, setting the company's strategy, driving execution and managing cash. What better way to learn than from entrepreneurs who have already navigated this complex journey to success themselves? In this regard, Sean Gallagher's *Secrets to Success* offers a myriad of practical tools and invaluable advice for those committed to growing their businesses. I highly recommend it.'

Verne Harnish, founder of the Entrepreneurs' Organisation and Gazelles, a global executive education and coaching company, and author of *Mastering The Rockefeller Habits* and *Scaling Up: How a Few Companies Make It and Why the Rest Don't*

'*Secrets to Success* is essential reading for existing business owners and budding entrepreneurs alike, with practical tips and hard-earned advice from an army of innovative business leaders who have succeeded in transforming ideas into reality.'

Norah Casey, entrepreneur and former investor on *Dragons' Den*

'Sean Gallagher's *Secrets to Success* is a compelling read. It highlights the importance of pursuing our passions and following our dreams if we want true success and happiness in our lives.'

Marci Shimoff, *New York Times* best-selling author of *Happy for No Reason* and *Chicken Soup for the Woman's Soul*

'In *Secrets to Success*, Sean Gallagher brings together incredibly inspiring stories from Ireland's leading entrepreneurs. Not only do we learn about how these people have succeeded in creating jobs, driving economic activity and building value, we also gain a new perspective on the valuable role that entrepreneurs and business-builders play in our economy. As a company committed to supporting, encouraging and fostering entrepreneurship through our EY Entrepreneur of the Year™ (EOY), I commend Sean, himself a member of the EY EOY™ alumni, for writing this book. A brilliant read.'

Kevin McLoughin, partner lead for
EY Entrepreneur of the Year™, EY Ireland

'With more than 250,000 small businesses in Ireland, Sean has done an outstanding job in selecting companies that represent such a diverse range of sectors and backgrounds. As all owner-managers are keenly aware, managing a business requires a wide range of skills and knowledge and can often be a lonely journey. In *Secrets to Success*, Sean demonstrates how applying these skills has helped those featured become successful and reassures all entrepreneurs that they are not alone. A must-read.'

Sven Spollen-Behrens, director, Small Firms Association

'Entrepreneurs are the lifeblood of our economy and make a significant contribution to job creation in towns and villages all over Ireland. Sean has done a great job of gathering and distilling the experiences of some of Ireland's most successful entrepreneurs in this book, which is an inspiration to the next generation of entrepreneurs to progress from start-up to the next global business success story.'

Julie Sinnamon, CEO, Enterprise Ireland

'There is only one Sean Gallagher. Indomitable and inspiring, he is as passionate about business as he is about life. Sean knows how to tell a good business story and in *Secrets to Success* he has used that skill to great effect in extracting the wisdom from each entrepreneur's struggle to succeed. A great read.'

Tom Lyons, deputy editor of the *Sunday Business Post* and author

'Sean Gallagher has an infectious interest in both Irish-owned and Irish-managed businesses. In *Secrets to Success* he gives a voice to Irish indigenous companies to share their experiences and their lessons. This is an important book for the country at this time.'

Paul McCann, partner, Grant Thornton

'Success comes from having the courage to be yourself and to play to your own unique talents and abilities. However, in business, as in life, it is often not our abilities but our choices that define our ultimate success. If you are thinking about starting a business or wondering how to take your existing business to the next level, then this book is an essential read. Full of inspiring role models and packed with practical advice and insights, you won't want to miss the valuable lessons it contains.'

Anne Heraty, CEO, Cpl Resources plc

'An honest insight into the highs and lows of true entrepreneurship, Sean's book captures the academic blueprint of how entrepreneurship should work and balances it brilliantly with real-life stories of the wonderful inspirational men and women that make up the Irish business landscape. A wonderful read.'

Bobby Kerr, former chairman of Insomnia Coffee Company,
presenter of 'Down to Business' on Newstalk radio
and former investor on *Dragons' Den*

'Sean Gallagher brings stories from the front. His work goes beneath the skin in a way only an entrepreneur can. He's been through a few battles himself and can spot the wheat from the chaff. Don't start a business without reading this book.'

Jerry Kennelly, founder and CEO, Tweak.com
and co-founder of the Junior Entrepreneur Programme

'Full of wisdom and insights, Sean Gallagher's *Secrets to Success* is essential reading for anyone with a desire to learn and a passion for success. It is like having your own board of experienced mentors who have already trodden the road you are now on.'

Frankie Sheahan, Pendulum Summit, Front Row Speakers
and former Irish international rugby player

'This book is a great read from a great guy. Full of business insights and real-life learnings, it will prove a valuable investment for anyone in business or thinking about starting a business.'

Gavin Duffy, Gavin Duffy & Associates,
investor on *Dragons' Den*

'The stories profiled in *Secrets to Success* all share a common thread and that is that being a successful entrepreneur isn't a personality type, it's about hard work, resilience, perseverance and the ability to stay focused on the end goal. A glimpse into the many roads that founders have travelled in their quest to succeed, this is a great read for anyone who wants to know what it takes to be successful.'

Nicola Byrne, CEO Cloud90, founder Call 11890
and president of the Irish Exporters Association

'Sean Gallagher continues to champion entrepreneurs, men and women, and to tell their stories in an interesting and engaging manner. While always positive in his approach, Sean describes not only the highs but the challenges that are an integral part of any entrepreneurial journey. Seeing how others have grown and developed their businesses inspires others to follow their lead and believe that they too can not only start but grow successful businesses.'

Paula Fitzsimons, national director of Going for Growth –
Supporting Female Entrepreneurship

'They say there is a book in all of us. Perhaps there is an entrepreneur in all of us too. If there is, then Sean Gallagher's *Secrets to Success* will help you identify it, nurture it, demystify it and give you the confidence and belief to "go for it".'

Ian Talbot, CEO, Chambers Ireland

'Being an entrepreneur himself, Sean Gallagher has a knack for identifying real achievers and, through his interviews, drawing out their experiences. Besides being a collection of fascinating insights into personal struggles, *Secrets to Success* distils an abundance of SME business wisdom.'

Nick Mulcahy, publisher, *Business Plus*

'Entrepreneurs are the lifeblood of our economy. From the trail-blazers of the past to the modern-day game changers, Ireland Inc. has produced some outstanding business leaders who have not only enriched Ireland but who have also left their footprints all over the world. As Warren Buffet remarked, "Someone is sitting in the shade today, because someone planted a tree a long time ago." In the same way, I believe Sean Gallagher's *Secrets to Success* will be instrumental in inspiring a new generation of business builders.'

Ian Hyland, president and publisher,
Business & Finance media group

'Too often the books we read on entrepreneurship are based on international experience. It is therefore refreshing to see so many inspiring Irish stories of entrepreneurship contained in one volume. Sean Gallagher has always recognised the gift that entrepreneurship is and has always believed in the contribution that the SME sector makes to the Irish economy. This book will provide great inspiration to both existing and aspiring entrepreneurs and is a must read for students in particular. I applaud him.'

Jim Power, economist

'Week in, week out in the *Sunday Independent*, Sean Gallagher captures the stories and back stories, the highs and lows, the struggles and the breakthroughs of Ireland's SMEs. The backbone of the Irish economy, these entrepreneurs' stories of courage under fire, risk-taking and vision are a touchstone for businesses, be they big or small. We are delighted that Sean Gallagher, Ireland's brand ambassador for the SME sector, has collated these stories to inspire us all.'

Dearbhail McDonald, Group Business Editor, INM plc

'In *Secrets to Success* Sean Gallagher has created a welcome and well-written compendium of varied entrepreneurial journeys complete with the maxims that drove their leaders' thinking as they grew.'

Ray Nolan, serial tech entrepreneur

'*Secrets to Success* clearly demonstrates what it takes to grow a successful business. Whether you run a different-sized business or operate in a different sector to the entrepreneurs profiled in this book, there are valuable lessons to be learned from these inspiring stories. A compelling read.'

Paul O'Kelly, international strategic consultant

'Sean Gallagher is an inspirational character. An entrepreneur himself, an investor on *Dragons' Den* and a writer in the *Sunday Independent*, he has his finger on the pulse of the nation when it comes to SMEs. So who better to write a book about secrets to success than Sean? This book is an important addition to entrepreneurship literature in Ireland.'

Mark Flood, director, Renatus Capital Partners

'As Ireland enters the most entrepreneurial era of its history there has never been a more important time to showcase stories from the world of Irish business. As a great storyteller, Sean has managed to bring stories that will not only interest and inform but intrigue and inspire. Bravo.'

Kingsley Aikins, CEO, Diaspora Matters

'*Secrets to Success* is an inspiring and thoroughly engaging read. It gets to the heart of what makes every entrepreneur tick, and is full of wonderful practical advice and real-world experience.'

Jack Murray, CEO, MediaHQ.com

'A perfect read for anyone with an interest in business and entrepreneurship.'

Pierce Casey, entrepreneur and chairman, Adelaide Capital Ltd

'Entrepreneurs are special people! They re-imagine the possible. They take on challenges that others don't recognise, or don't have the appetite to tackle. But this is not easy. It requires self-belief, emotional resilience, focus, discipline and unrelenting personal commitment. Sean's book shines a light on Ireland's entrepreneurs and captures what it takes to start and grow a successful business. It is a great read and there is much to learn here.'

Feargal O'Rourke, Managing Partner, PricewaterhouseCoopers

'This book should be required reading for every 2nd- and 3rd-level business student in the country. Indeed, every business teacher in the country should read it to enable them to have a much deeper appreciation of the successes and challenges faced by modern-day entrepreneurs.'

Thomas Cooney, Professor of Entrepreneurship,
Dublin Institute of Technology

I dedicate this book to all those who have ever had the courage to follow their dream of starting their own business. And all those who have a desire to follow in their footsteps.

I also dedicate it to my wonderful wife, Trish, and our children, Bobby and Lucy. You show me every day what real success looks like.

CONTENTS

ACKNOWLEDGEMENTS

Writing a book, like running a business, is a team effort. I wish to acknowledge the help and support of everyone who has played a part in turning the idea for this book into the reality of what you are now holding in your hands. Particular thanks must go to the following:

My publisher, Mary Feehan, and your team at Mercier Press – Deirdre Roberts, Noel O'Regan, Sarah O'Flaherty, Patrick O'Donoghue and Wendy Logue – for believing in the book from the very outset and for your support and encouragement throughout. You are true professionals.

Best-selling author and journalist Emily Hourican for doing the initial edit and helping me reduce the word count of my initial draft without losing any of the important content from the contributors. You are a pleasure to work with.

The entrepreneurs whose interviews and stories are the heart of this book. You are exemplary role models to all of us and I want to acknowledge you for your willingness to be included in this book and for the honest and frank nature of your sharing, which makes these stories so insightful and inspiring.

The hundreds of other entrepreneurs that I have interviewed over the past five years. Your stories are equally inspiring and were it not for the need to keep this book to a required length, I would have happily included every one of them.

The *Sunday Independent* and the staff and management at INM for your willingness to allow me to update the original stories that appeared in the paper and include them here. Thank you too for the opportunity to contribute to the paper over the past five years. It has been a wonderful experience working with you and for that I am extremely grateful.

The many entrepreneurs and business owners with whom I have worked, invested in or mentored over the past twenty-five years. I salute you for your great courage in doing what you do and I acknowledge all that I have learnt from you. You have been as much my coaches and mentors as I have been yours.

Larry Bass from ShinAwiL for the opportunity to be part of *Dragons' Den* (*Shark Tank* in the US) and for the many positive experiences and opportunities that followed as a result.

Jack Canfield, America's No. 1 Success Coach and world renowned author of *The Success Principles*, the *Chicken Soup for the Soul®* series and countless other best-selling books. Thank you for your wisdom, your authenticity and for being such an encouraging mentor and friend.

Derek Roddy for our enduring friendship over the last twenty years and for being an exceptional business partner in Smarthomes for over a decade. Your honesty, focus and problem-solving abilities are unmatched.

Colm Piercy, my long-time friend and business partner in Clyde Real Estate. Your business acumen, entrepreneurial expertise and big picture thinking are awesome.

Cathal Lee for your friendship and guidance in the area of communications. Gerry Carolan for ensuring that I got to all the interview locations in this book on time.

My brother-in-law, Bernard O'Connor, for reviewing the initial draft of this book and for sharing your many helpful insights.

My siblings, Gerry, Breda and Noeleen, and all my friends, way too many to mention here, for your constant love, loyalty and support.

Finally, my wife, Trish – an amazingly authentic, loving and supportive partner. I thank you for your patience, unwavering love and support during the writing of this book (and indeed all the many other projects I have been engrossed in over the years). For putting up with long absences, missed holidays and for me not being present even when I have been around. You and our children, Bobby and Lucy, inspire me more than anything else and make it all worthwhile. I feel grateful and truly blessed to have you in my life.

FOREWORD

Not all readers are leaders, but all leaders are readers.

Harry S. Truman

I am delighted to introduce this book to you. Written by my good friend Sean Gallagher, it contains many valuable lessons about what it takes to become successful – not only in business but also in life.

It is now more than forty years since I first began teaching on the topic of what makes people successful. Like many of you reading this book, my life started out in a very average way, without wealth or privilege. I worked part-time jobs to make my way through school and college until I became a high school teacher. When I later met my mentor, the self-made multi-millionaire W. Clement Stone, he hired me to work in his foundation and trained me in the fundamental principles of success. Applying these principles in my own life has enabled me to enjoy phenomenal levels of success, fame, wealth and happiness.

But these principles and techniques have not only worked for me; they have also worked for the many hundreds of thousands of people I have taught around the world through my books, speeches, seminars and workshops.

What I have learned is that success leaves clues. Anyone can learn to become successful so long as they understand and apply key principles and techniques, such as those used by the successful entrepreneurs in this book. Like a combination lock, once you discover the right numbers you can achieve whatever you want in life. The principles work but only if you are willing to work them.

I first had the pleasure of meeting Sean when he attended one of my seminars in Dublin's Mansion House in 2008. Like many others he stood in line to meet me after the event and I signed his copy of my book *The Success Principles: How to Get from Where You Are to Where You Want to Be*. I was immediately taken by Sean's positivity, his engaging nature and his commitment to coaching and mentoring others – especially those in small and medium-sized businesses.

Like all entrepreneurs, Sean is also a man of action. Soon he was on a plane to the US to take part in my five-day intensive 'Breakthrough to Success' event in Phoenix, Arizona. Over the next few years, I personally mentored Sean and was delighted when he completed my 'Success Principles Train the Trainer Programme', so that he, too, could teach the lessons I spent decades learning.

In recent years, Sean has joined me in facilitating my week-long private retreats in Europe and the US, where he draws on his diverse and extensive business experience to help mentor and coach those looking to take their lives and their businesses to the next level. A gifted leader and trainer, Sean's natural and authentic style make him a powerful force when it comes to empowering others to achieve their personal and professional goals. His work in compiling these inspiring stories into a book for others to learn from is an example of his heartfelt desire to help others.

So whether you are an existing business owner or an aspiring entrepreneur, there is much that you can learn from the lessons shared by the successful entrepreneurs featured in this book.

Success, however, takes time, effort and perseverance. The motivational philosopher Jim Rohn put it well when he said, 'You can't hire someone else to do your push-ups for you.'

As writers and coaches our job is to provide you with the principles for success, a road map and an invitation to step into your own greatness. It is up to you to apply these in your own life, so that you too can achieve the results you desire.

I encourage you to believe in yourself, and armed with all that you will learn in this book, I invite you to pursue your dreams with confidence, vigour and determination.

To your success,
Jack Canfield.
(*New York Times* best-selling author of *Chicken Soup for the Soul*®
and *The Success Principles,* and America's #1 Success Coach)

INTRODUCTION

Welcome. If you have bought this book or perhaps been given it by a friend, family member or work colleague, then it is likely that you have an interest in business.

If you are someone who runs your own business, whether a hair salon in Manchester, a construction company in Sydney, or a hi-tech start-up in Dublin or San José, then you will know all too well the satisfaction this brings. But equally, you will know the constant challenges you face and the loneliness that is often part of the journey.

Perhaps you are someone who has long craved – even obsessed over – the idea of one day owning your own business, but haven't, up to now, known where to start, or had the courage to take that important first step.

Maybe you are a student who is reflecting on what to do with your life. Wondering which of the many career options to pursue. Trying all the while to weigh up what will provide you with a living and at the same time bring you joy and fulfilment. Wondering, above all, what will make your heart sing.

Well, this book is for you.

Even if you work for a large corporate organisation, government department or multinational company, there is much you can learn from the stories in this book that can help in building a culture of creativity, innovation and enterprise within your organisation.

Drawn from articles written for the *Sunday Independent* (Ireland's largest newspaper) over the past five years, this book is a compilation of inspiring stories of successful Irish entrepreneurs and business leaders. Representing a variety of sectors and located in different parts of Ireland, their stories are as diverse and as interesting as the businesses they lead. They are, for the large part, ordinary men and women. One thing they all share, though, is that they have dared to dream. But more than dream, they have taken action. They have stepped out from the crowd and from the familiarity that is their comfort zone. And they have triumphed.

Now more than ever, as we emerge from one of the worst recessions the world has ever experienced, it is important that we acknowledge and celebrate the vital role that entrepreneurs and business-builders play in our society. They are the unsung heroes who, through their risk-taking and ingenuity, create jobs. They are the driving force behind our economies and the glue that helps hold our communities together.

You may wonder what you can learn from these stories about Irish entrepreneurs. As you are about to discover, Ireland is a hotbed of entrepreneurial activity. Its can-do attitude and progressive mindset supports a thriving start-up culture that is creating economic activity far beyond what would normally be expected from a small island on the edge of the Atlantic. A hub for foreign direct investment, Ireland's performance is unrivalled, with more than 1,200 companies, from true global giants to the hottest names in everything from IT, life sciences and finance having already chosen Ireland as their strategic European base.

Having travelled extensively as a long-term student and now trainer in the areas of success, positivity and entrepreneurship, I am convinced that what can be learned from Ireland's microcosm of entrepreneurial endeavour can be applied anywhere in the world.

Contained within these stories are valuable lessons that each entrepreneur shares about their journey from start-up to success. We learn about their backgrounds and what shaped them, how they came up with their killer business idea, as well as the significant challenges that confronted them along the way. We learn too that while they have enjoyed the sweet taste of victory, all, without exception, have known times of bitter defeat.

But above all else, we learn that it has been their incredible tenacity and resilience that has helped them turn obstacles into opportunities and adversity into success. Perhaps their greatest achievement, though, is that by their very example they inspire the rest of us to pursue our own dreams.

I hope that you will find their stories as enjoyable to read as I have found them to write. I hope too that they will help demonstrate just how powerful an idea can be. How important is it to believe in yourself, and how an indomitable spirit – combined with unwavering determination – can help make dreams come true.

PART I

CHAPTER 1

WHY ENTREPRENEURS ARE IMPORTANT

THE POWER TO CHANGE THE WORLD

> *The reasonable man adapts himself to the world; the unreasonable one persists in trying to adapt the world to himself. Therefore, all progress depends on the unreasonable man.*
>
> George Bernard Shaw

I have chosen not to write this book as a how-to guide to starting or running a successful company. This is because I have found that information alone is seldom enough to change our human behaviour. If it were, we would all be living healthy and balanced lives. Most of us do not need more information – we need more inspiration.

Each of the entrepreneurs featured in this book has an inspiring story to share. Woven into their stories are their individual whys – what motivates them to do what they do. Some started their businesses because they were made redundant, others because they had a vision of something they wanted to create or a passion for something they loved to do. Others are family businesses passed on from one generation to the next.

One thing is certain in business; no one ever starts a big company. Each of the businesses here started out small and, through hard work, perseverance and the occasional helping of good luck, grew to where they are today.

My reason for writing this book and for sharing these stories is to help others realise that – irrespective of where we come from, our age, gender or educational background – we all have within us the ability to achieve whatever we set our minds to.

Over the last twenty-five years I have become an avid supporter and champion of entrepreneurship. Throughout that time, I have trained, mentored or invested in hundreds of emerging businesses, have founded a number of successful businesses in the consulting, technology and real estate sectors, and, for the past five years, have interviewed more than 250 successful entrepreneurs for my weekly newspaper column. During that time, I have come to realise that these entrepreneurs all share common traits that have helped them become successful. Importantly, too, I have come to understand that these same traits can be developed and nurtured in those seeking to follow in their footsteps.

What excites me most about entrepreneurs is that they have the power to literally change the world for the better. They create jobs, transform communities, drive economic growth and tackle global challenges. From the founders of exciting start-ups to the leaders of global businesses, entrepreneurs are constantly seeking out new ideas and new ways to push the boundaries of possibilities. In doing so, they draw on their optimism, creativity and their determination to improve both their own lives and the lives of those they serve.

Entrepreneurs are visionaries who see the future and then work to create it. Their only limit is their own imagination. They are the dreamers and the trailblazers, the ones drawing their own maps and making their own rules. We can all think of well-known examples, such as Bill Gates of Microsoft, Steve Jobs of Apple, Mark Zuckerburg of Facebook or Sir Richard Branson of Virgin, whose products and services impact the lives of millions of people around the world on a daily basis. However, in every corner of every country in the world there are countless other, less well-known entrepreneurs who have dedicated their lives and their talents to coming up with solutions to many of the world's problems. Together, they are developing and bringing to the market everything from electric cars and solar energy products to breakthrough drugs and medical devices that are literally saving millions of lives.

We may have a tendency to take for granted some of the products and services we use every day. What of the local hotelier, neighbourhood shop owner or car mechanic who all run their own businesses? Or the farmers who grow the food we eat. They too are entrepreneurs. How would those of us who live in cities and towns ever manage to feed ourselves and our families if it weren't for their effort and their enterprising spirit.

While the priority for entrepreneurs must be to ensure the survival and long-term sustainability of their businesses, many are driven not by the desire to make money but by the desire to make a difference.

CREATING JOBS AND GENERATING WEALTH THROUGH TAXES

If we want to live in a society that is both caring and economically sustainable, we need to invest in building schools for our young people, hospitals for our sick and elderly, and roads and other critical infrastructure. We also need to provide support to those who cannot find work or who, for one reason or another, are not able to work. In short, we need to make sure that no one gets left behind.

To achieve this, governments everywhere need money and lots of it. Most of this money comes by way of taxes, whether income tax, value-added tax (VAT) or corporation tax. But who creates this wealth in the first place? And how is it created?

In addition to large multinationals and corporations, wealth is created by business owners and entrepreneurs who – through their own ingenuity, risk-taking and hard work – start businesses. In the process of manufacturing their products or delivering their services, these business owners hire staff to whom they pay wages. Of these wages, in many cases almost half goes straight to the government in the form of taxes. Furthermore, most of the goods and services that these businesses sell have VAT or other taxes attached to them, and that money also goes directly to government. If, after all their hard work and effort, entrepreneurs actually end up making a profit, then that too is taxed.

Whatever disposable income employees have left over at the end of the month is largely spent on paying mortgages on their homes, buying food for their families, providing education for their children, as well as being spent in local shops, bars and restaurants within their communities, thereby helping to support other businesses and maintain the jobs of their employees.

And therein continues the circular flow of money.

Many people forget that ultimately it is our entrepreneurs and business builders who actually generate much of the wealth that goes to fund public services and to keep society and our economies functioning effectively.

In short, the more entrepreneurs we have, the more jobs are created. And the more jobs we have, the more revenue governments have to spend on essential services.

OPPORTUNITIES FOR PERSONAL FULFILMENT AND ECONOMIC INDEPENDENCE

As well as realising their own dreams and ambitions, entrepreneurs create opportunities for others to fulfil their potential. There are many who do not wish to be self-employed but who do wish to work. Through the jobs that entrepreneurs create, they give others the opportunity to use their skills and talents to make a contribution to society. In turn, the salaries they receive enable them to provide a good and secure standard of living for themselves and their families. Their children grow up in an environment where they have positive role models and where they are encouraged and supported to pursue their own career aspirations. In short, employment is the only real and long-term solution to poverty, disadvantage and social exclusion.

THE GLUE THAT HOLDS COMMUNITIES TOGETHER

Communities and businesses are so inextricably intertwined that neither can exist without the other. In every town, village and rural community across the world, entrepreneurs and business owners can be found running every conceivable type of business. They do so in locations where large multinational firms never can. These businesses depend on their local community for business as well as to provide employees. The communities in which they are located rely on them in turn for employment – the type of jobs that are grounded and rooted in these local areas. Without them, there would be terrible repercussions. Local people would be forced to emigrate or move to larger cities in search of work. Shops would close. The local post office and local school would close. Football clubs and other sporting organisations would struggle to field teams. And the older population would face the prospect of being left behind, alone and isolated.

Keeping communities alive, however, requires that we invest in them. It means encouraging and supporting more entrepreneurs to set up businesses and to create more jobs in these areas. If we can achieve this, we can help stem the flow of young people from their communities and help retain a vibrancy that might otherwise be extinguished.

Moreover, entrepreneurs and business owners everywhere generously give back to their communities. Many like to support the area in which they grew up or where they initially started their businesses. Most have active corporate social responsibility practices where they support sporting, charity, educational or community-based initiatives. Without their philanthropic support, many of these initiatives simply could not continue to exist.

Given the important role entrepreneurs play in the world and in their local communities, it is time now that we acknowledge and recognise their contribution.

But what is it that makes these entrepreneurs successful?

CHAPTER 2

SUCCESS LEAVES CLUES

– The Top Ten Traits of Successful Entrepreneurs

If you are not willing to learn, no one can help you. If you are determined to learn, no one can stop you.

Zig Ziglar, American author and motivational speaker

There has been much debate over the years as to whether entrepreneurs are born or whether, instead, it is possible to teach someone to become an entrepreneur. Research the subject and you soon discover that there are as many answers as there are people who write on the subject. In reality, there may not be a simple answer to this enduring question.

What is clear, however, is that deciding to launch a business takes courage. And managing its growth requires a combination of the right skill set and the right mindset. The good news is that, in my experience, this skill set can be learned and this mindset developed.

THE ESSENTIAL STEPS TO SETTING UP AND GROWING A SUCCESSFUL BUSINESS

Running a business is not rocket science. People of all ages, backgrounds and nationalities do it. Put simply, it is a process – a complex one, but a process none the less. Each step in this process is important and has the potential to either contribute to the advancement of the business or its ultimate demise. And each one could in its own right fill the syllabus of a lengthy college degree.

While it is not the intention of this book to go into these steps in great detail, here are some of the most important ones:

1) Identify a need or gap in the market.

2) Develop a product or service that meets that need and for which a sufficient number of customers are willing to pay.

3) Be able to sell your product or service at a price that not only covers your costs but also generates enough profit to enable you to reinvest in growing your business.

4) Find the fastest and most effective route to market and then build a brand that outlines your value proposition and how your business will be perceived in the market.

5) Hire motivated and talented staff who are committed to your company's vision and then align their individual roles and behaviours to your company's objectives.

6) Ensure you have sufficient capital to set up the business in the first place and enough working capital to support it through its continued expansion.

7) Have systems in place to collect any debt that is owed to you and to make sure you pay whatever debt you owe to your creditors.

8) Protect any intellectual property you have developed within the business to safeguard against 'copycat' or 'me too' competitors.

9) Constantly innovate so that you stay relevant to the market and to changing trends and evolving customer preferences.

10) Finally, increase the size and scale of your business, through either organic growth or through merging with or acquiring other similar or related businesses, until you reach a point where you are satisfied – or until you decide to exit by way of sale, merger or initial public offering (IPO).

All sounds fairly straightforward, doesn't it?

While many of the above steps require knowledge and skills to execute effectively, these can either be learned by an entrepreneur or acquired by hiring the services of those who already possess them – such as employees, contractors or external consultants. You may even wish to partner with someone who already has the skills that you lack.

The challenge for most founders in launching their businesses is that they are undertaking many of these steps for the very first time. It is for this reason that serial entrepreneurs often find it easier to start new businesses or secure financial backing for their ideas, as they have already mastered the process.

THE MINDSET AND THE PSYCHOLOGY OF SUCCESS

It has been my experience that success in business has less to do with intelligence and more to do with psychology. For that reason, school or college results alone are not the best predictor of entrepreneurial capabilities. There are any number of examples of entrepreneurs who didn't go to college or who left school early and still went on to be successful. At its core, success is about the ability to recognise a good opportunity when you see it and then to pursue it with drive, focus and determination.

But there are also a number of other traits and characteristics that are to be found in nearly all successful entrepreneurs. The following are ten of these top traits and while they are not, of course, a definitive list of the make-up of every entrepreneur, they can certainly be found in those who you will read about later in this book.

1. They have a Belief in Themselves and are Optimistic by Nature

> *A pessimist sees the difficulty in every opportunity. An optimist sees the opportunity in every difficulty.*
>
> Sir Winston Churchill

Entrepreneurs are natural optimists. They expect things to work out and have a tendency to look for the positive in any situation. They focus on solutions and see opportunities where others see only problems. Their language is always about what they can do, not what they can't. They see setbacks as opportunities to learn and obstacles as something to be got around rather than a reason to give up.

Entrepreneurs have no more control over their environment or situation than anyone else, but what they do have is a belief in themselves and their ability to respond to whatever challenges arise. In short, entrepreneurs tend not to worry overly about the future because they are too busy creating it.

2. They have a Positive Attitude to Risk and Failure

> *A ship in harbour is safe, but that is not what ships are built for.*
>
> John A. Shedd, American author and professor

Many people long for the security of a guaranteed monthly

pay cheque or a permanent and pensionable job. However, for the entrepreneur, the very idea of being constrained by the predictability that some jobs impose can be terrifying. Entrepreneurs long for a world of adventure where they are free to pursue their goals, implement their ideas and follow their dreams.

They accept, too, that risk is a natural part of this process and that the degree to which they succeed will be proportionate to the degree to which they are willing to fail. The higher the risk, the greater the potential reward. Moreover, while they do not wish to fail, they know that – should it happen – they will find a way to embrace such failure and turn it into a valuable source of learning.

3. They are Visionaries and Strategists

Effort and courage are not enough without purpose and direction.

John F. Kennedy

Entrepreneurs usually start out with a compelling vision and a sense of clarity about what it is they want to achieve. They see gaps in the market that they believe they can fill. Most will build their businesses around solving problems, either their own or other people's. Their vision is often to create something bigger and more enduring than themselves. They see this as an opportunity for them to make their mark in or contribution to the world.

While they have the capacity to see the bigger picture, entrepreneurs are not simply dreamers. They know how to develop a strategy to take their idea from concept to launch – and beyond. They know what resources to marshal. And they know how to lead others. Their sense of purpose and passion inspires action and loyalty in those around them.

4. They are Excellent Communicators and Storytellers

The goal is to provide inspiring information that moves people to action.

Guy Kawasaki, author, speaker, entrepreneur and evangelist

Successful entrepreneurs are good communicators. Some may be evangelical about their message while others are more low-key. All, however, understand that to succeed they must engage and enrol key stakeholders in helping them to achieve their ambition – from their employees and customers to their investors. Most will seek to involve these stakeholders in decision-making processes in the certain knowledge that people will best support that which they help to create.

Many increasingly draw on the power of storytelling to connect, not only with the intellect of their audiences, but also with their emotions. They use stories as a way to tap into their audience's hopes and fears as well as their aspirations. And they find ways to distil their message into absorbable bite-sized pieces on the understanding that such messages must first be understood before they can be championed.

5. They Take Action

You will never plough a field by turning it over in your mind.

Old Irish Proverb

Entrepreneurs are goal-focused and target-driven. Not content to sit around talking and planning, they are eager to take action. The more they act, the more confident they become in themselves, and the more they empower and inspire others around them.

They have also learned the art of goal setting. They realise that what they want usually exists on the other side of their comfort zone and so their goals involve a significant stretch for themselves, their teams and their companies.

Once committed to an idea, they are also willing to make major sacrifices in terms of time, resources, personal relationships and sometimes even their health. To others this may look like obsession rather than commitment, but to the entrepreneur it is as if they feel compelled to see their idea through to completion.

6. They are Great Leaders

Before you are a leader, success is all about growing yourself. When you become a leader, success is all about growing others.

Jack Welch, former CEO of General Electric

After setting up their businesses, entrepreneurs quickly discover that their roles change. They find themselves managing people, often for the first time. They realise the importance of developing a company culture that supports the development of their staff. And, as additional layers of middle management are introduced, they finally get to adopt a more strategic leadership role where they can begin to work *on* their business rather than *in* their business.

Most will come to the realisation, too, that management is different to leadership. The distinction, as management consultant Peter Drucker put it, is that: 'Management is about doing things right whereas leadership is about doing the right things.'

However, few entrepreneurs ever start a business properly trained or adequately prepared for their newly acquired leadership roles. Over time, most will develop their own distinct approach and authentic style of leadership. The wise ones will go on to invest in their own development, study leadership techniques and bolster this with a mix of advisors, non-executive directors and mentors.

7. They are Good Networkers and Excellent Team Builders

You are the average of the five people you spend the most time with.

Jim Rohn, entrepreneur, author and motivational speaker

Entrepreneurs are a tribe. They are drawn to others like themselves, where they feel supported and understood. They enjoy being around other like-minded, outward-looking and forward-focused business leaders. They regularly benchmark themselves against others, less for the purpose of competition and more as a motivation to do better.

They are smart people. Smart enough to understand that they can never grow or scale a business on their own. Many are generalists who play to their personal strengths and hire others who have skills and core competencies in areas where they do not.

They know too that the size of their network matters. They join networking groups or membership organisations, and go to conferences and trade shows in an effort to learn, to look for new opportunities and to extend their reach.

They are not afraid to ask for help – even the really successful ones – and most are equally happy to give such help and advice to other business-owners or would-be entrepreneurs.

8. They are Willing to Embrace Innovation and Change

It is not the strongest of the species that survives, nor the most intelligent, but rather the one most adaptable to change.

Charles Darwin

Most people do not like change. Instead, they prefer the comfort that comes from certainty and predictability. However, we are now living in a time of unprecedented change, where entire industries are being disrupted and whole sectors turned on their head. Over the next twenty years, many of the young people of today will be working in jobs not yet created and in industries not yet conceived.

Entrepreneurs realise that to succeed, not only do they need to be comfortable with change, but they need to be the drivers of that change. They understand the need to constantly innovate or run the risk of being left behind and becoming irrelevant. They have a willingness to embrace experimentation and risk possible mistakes in the certain knowledge that their failure to innovate – if not pursued – may turn out to be their greatest mistake.

9. They are Committed to Continuous and Never-ending Improvement

When we strive to become better than we are, everything around us becomes better, too.

Paulo Coelho

Successful entrepreneurs, by their nature, are committed to what the Japanese call *kaizen*, meaning continuous and never-ending improvement. This applies not only to their businesses but also to themselves. They know that to do better, they have to be better. They are committed to investing in their personal development as well as constantly seeking new ways of improving everything they do. They do courses, attend seminars and hire mentors and coaches. Some join mastermind or peer-to-peer support groups, while others work regularly with accountability partners, holding each other accountable for achieving the goals they have set for themselves and their companies.

And they understand that, while they have many competitors in their businesses, their greatest competition is always against themselves – doing better today than they did yesterday.

10. They Persevere

Success seems to be largely a matter of hanging on after others have let go.

William Feather, American author

Entrepreneurs typically have as many fears and insecurities as everyone else. However, they possess an unwavering determination to see things through. They are tenacious and often uncompromising. Even in the face of obstacles that, to others, may seem almost insurmountable, they find the inner strength and conviction to push ahead relentlessly. They hang on when lesser mortals, maybe even wiser ones, might have let go.

They may adapt their dreams, update them, even suspend them for a period, but they are seldom prepared to abandon them. It is often such resilience and determination that leads them to ultimate success.

CHAPTER 3

THE WILL TO SUCCEED

Nothing splendid has ever been achieved except by those who dared to believe that something inside of them was superior to circumstance.

Bruce Barton, American author, businessman and politician

While all entrepreneurs may have certain traits that help them become successful, the environment and culture to which they belong can also contribute to the realisation of their potential. Nowhere is this more evident than the island of Ireland, which has always succeeded in punching well above its weight when it comes to the world of business and entrepreneurship.

With just 4.8 million people living in the Republic of Ireland and a further 1.8 million in Northern Ireland, Ireland has a relatively small population compared to other countries and yet its global reach is immense, with an estimated 70 million people across the world claiming Irish ancestry, half of these in the US alone.

Irish people love to work. Entrepreneurial by nature, they have a work ethic that is second to none. Over the years, the country has produced many companies that now compete in the world of global business. Brand names such as Jameson Irish Whiskey, Guinness, Kerry Group, Glanbia, Smurfit Kappa, Primark, CRH, Ryanair and Alltech are famous the world over.

Ireland's entrepreneurs, too, have proved themselves to be some of the smartest and most successful in the world in their chosen fields. Names such as Denis O'Brien of Digicel; Eugene and Gene Murtagh of Kingspan; J. P. McManus and John Magnier, racehorse owners with various property and business interests; Martin Naughton of Glen Dimplex; Sir Michael Smurfit of Smurfit Kappa; the late Tony Ryan, co-founder of Ryanair, and that firm's CEO, Michael O'Leary; financier Dermot Desmond; Dr Pearse Lyons of AllTech; and brothers John and Patrick Collison of mobile payment firm, Stripe, who in 2016 became the world's youngest ever self-made billionaires at the ages of twenty-six and twenty-eight respectively.

So what is it that makes this little island and its people so unique in the world of industry and enterprise?

Having faced centuries of occupation, repression and economic hardship, which has seen millions of the population forced to scatter to the four corners of the globe in search of a better life, the Irish have developed a spirit of resilience and self-determination. Perhaps it is this background of adversity that has helped give Irish people their can-do attitude and a propensity for innovation. They know that if they want success they have to earn it and pursue opportunity where they find it, whether in Ireland or in one of the many countries that the Irish diaspora has spread to.

Like many other countries around the world, Ireland suffered badly as a result of the economic crash of 2008. This, together with the collapse of the banking system and the country's over-reliance on the construction sector, resulted in hundreds of thousands of jobs being lost and the floodgates of emigration flung open once more. However, drawing on their innate strength of character, Irish people dug deep to endure a long period of sustained government cutbacks and austerity measures. Thanks to their enduring spirit, a thriving SME sector and the presence of over 1,200 foreign direct investment or multinational firms, Ireland not only survived the recent downturn but has once again begun to flourish. Now, a decade on, the country is fast approaching full employment and has regained its position as the fastest growing economy in the European Union.

With a first-class educational system, Ireland continues to produce highly educated, creative and resourceful individuals who are recognised around the world for their adaptability and creativity. This island economy also attracts gifted and resourceful immigrants to its shores, creating a multi-cultural melting pot of talent that has attracted levels of foreign direct investment (FDI) far beyond what might be expected of a country of its size. In fact, Ireland is the second most attractive country globally for FDI – after Singapore – with true global giants and the hottest names in everything from IT, life sciences and finance having chosen the country as their strategic base or European headquarters.

Apart from this strong multinational sector, Ireland continues to have a vibrant and export-led indigenous sector. According to the country's Central Statistics Office (CSO) figures, there are nearly 249,000 active businesses in Ireland, an astonishing number considering the size of the country. Of these 99.8% are small and medium enterprises (SMEs), which together employ almost 970,000 people or 69.1% of all those employed in business in Ireland. These are the backbone of the Irish economy and key to the country's economic future. A thriving start-up culture supported by an active investment community and an attractive range of government-backed incentives, continues to result in approximately 35,000 people becoming new business owners each year according to Global Entrepreneurship Monitor Ireland figures.

Every entrepreneur the world over has their own compelling reason for wanting to start their own business and their own unique vision for what it is they want to achieve. For Irish entrepreneurs in particular, it is their unique heritage and history that helps give them the drive, the imagination and the tenacity to follow their dreams.

Before sharing the stories of some of Ireland's most inspiring entrepreneurs, first let me share my own story and what led me to write this book.

CHAPTER 4

MY STORY

> *Everyone who gets to where they are, first had to start where they were.*
>
> Unknown

Like seeds, we all grow where we are planted, each of us shaped and moulded by our families and the communities in which we grow up. While we don't choose these roots, they give us our accents and our values.

My career certainly did not start out in a boardroom. It started, instead, in a small rural village in the north-east of Ireland – Ballyhaise in County Cavan. For all its many attractions Cavan could never boast of being a wealthy county. Farms are generally small and many farmers work part-time jobs to survive. What they do have, however, is a strong work ethic and an enterprising spirit. Growing up, the emergence of intensive farm enterprises, such as pig, poultry and mushroom farming – activities that required very little land on which to operate – became, for me, a symbol of how innovative people can be when they have many needs but few resources.

A friendly and down-to-earth community, Ballyhaise was full of the usual mix of small farmers, shopkeepers, publicans, builders and carpenters. They never called themselves entrepreneurs, but that's what they were. They worked hard, paid their taxes, spent their money in the local community and kept the village alive. To me, they epitomised what working for yourself is all about.

Ballyhaise was also where I learned the value and impact that having a part-time job can have on a young person's attitude to business – something I have since learned is common to many would-be entrepreneurs. Working in the bar next door to where we lived from about ten years of age taught me my first valuable business lesson and one that has stayed with me ever since – it is not your employer who pays your wages, but the customer.

LEARNING TO BELIEVE IN MYSELF – MY PERSONAL DEVELOPMENT JOURNEY

Every adversity, every failure, every heartache carries with it the seed of an equal or greater benefit.

Napoleon Hill

From a young age I came to the realisation that life doesn't happen to us. Instead we create it, by the decisions we make and our responses to the challenges we face.

I was born with congenital cataracts in both eyes, congenital simply meaning that they developed before I was born. A form of cloudiness that obstructs the passage of light through the lens, cataracts make it difficult to see clearly. Back then, there was little understanding of the potentially adverse effects these cataracts would have on a child's learning ability, personality or self-esteem.

Going to school posed major problems for me. Simply trying to keep up with those around me often left me feeling exhausted and there were times when my inability to see the blackboard properly created such a sense of panic in me that I wanted to run away from school and never go back. Because I couldn't read small print, I read slowly and awkwardly. Extreme sensitivity to light didn't help either. During my late teens, when I eventually developed the confidence to wear sunglasses, I did so against the backdrop of jeering comments about trying to look cool. As a result, I often ended up enduring the pain of the day's glare rather than deal with those taunts.

Words of encouragement from my fifth-class teacher and then school principal, Tom Gawley, helped boost my confidence and change my view of my future. During a role-playing exercise in class where I wasn't required to read, he noticed a confidence in me that he had not seen before. At break he called me aside and, in a sympathetic voice, counselled me, saying, 'You know, Sean, you have your own unique talents and while you may not be able to keep up with others in some areas, never allow that to defeat your spirit. Concentrate instead on your own strengths and if you do that you can achieve anything you want in life as long as you are prepared to work really hard at it.'

At the time I didn't fully grasp the significance of his words or the ultimate impact they would have on my life. But I remember leaving the classroom that day feeling more confident than I had ever felt before, proof that sometimes we have to discover other people's belief in us before we can believe in ourselves.

As the years passed, I found ways of compensating for my limitations, determining never to allow them to define my ambitions or me. In fact, I came to realise that while being born with congenital cataracts created many challenges during my early life, it also developed in me a sense of resolve and determination that I might not otherwise have cultivated – traits that would prove invaluable to me in later life.

Another boost to my confidence came when I became chairman of my local Foróige Youth Club in my late teens. Foróige is the leading youth development organisation in Ireland, the purpose of which is to involve young people consciously and actively in their own development and in the development of society. Their philosophy of personal development, self-determination and self-empowerment immediately resonated with me. The idea that each of us is unique, that we have our own talents and abilities and that all of us have a choice in what we think, do and become, were principles I took on board in my teens and which have stayed with me ever since. It was also there that I learned how to chair meetings and speak in public for the first time. Looking back now, I realise that much of what has helped me in life, I learned from Foróige.

OUT OF A JOB AND ALMOST OUT OF HOPE

I have long been a supporter of entrepreneurs, largely because they create jobs, and job creation is the only long-term solution to the scourge of unemployment. You simply cannot understand what it is like to be unemployed unless you have first been unemployed. I got my first taste of what it felt like in 1984. I had finished agricultural college and was working in the local agricultural co-op by day and in the bar at weekends. I had also just bought a small farm with my father and had stocked it by painting sheds for local farmers, who paid me in calves instead of cash. Things were going well until I was involved in a car accident that left me with neck and back injuries. These resulted in me being unable to work for most of the following year. Once recovered, I found myself out of work and struggling to get my life back on track.

When you are unemployed, you don't just lose your job, you lose your status and your income. You become withdrawn from the very network that will most likely provide your next opportunity. But more than that, you lose your self-confidence and your self-esteem. You begin to feel gripped by the fear, real or otherwise, that you might never work again; that you might never get to become the person you know you are capable of becoming.

A DIFFERENT SORT OF MISSION

During this time in my life I took daily sanity walks on the country roads around our village. On one of these walks I was joined by my former teacher Tom Gawley. Recognising that I was struggling, he wrote *Tabula Rasa* in the journal I was keeping at the time. 'It's the Latin for "clean slate",' Tom said. 'It's what you do with it now that counts.'

His words helped strangle the negativity that had taken hold in my mind. They became a constant reminder that we are in control of our own destiny. That, irrespective of what has gone before, we are not our past, and that we can at any time begin to write a new future for ourselves.

It was then that I took up judo to help me recover from my injuries. Having committed myself to training hard, I received a black belt in less than five years, fulfilling a long-held ambition to become proficient in martial arts. The outcome of the accident ultimately led to me developing greater flexibility, agility and strength than I might otherwise have had.

Once I'd fully recovered from my injuries I considered heading to Africa to work on the missions, but an invitation to address a local youth group in my home town changed my mind. Made up mostly of sixteen-year-olds, these young people had fallen through the cracks in the formal education system. But rather than talk, I listened. Most were from homes where their parents were unemployed. When I asked what hopes and aspirations they had for their future their answers shocked me.

They didn't have any – they assumed they were destined for a life on welfare.

Before long, I had abandoned any thoughts of going to Africa and returned instead to full-time education to become a professional youth and community worker. The more I studied – and the more time I spent working with young people from varying backgrounds, including the inner city, young offenders and members of the travelling community – the more convinced I became that the only solution to long-term disadvantage was a combination of access to education and meaningful employment.

It was then that I first got involved in politics, joining the local branch of the country's largest political party, Fianna Fáil. My focus was to raise awareness of the challenges faced by young people throughout the country and the need for better leisure facilities and a properly funded national youth service. Before long, I found myself elected as one of four youth members to the party's national executive.

The next two years were spent working with the National Youth Council of Ireland, developing the country's first life-skills-based national alcohol education programme for young people. This, in turn, led to an offer of a job as political secretary to the then Minister for Health, Dr Rory O'Hanlon. While exciting and interesting, it didn't last. Two years later, the then Taoiseach (Prime Minister) Charles Haughey was ousted and his replacement, Albert Reynolds, immediately proceeded to dismiss most of his ministers. And with them went their secretaries – me included.

I was once again unemployed. Determined never to be in this position again, I decided it was time to take control of my own destiny. So I resolved that I was going to work for myself.

WHO WANTS TO BE AN ENTREPRENEUR?

I was, however, faced with a few challenges. I didn't have any money. I didn't have very much business experience, nor did I have a definite business idea.

'I need some stepping-stones to get into business,' I thought. So I got a job in a community partnership project developing training initiatives for those who were long-term unemployed. While short term, this led to me being offered the role of assistant CEO with a local enterprise agency, where I began to specialise in delivering 'Start Your Own Business' programmes and mentoring emerging entrepreneurs. During the next five years I read everything I could about business, as well as interviewing every successful entrepreneur I could think of. I also went back to college at night and completed a Masters of Business Administration (MBA).

All I was missing now was an idea. And that came next.

In 1997, while co-leading a trade mission of local businesses to the United States, I met my future business partner, Derek Roddy. It was a time when house building was on the rise in Ireland and technology was becoming more a part of our daily lives. Both Derek and I had recently bought new houses and were appalled to find that most rooms had not been cabled for access to basic phone, Internet or TV services. Having both gone through the frustration of having to drill holes in our brand new homes in order to bring cables to each room, we developed a central cabling system that could be installed during construction that would future-proof new homes for these services, as well as home office, home cinema systems multi-room audio and security cameras. Pioneering for its time, our company, named Smarthomes, grew to become Ireland's largest home technology company, scooped multiple awards for innovation and was selected as a finalist in the Ernst & Young Entrepreneur of the Year Awards.

Derek and I experienced some great highs during those years, such as winning the contract to install our technology in thousands of homes in Adamstown, Ireland's largest housing development at the time. But we also experienced crushing lows, such as when the crash of 2008 left many developers and contractors unable or unwilling to pay us. While difficult, we dug deep, emptied our reserves and managed to survive. Like many other businesses at that time, survival became the new benchmark of success.

With a ninety per cent fall off in the number of new homes being built, we decided to pivot the business and focus instead on developing controls that could be installed in existing homes to enable home owners to better manage their home heating systems and reduce their energy costs. When I later exited the business prior to running in the presidential election of 2011, Derek – himself a hugely innovative and talented entrepreneur – took it over and immediately set about creating Climote, an award-winning remote heating control system that is going from strength to strength.

I had become disgusted by the appalling treatment of thousands of sub-contractors like ourselves by some developers and construction firms, who used anomalies in the law to avoid paying for goods supplied to them. Claiming that these were now part of the fabric of the buildings in which they were installed enabled banks and receivers to sell off the developments to discharge the debts of the developers and construction firms, while leaving a myriad of plumbers, carpenters, electricians, painters, tilers and window suppliers high and dry. The result was the loss of thousands of jobs due to these sub-contracting businesses being forced to close. Seeking to address this, I launched a campaign calling for new legislation to be introduced. Senator Feargal Quinn was the first to respond to my call and courageously championed new legislation in the area. With the backing of the Construction Industry Federation (CIF), we eventually succeeded in changing the law through the introduction of the Construction Contracts Act 2013, which provides statutory payment protections for subcontractors.

ENTER THE DRAGON

A write-up on Smarthomes in a 2008 book by KPMG called *That'll Never Work* led Larry Bass of ShinaAwiL Productions to approach me about becoming one of the investors on the Irish version of the popular TV show *Dragons' Den* (*Shark Tank* in the US), which was about to be launched. The programme provided a platform for entrepreneurs to pitch their business ideas to a panel of five investors, or 'dragons', in an effort to convince us to invest our own money in return for a negotiated percentage equity in their businesses. A great success, the show did much to increase awareness of entrepreneurship in the country. For me, it resulted in a higher profile and opened the door to a world of speaking opportunities.

From a young age, I had always enjoyed public speaking. Now I had audiences who wanted to hear stories from 'the Den', tips from the world of business and how they too could become entrepreneurs. I began to address local chambers of commerce who were struggling with the closure of businesses in their areas, neighbourhood organisations looking to breathe new life into their jaded communities, and unemployment groups seeking encouragement and support in finding a way out of their joblessness. I became the ambassador for the Irish Association of Supported Employment – drawing on my own childhood struggles with my sight to help promote the right of those with disabilities to find both dignity and purpose through training and employment, particularly given that in times of recession those with disabilities suffer even higher unemployment than others.

Increasingly, I was invited to speak in schools and universities throughout the country. Everywhere I went I began to notice a real hunger for hope, positivity and leadership.

With the media choosing to constantly focus on everything that was wrong, a blanket of negativity had fallen like a fog over the country. Fear had percolated into the psyche of the general population and failure became the word on everyone's lips. Whatever money there was in the country was now being hoarded as a result of this fear, further compounding an already difficult situation.

My head and my heart were screaming that this was the very time that Ireland needed to focus, not on our weaknesses but on our strengths, not on our problems but on possible solutions to those problems. We could not afford to be constantly pulling against one another; instead we needed to start pulling together. And we certainly could not keep lambasting our nation across the airwaves of the world. Instead I felt we had to call on all those around the world who loved Ireland to rally in our time of need.

By this time I had become a student of Jack Canfield. A famous author and internationally recognised leader in the area of personal development and peak performance strategies, Jack has spent over forty years teaching the proven principles of success to entrepreneurs, corporate leaders and CEOs from some of the world's largest companies. He is also one of the authors featured in the best-selling book and film, *The Secret*, and is co-author of the phenomenal *Chicken Soup for the Soul®* series, which has sold literally hundreds of millions of copies around the world.

Meeting Jack for the first time at a seminar in Dublin in 2008, I found his approach authentic and his message refreshingly positive. It was inspiring to be in the company of someone who was as goal-driven and as solution-focused as I was, and who shared my same optimistic vision of the world. I began travelling to meet him in California where he lives, and before long Jack had become my mentor.

As I worked with Jack, my confidence grew and with it my resolve to do something positive for Ireland. It was then that I decided to run for election to become the president of Ireland.

RUNNING FOR PRESIDENT

If not me, who? If not now, when?

Version of an old Jewish saying attributed
to Rabbi Hillel the Elder

The decision to run for president was the toughest decision of my life. To many it came as a surprise. But I knew that if I wanted to change what was happening around me, then it was up to me to step forward. And running for president seemed the right thing to do. I ran independently of my Fianna Fáil background. Although proud of it, it was not part of my message at the time. I stood as an independent so as to be above and outside party political rivalry. There had been enough of that.

Looking at the change that previous incumbents had brought to the role, and given the economic challenges that Ireland now faced, I felt that the time had come for someone from the world of business to fill the role. Apart from the significance of this at home, I felt it would also help in projecting a positive image of Ireland abroad as a country that was modern, dynamic and open for business. Given that the modern media only deals in sound-bites, I distilled my many messages into one easy-to-understand mantra – the need to get Ireland back to work, stem the flow of emigration and offer a future to our young people.

Before I could ever hope to win the election, I first had to get into the race. Rather than the traditional route of getting a nomination from a political party or twenty TDs (members of parliament) and senators, I chose the less travelled road of seeking the support of four local authorities. This was not an easy route, given that most of these local authorities are controlled by one or a number of the political parties. But for me it represented a clear message that mine would be a truly bottom up, community-based and grass-roots campaign.

With this in mind, I recruited a small team of staff supported by volunteers from many of the universities, institutes of technology and community groups I had previously addressed. Together with my family, my wife Trish's family and our wide circle of friends, we worked tirelessly to get my campaign off the ground.

I appointed Cathal Lee as my campaign manager. Smart and politically astutc, Cathal had previously worked in the Oireachtas (Houses of Parliament) before taking up a public affairs role with the CIF. It was there that we first worked together in advancing the Construction Contracts legislation.

While Cathal's family had lived next door to me when I was growing up and we shared many of the same values, the most important consideration in choosing him was that I trusted him completely.

Having launched our campaign on the TV programme *The Late Late Show*, we spent the following months meeting councillors in their own homes and addressing council meetings all across the country. Challenging as it was, we eventually secured the support of four local authorities: Clare, Leitrim and Meath County Councils and Cork City Council.

I was now in the race.

During the same period, and with Trish at my side, I embarked on a listening tour, visiting youth, community and business groups in every part of Ireland. In less than three months we succeeded in building a grass-roots organisation consisting of more than 2,500 volunteers. Every single one had their own story to tell, their own reason for joining, and every one believed in the need for change.

Our approach to the election was different to that of the other candidates and parties. We refused to speak negatively of the six other candidates but instead welcomed them into the race. We didn't waste money on the customary campaign bus nor did we litter the countryside with election posters, relying instead on our volunteer network and an innovative social media strategy. From a rank outsider initially, I rose to top the opinion polls at forty per cent just three days out from voting.

However, Monday 24 October 2011 changed that.

That evening I took part in the final televised presidential debate on the *Frontline* programme on RTÉ (Ireland's national broadcast network), an experience that would ultimately cost me the election. The presenter of the programme, Pat Kenny, put a tweet to me live on air, challenging my recollection and previous statement about my involvement in a legitimate fund-raiser for Fianna Fáil back in 2008. It would later transpire that this tweet was a hoax and had come from a completely fake account, the source of which had not been verified by RTÉ before being put to me. Moreover, RTÉ later received a corrective tweet almost thirty minutes before the end of the programme, which clarified that the previous tweet had indeed been a hoax. This was never made known to the audience in the studio, nor to the almost one million viewers watching the programme at home – even though there was ample time to do so. The matter was further compounded when, during an interview with Pat Kenny the next morning on his show on RTÉ Radio 1, the bogus nature of the tweet was once again not revealed.

This fake tweet and my reaction to it became the headline in all the newspapers and media outlets the following day. And with only forty hours before an election moratorium on media coverage, there was insufficient time to recover from the fallout.

Ultimately, I went on to receive over a half-a-million first preference votes, putting me in second place out of a field of seven candidates. It was an incredible result. People regularly ask me now, given everything that happened during the final days of the campaign, if I ever regret standing for election. The answer is absolutely not. Regrets more usually come from wanting to do something but not having the courage to go for it. For me, this had been an amazing journey.

While our campaign has been credited by many as being one of the most dynamic and effective election campaigns in Irish political history, it would not have been possible without the many thousands of people who supported me and canvassed for me in every part of the country. I remain as humbled as I am proud of what we achieved and I will be forever grateful to those people and to the hundreds of thousands of people who voted for me.

It took me quite some time to reconcile myself to the outcome of the election. Not because I hadn't won the election, but because of the nature of the ending. The impact that *Frontline* had on the outcome of the election, and RTÉ's total unwillingness to accept that the programme had been unfair, led me to take a case against them to the Broadcasting Authority of Ireland (BAI), the broadcasting regulator in Ireland. The BAI ruled in my favour, that both the *Frontline* programme and the following morning's Radio 1 programme had indeed been unfair. I subsequently took a legal case against RTÉ, not just because of the fake tweet but because of a myriad of additional failings in the planning and production of the programme.

Four years later, on 19 December 2017, the case was finally settled. RTÉ read out an apology in the High Court in Dublin and paid me substantial damages. In the apology, RTÉ acknowledged that mistakes had been made and that it had failed to comply with its statutory duty of fairness to me under the country's broadcasting laws. In particular, it acknowledged that the fake tweet should not have broadcast and, when it became apparent during the course of the programme that it was false, that fact should have immediately been broadcast. RTÉ also acknowledged its failure to clarify the issue of the fake tweet on the following morning's Radio 1 broadcast.

Importantly, the apology went on to acknowledge and fully accept the findings in the BAI's ruling of March 2012 as well as the findings of RTÉ's own internal review, published in November 2012, which identified numerous significant failings in the broadcast separate to that of the tweet. These included concerns about the format of the programme, the lack of editorial supervision, the selection of audience members, the selection of specific questioners, the drafting or redrafting of questions by the production team and the lack of a single direct question from the audience to the next highest-polling candidate, Michael D. Higgins. In summing up, RTÉ acknowledged that the production of the programme had fallen significantly short of the standards expected by the public and required by law.

In accepting RTÉ's apology, I reiterated, through a statement issued by my solicitor Paul Tweed, that my motivation in taking this case was not just about addressing the unfairness shown to me, but also about ensuring that what happened to me would never be allowed to happen again.

I am satisfied now that this case, challenging as it was, has led to the introduction by RTÉ of a number of very significant changes in policies, procedures and protocols, which will help ensure that every candidate who stands for election in Ireland in the future will be treated with fairness, objectivity and impartiality by the state broadcaster, something that is an essential part of the integrity of the democratic process.

BACK TO BUSINESS

Before running in the election, I had stepped away from all my business interests. I had also invested a lot of money, time and energy into the campaign, but now it was time to move on. I found myself having to draw on everything I had learned throughout my life in order to start afresh. Although it wasn't easy, the words *tabula rasa* echoed in my head.

My phone hardly rang for the next eighteen months, except for close friends and family. There were no business opportunities and no invitations to speak. I had fallen into no man's land – somewhere between the world of business and the world of politics. The one exception was the *Sunday Independent* – Ireland's largest-selling newspaper. They invited me to write a weekly column profiling successful entrepreneurs and it is these stories that form the heart of this book.

In 2014 I started a new company providing office and industrial accommodation to expanding indigenous businesses and multinational firms throughout the country. Teaming up with long-term friend and tech entrepreneur, Colm Piercy, this business, Clyde Real Estate, now includes among its many tenants names such as Intel, Nokia and Citi. I continue to support as many other emerging entrepreneurs as I can, as well as speaking at and chairing all manner of business, personal development and leadership conferences and seminars.

For the past three years I have also been working closely with my former mentor, and now good friend, Jack Canfield, co-facilitating private retreats with him in the US and Europe where we work with people from around the world who want to take action to achieve their most ambitious goals and dreams. And, five years on from when I first began writing for the *Sunday Independent*, I continue to profile successful entrepreneurs in the hope that their stories will help inform and inspire the next generation of business leaders.

PART II

INTERVIEWS

CHAPTER 5

LIVING THE DREAM
– The Story of Matthews Coach Hire

Matthews.ie

www.matthews.ie

'I'm living the dream, Sean, I'm living the dream.' So says Paddy Matthews when I ask how he is doing. Sitting in his office in his company's headquarters in Inniskeen, County Monaghan, Paddy tells me that every morning he has to pinch himself to see if his life now is real.

Paddy never set out to become an entrepreneur but today he owns one of Ireland's largest private bus companies, Matthews Coach Hire. With a fleet of forty-four coaches transporting over 4,500 passengers every day, his company currently employs eighty-five staff and has an annual turnover of more than €9 million.

Life hasn't always been this good for Paddy. Years on the road as a truck driver took its toll on his health, leaving him with such severe back pain that he ended up out of work and on disability benefit for almost six years. Paddy's story, however, is one of triumph over adversity; a story about the power of possibility and a strong reminder to us all of our potential to overcome whatever life throws at us.

Paddy Matthews grew up in Dundalk, County Louth. His father worked as a driver with Ireland's national public transport provider, CIÉ, and Paddy's first memories are of helping him deliver flour and sugar, which had just arrived into the area by train, to local shops. After school he worked with the customs service along the border, and later with an American electronics component plant in the town. But Paddy quickly learned that being indoors all day wasn't for him.

'I didn't like the idea of being confined, so I left,' he says with a smile.

He followed his father's footsteps and became a driver, mostly delivering building supplies to local construction sites. Before long he had progressed to more gruelling work as a long-distance truck driver. Working across Europe meant being away a lot from home and family. The following eighteen years were difficult for Paddy. The work was demanding and the lifestyle unhealthy. So much so that he ended up doubling his weight to more than eighteen stone. The effect of the extra weight, as well as long hours behind the wheel, led to severe damage to the discs in his back.

'Both the doctors and myself feared that I was heading for life in a wheelchair,' he says solemnly.

During that time, Paddy visited his local Rehab Training Centre, where it was suggested he consider a course in transport management. He had just finished that when he was approached by a local bus owner, who offered to sell him his sixteen-seater minibus.

'At the time we had six children: three of our own and three foster children. Getting the eight of us to mass on a Sunday morning was a bit of an ordeal. So we decided to buy the minibus, partly for our own use but also with the idea that we might set up a small sideline business doing school runs and the like,' explains Paddy.

The man who sold him the bus agreed to continue to drive it, while Paddy and his wife Mary would look after bookings and the business side of things. Word soon spread of Paddy's new venture and local football teams began to ask if he would transport them to and from matches around the county.

Paddy soon realised there could be the basis of a good business there. However, he also realised that his sixteen-seat mini-bus wasn't big enough. He bought a bigger bus, which meant he could get work from Bus Éireann (the state's official bus company) doing school bus runs. He expanded as demand grew and, before long, had a fleet of eight buses.

Realising that the buses were mainly being used in the mornings and evenings, Paddy came up with the idea of a daily service from Dundalk to Dublin along the new M1 motorway. 'We had to apply for a licence for the route and had to compete with the state bus service, which was heavily subsidised,' says Paddy.

Undeterred, he pushed ahead and eighteen months later his licence was granted. This was a move that proved pivotal for the business, and one that gave Paddy the confidence to start a new and more ambitious chapter for Matthews Coach Hire.

But the next few months were challenging and severely tested both that decision and Paddy's resolve.

'In the beginning, the buses went up and down the motorway to Dublin every day almost empty. At the time, many people felt it wasn't cool to travel on a bus and preferred to take the train instead,' says Paddy.

The unfortunate collapse in August 2009 of a section of the viaduct at Malahide estuary on the main Dublin to Belfast train route changed that. Trains could no longer make the complete journey from Dundalk and Drogheda to Dublin, so passengers had no option but to finish the journey by bus. A growing number chose to use the bus for the entire journey rather than swap in Malahide, and so Paddy's coaches got the opportunity they needed to prove their worth.

'We began to market our service aggressively, emphasising that the price was half that of the train; that customers would always be guaranteed to get a seat; that all our buses had air conditioning and that they were twenty minutes faster than the train. In addition, we became the first bus company to offer free WiFi,' explains Paddy.

Paddy's business began to prosper. Even when the recession kicked in, it could not defeat his positive attitude and problem-solving capability.

'When the Celtic Tiger died in Ireland, our business took off,' explains Paddy. 'The downturn saw many workers suffer a drop in wages, which meant many were forced to get rid of their second car. And so more and more people who had been driving to Dublin every day, decided to take the bus.' Doing so meant they no longer needed to fund the costs associated with running a car such as insurance, tax, tyres and servicing, as well as rising parking and toll charges. Even better, the introduction of the government's new annual Taxsaver ticket meant that bus passengers could recoup half the cost of their annual ticket.

'Apart from increased business, the Taxsaver ticket meant that we were now getting a significant amount of our annual turnover paid upfront at the beginning of the year, a godsend in terms of cash flow,' says Paddy.

The downturn also brought a dramatic change in the number of college students who could afford to live in Dublin full time. Instead, it became cheaper for them to move home and travel to college by bus on a daily basis, rather than pay for rent and food in the city. To cater for this growing student market Paddy began running daily services to Dublin City

University, University College Dublin and a number of other city centre colleges.

Again Paddy realised that because colleges were closed during the summer months, he had to find alternative ways to utilise his fleet during this period. So he began targeting sporting organisations, corporate conferences and music events. From there, he started his own tour company, initially organising day shopping trips to Belfast, and later sightseeing tours of places such as Glendalough and Kilkenny city.

In 2012 Paddy expanded this part of the business and began targeting the USA with authentic Irish-themed tours focused around history, horses, music and whiskey tasting. More recently, he launched Matthews Golf Tours.

There have been many bumps along the road for the Monaghan entrepreneur. Up to 2008 the government had been operating a fuel rebate scheme that provided excise duty reliefs on fuel used for scheduled transport services, school transport services and tour group rates. At the time the rate of excise duty on road diesel was 36.8 cents per litre of which 34.5 cents per litre was refunded to qualifying public transport service providers. However, in 2008, the government discontinued this scheme for private operators as it was seen not to be in compliance with EU regulations. The loss, which amounted to almost €350,000 a year for the company, had the potential to damage the business.

Instead, Paddy took a different approach. 'I divided the number of buses we had and the number of trips we made every year. I worked out that if we were able to increase our passenger numbers by just two per trip, we could make up for the deficit,' he explains.

The size of the loss seemed almost insurmountable at first,

but once Paddy had broken it into what he felt were achievable goals, the entire company worked together to increase passenger numbers.

'What started as a potentially damaging blow to the company actually ended up becoming a positive motivating factor in growing our business,' says Paddy.

Innovation has also been key to Paddy's long-term strategy. Setting out to become Ireland's cleanest and greenest passenger transport service, Paddy fitted all his coaches with the latest fuel saving technology, while each driver was trained to reduce fuel consumption and CO_2 emissions.

'The real success came, however, when I introduced a leaderboard system where drivers were rated by the amount of fuel they used. We then linked their annual bonus to their success in achieving greater fuel efficiencies. This created a competitive environment where drivers were challenged to improve their own performances against the performance of other drivers.'

In a stroke of genius, Paddy had found a way to reward his drivers for the very behaviour he wished to promote.

Paddy is also quick to credit his staff for their friendliness towards passengers, something he believes has been key to the company's ongoing success.

Twenty-five years ago Paddy Matthews faced the real threat that he might never work again. Since then, he has consistently demonstrated the characteristics of a great entrepreneur: a determination to succeed, resilience in overcoming adversity and a commitment to innovation and continuous improvement.

It's easy to understand what Paddy Matthews means now when he says he is living the dream.

Paddy's Advice for Other Businesses

Trust yourself

Trust yourself and your instincts, even in the face of what seems like contrary advice. It may take time for your ideas to work out but if you know your business and believe in what you are trying to accomplish, success will come.

Create the right ethos and company culture

It is important to establish the correct culture in your company. You achieve this by setting and following high standards and always trying to improve. Always try to be better tomorrow than you were yesterday.

Set goals constantly

Continuously set goals for yourself, your company and your team. This keeps the business moving forward and your staff motivated.

CHAPTER 6

FROM LITTLE ACORNS DO MIGHTY OAKS GROW

– The Story of Avoca

AVOCA

www.avoca.com

What started in 1723 as a small hand-weaving mill in the village of Avoca in County Wicklow has grown to become one of Ireland's best-known and most-loved retail companies. Known simply as Avoca, the company employs 1,000 staff, operates outlets in twelve locations throughout Ireland and this year will see its turnover top more than €75 million.

It is difficult to sum up the business in a single sentence, but Simon Pratt, the company's former managing director, describes Avoca as a blended mix of retailer, wholesaler, manufacturer and food producer.

'A customer once described the experience of browsing through our stores as being similar to exploring a treasure trove. You find something new every time,' he says.

There certainly is an eclectic feel to the place, with shoppers buying everything from fashion, knitwear and jewellery to homeware, ceramics and the company's now famous rugs and throws. There's even a bookstore where you can buy, among other things, the company's own cookbooks.

No wonder Avoca was recently voted Ireland's Store of the Year, as well as being selected by international trade magazine *Retail Week* as one of the '100 Most Inspirational Stores' in the world – right up there with Bloomingdales in the US.

'The company dates back to 1723,' explains Simon. 'The village of Avoca was, at that time, home to Europe's largest copper mine. A mill was set up locally to grind corn for the workers. Over time the mill began weaving fabric, by hand, to make clothing for the workers and their families. That's where the name Avoca Hand Weavers originally came from.'

In 1974 Simon's parents, Donald and Hilary Pratt, bought the old mill which was, by then, almost defunct.

'My father had been a lawyer up to that point. He was more of a risk-taker than my mother and she often reminds him how she thought he was out of his mind to buy the place,' laughs Simon. 'However, once the decision was made, they both threw themselves into the business.'

The enterprising couple began selling fabric from the back of their car. When efforts to attract international wholesale buyers to their mill failed, they decided to open a purpose-built showroom closer to Dublin, in Kilmacanogue. The outlet became a great success, attracting not only wholesalers but local shoppers as well.

With their business taking off, the couple decided it was time to diversify, and began manufacturing clothing from the fabric they wove. As more customers arrived, they began introducing more products, such as ceramics and knitwear sourced from other producers.

Over time Donald and Hilary came to the realisation that in order to differentiate themselves from other craft shops, they would have to start developing their own branded products. 'In that way they were able to build their brand while becoming masters of their own margin,' explains Simon.

Simon joined the business full time in 1990, having studied

business and politics in Trinity College Dublin. He was joined soon afterwards by his sister Amanda. She had a flair for design and helped develop the company's own range of products, including fashion, rugs, scarves, candles, soaps, ceramics and knitwear.

'It's always been our philosophy to follow the light,' explains Simon. 'We try new things and if they work, we keep doing them. If they don't, we stop and move on.'

One thing that did work was their decision to introduce food into their stores.

'Most women like to shop, but we realised that, by offering food, we could create a place where men would also come,' explains Simon. 'Food became integral to our stores. In fact, it was the game changer.'

The store in which I meet Simon, Rathcoole, has two restaurants offering table service and self-service, and, at peak time, can cater for 400 customers. The store has its own bakery where bread is baked fresh every morning from 5 a.m. onwards, a fresh fruit and veg section, and an area selling ready-to-go meals. These ready-to-go meals were being made in the individual stores until Simon realised this was no longer cost effective and so invested in a new purpose-built central kitchen to service all the company's outlets.

'We were determined to retain the authenticity and quality of our produce and so we moved some of our very best chefs and bakers to work in this area of the business,' he explains.

Although a relatively new phenomenon in the retail trade, there are now a number of food concession businesses that have become an integral part of the Avoca success story. These operate as separate businesses under their individual brands and instead of rent, pay a percentage of their turnover to Avoca.

These include James Whelan's Butchers, the Poulet Bonne Femme Chicken Rotisserie, the Michie Sushi Bar, the Sprout Juice and Salad Bar, and Nature's Gold health food store. The upside for the company is that they add a wide range of food options for Avoca customers.

'The key challenge is definitely the labour-intensive nature of the business,' Simon explains. 'We do things the long way here, like using real flour when we make bread or peeling potatoes from scratch. This gives us a lot more work to do and a higher labour requirement but the positive aspect is that it gives us full control of the production process.

'It's hard to grow a family-run business like ours without access to external capital for investment and expansion. Big businesses can issue bonds, whereas smaller businesses rely on access to bank borrowings. Trying to fund the opening of a new store from retained profits definitely makes expansion a much slower process,' he admits.

To counteract the recent downturn in the economy, when discretionary incomes were hit, Simon made sure that each store stocked product ranges that were in the more affordable category. The result ensured that footfall held firm.

Not content to stand still, and continuing to see opportunities in the market, the company recently opened Salt, a food-only, stand-alone store in Monkstown, south Dublin. Simon talks excitedly about how he envisages such food markets and cafés becoming a part of the company's future growth strategy.

Avoca has retained all the hallmarks of a family-run business. Until recently, Simon's parents, Donald and Hilary were still involved, as were his sisters Amanda and Vanessa and his brother, Ivan. Together, they succeeded in building an iconic

Irish brand and a winning formula for retail success that would be at home in just about any part of the world.

In January 2016 the Pratt family sold the business to US multinational Aramark for €65 million. Aramark has committed to continuing to grow Avoca as an independent business both in Ireland and overseas. Only months later the biggest Avoca store to date was opened in Dunboyne, County Meath, costing over €3 million and spanning 35,000 square feet of retail space.

The company's journey has seen Avoca grow from a tiny business with just a handful of staff to a national and now globally recognised brand. Central to its continued growth has been the relentless focus on innovation and the willingness to embrace new ideas. It was one of those ideas in particular – the introduction of food into its product offering – that eventually helped propel Avoca to the great success it has now become.

Simon's Advice for Other Businesses

Business is not about the single sale

Retail is generally a low-margin business. For that reason, success is not about getting a single sale; it is about building a long-term relationship with your customers. Developing repeat business is one of the most important goals for any company to focus on.

Treat your staff well

It is important to treat your staff with respect and thoughtfulness – the way you would like them to treat your customers. People learn more from example than from preaching. Set your own best example so that staff both know and feel the experience of being treated well.

Learn to make decisions quickly

If you know in your heart that a tough decision has to be made, then, after giving it due thought and consideration, do it quickly and do not prevaricate. Dithering in the face of difficult decisions often allows a problem to get worse and does little to build other peoples' confidence in your leadership and management abilities. Gather the facts and then act.

CHAPTER 7

NEVER GIVE UP ON YOUR DREAM

– The Story of Timbertrove

www.timbertrove.com

Henry and Shirley O'Kelly from the company Timbertrove are wonderful examples of the resilience required to run a small business. Established in 1986 and located just below the Hellfire Club in Rathfarnham with magnificent views over Dublin, Timbertrove started out making garden sheds, before diversifying into other timber products such as fencing, playground equipment and wooden furniture. More recently, they added a country store and café, and now employ thirty-five staff with an annual turnover of over €2.3 million.

Like many other businesses, the last few years have brought incredible challenges. The couple saw their turnover all but disappear and lost their family's savings in an effort to keep their business afloat. Through it all, their indomitable spirit and absolute determination to survive has seen them reinvent their business and find new opportunities for growth.

Henry O'Kelly grew up on a small farm close to where the business is now located. His father also ran a local plant hire business to make ends meet. At the early age of fifteen, having developed a love of machinery, Henry left school to join the family business. In his spare time and to make extra money he cut silage for local farmers and dug foundations for new houses being built in the area.

'Because I had grown up surrounded by trees, I decided to combine my interest in machinery with my love of timber and in 1986 I set up a small sawmill business,' explains Henry. 'I had very little money and the only thing I really owned at the time was an old red tractor.'

Henry's business model was simple. He bought trees from Coillte (the government's commercial forestry business), cut them into planks and sold them to local contractors involved in the building business. The problem was that he wasn't making much profit.

'Eventually it dawned on me that if I made something out of the timber myself first before selling it, I would make a much higher margin than simply selling planks. That's when I started to make my own range of quality garden sheds. Instead of getting €20 or €30 per sale, I was now getting up to €500.'

Shirley grew up in Churchtown in south Dublin, where her family ran a well-known motorcycle shop. She, too, left school at fifteen, to take up a job in a local motor company. There, she worked her way up from a role in sales to become transport manager and, eventually, general manager of the business. Having met Henry, she left to join his business full time. She looked after the finances while he concentrated on operational matters. Over time, Henry's natural flair for design led him to diversify into other products including fencing, dog kennels, garden furniture, wooden gates, decking and customised timber features. The business was growing steadily.

By the early 2000s the house-building boom was also in full swing.

'We began building up a strong customer base among many

of the country's top builders and developers,' explains Henry. 'In addition to garden sheds, we were supplying the fencing that separated the houses on sites – up to as many as 500 homes on a single site. We even began making playground furniture, winning major contracts with the likes of Dublin Zoo and Fota Wildlife Park. Everything was going well. And at that point, we had fifty employees and a turnover of more than €4 million.'

However, the collapse of the construction sector in 2008 saw sales evaporate almost overnight.

'We fought hard but eventually had to make redundancies, which was heartbreaking,' admits Henry. 'I went back on the tools and back into the workshop where I had started all those years earlier. But that's what we had to do to survive.'

In an effort to sell the sheds they had already made, as well as drum up orders for new ones, they booked a small stand at the annual Ploughing Championships, where Henry focused on selling the sheds, while Shirley and their now three young children sold a range of gifts to make sure that at least the costs of the show were covered.

'As hard as we tried, people just weren't in the market to buy garden sheds. With discretionary income tight, they weren't seen as essential items,' explains Shirley.

However, they were determined to keep on fighting. In the run-up to Christmas that year, Henry and Shirley decided to put on a magical Santa experience – building a Christmas Village from the garden sheds they had made and couldn't sell. While it turned out to be a roaring success and helped them get through the winter season, the business overall was still leaking cash. At that point they made the tough decision to invest all their savings in an effort to continue to pay staff and keep the business afloat.

'Ultimately, we ended up losing everything,' admits Shirley solemnly.

It wasn't just their business that was badly affected. The whole experience affected Henry and Shirley personally. Married with three young children and working 24/7, they spent years living in constant fear and trepidation.

'It changes your personality,' admits Henry honestly.

By 2012 and with the business on its last legs, Henry and Shirley knew that they had to make one last-ditch effort if they were to turn things around.

'That's when we decided to turn off the TV and stop listening to the news,' explains Shirley. 'Instead, we began reading business management and personal development books and focused only on what we could do to change our own situation,' she adds. 'Given the scenic area in which we are located, we decided to open a café to service the growing number of walkers, cyclists and tourists. It was this that eventually saved the business. Who would ever have thought that a café could turn around a sawmill? But it did and now our top-selling product is a scone.'

More recently, the pair set up a country store and gift shop on the site. The combined result is now a thriving retail destination that opens seven days a week, attracting as many as 4,000 customers a month. They are excited too that their eldest daughter, Danielle, has recently joined the business as Business Development Manager. With a business degree and a year spent working in San Francisco in a similar retail company, she is now bringing her own flair to the business.

Their mood is different now and their outlook brighter. The recent increase in new house building has brought about a welcome increase in sales of their garden sheds and timber products. Life hasn't gotten much easier for the pair, but things have at least stabilised and they can now see a future for themselves and the business.

'I came across this quote recently which I think really sums up our own story,' explains Shirley. It reads: 'One of the best feelings in the world is watching things finally start falling into place having watched them fall apart for so long.'

Henry and Shirley's Advice for Other Businesses

Positivity and self-improvement

Don't engage with negative people. Instead, focus on developing your own positivity. Learn to be optimistic in the face of challenges and train yourself to look for solutions rather than focusing on problems. Study and learn from other successful entrepreneurs who have been where you now are.

Quality

Strive to be unique in the level of product quality and customer service you provide. This will deliver results in the long term through increased loyalty and repeat business from satisfied customers. It will also help with generating new business through referrals.

Change

Business, like life, is constantly evolving and changing. To survive, you have to learn to innovate and adapt to the market. When things go wrong, you have to be willing to think outside the box in order to find new opportunities and new ways forward.

CHAPTER 8

THE CREAM ALWAYS RISES TO THE TOP

– The Story of Glenilen Farm

www.glenilenfarm.com

Alan and Valerie Kingston's family farm is located in Drimoleague in beautiful West Cork. It is here that the couple run Glenilen Farm, a farm-based business specialising in the production of yoghurts, cheesecakes, desserts, creams and butter.

'It's an idyllic location for dairy farming,' says Alan. 'The lush hills of Drimoleague offer our cows a rich supply of nutritious grass, and they supply us with the rich tasty milk that goes to make our delicious products.'

The farm has been in Alan's family for generations. While he loved farming, Alan was always open to exploring other opportunities. And one such opportunity came along when he met and married Valerie. Valerie was a farmer's daughter from Macroom in County Cork. Having studied Food Science Technology at University College Cork, she worked for a number of years with Dairygold in their research and development division. It was during a two-year stint volunteering in the poorest areas of West Africa, however, that Valerie was first introduced to small-scale butter, cheese and yoghurt production. There, she helped manage a food development project encouraging local farmers to start small dairy enterprises as a more sustainable alternative to their traditional nomadic way of life and one that created a more stable environment and allowed children to attend school more regularly.

The couple married in 1997 and Valerie decided to be a stay-at-home mom. To facilitate this, she started a business from her own kitchen, using milk from the farm to make yoghurt and cheesecakes, which she sold in local markets. Alan didn't pay much attention to her enterprising skills until one August bank holiday weekend when he realised the potential of her endeavours. That weekend she returned from the farmers' market in Bantry having turned two large saucepans of milk into €110 cash.

'It was only then that I fully realised the potential for adding value to the milk we were producing,' says Alan. 'From that moment on, I fell in love with my cows all over again.'

'And from that moment on I was no longer on my own,' says Valerie.

In 2002 the couple began supplying local shops such as SuperValu and Spar. 'Things grew steadily from there,' she adds.

Because they couldn't afford expensive marketing campaigns, they relied instead on word of mouth to spread their reputation.

'Our growth was more reactive than proactive because we were responding to demand rather than driving it,' explains Valerie.

'We found local farmers' markets a valuable outlet and a great way to get customer feedback, which helped us decide on new products,' adds Alan.

'The River Ilen runs through the farm and we also have a glen which can be seen from the house. While we were trying to come up with a name for the business, we looked out the window and decided to put the two together to create Glenilen,' the pair explain.

In 2008 Alan and Valerie took the courageous step of building a new 12,500 square-foot food unit on the farm. The move enabled them to bring together all components of their rapidly expanding business, including production, packaging, storage and office administration.

'It was also great for our children to get the kitchen back as a family space,' laughs Valerie.

With this new facility in place, the business was able to scale up production. As a result, they soon got their next big break when they were listed with many of the country's large multiples (supermarket chains). This meant that their products were added to the central list of products that any store in a group or chain of stores could order from their central distribution. (While independent store owners can largely stock what they like on their shelves, those in a group or branded chain of stores are mostly required to order through this central distribution system.)

In 2010, with the help of Bord Bia (Ireland's state-run food board), the company launched into the UK, where they began by focusing on high-end stores such as Selfridges, Harvey Nichols, Waitrose, Booths and Whole Foods Market. From just twenty Waitrose stores initially, they now have listings in over 220. They went on to launch other successful ranges including single serve desserts and 'Thick & Fruity' yoghurts.

'Our products are authentically farm-based and the taste reflects the fact that the milk is from our own and neighbouring farms,' Valerie says. 'We don't use any additives. Simplicity is at the heart of everything we do.'

But such growth can bring challenges.

'Scaling a business like ours is a balancing act,' says Alan.

'We work to achieve growth, but we also have to retain the quality that is an integral part of our core ethos as an artisan farm-based business.'

Today the couple employ forty staff and have a turnover of over €5 million.

'A brand like ours is like an iceberg,' adds Valerie. 'What most people see is only a small portion of the operation. The real success lies in what people don't see; the passion of our staff, the attention that goes into making our products and the integrity we strive for in dealing with all our staff, suppliers and customers. And finding the right people is crucial. In the beginning, we couldn't really afford to hire them. Now, we couldn't afford to be without them,' she says.

They have set a target that ten per cent of each year's turnover will come from new products developed in that year.

'There's no room for sitting still,' insists Alan. 'Customers and retailers are constantly looking for new products and, as a result, innovation has become a key part of our operation.'

The many awards and accolades that decorate the walls of their offices demonstrate the success of Glenilen Farm, including being one of the finalists in the Ernst & Young Entrepreneur of the Year Awards in 2012. The couple are expanding the factory again, adding a new administration block and viewing facilities for group tours keen to learn about food production in the most authentic of settings.

'We just received news of our largest single listing to date of 150 Sainsbury's stores in the UK,' says Valerie excitedly. 'And we are also investing a further €1 million in new packaging equipment which will allow greater efficiencies as well as an extension of our shelf-life – something that will allow us to enter new markets.'

Alan and Valerie's faith is important to them. It guides them and provides a greater purpose to everything they do. They feel honoured to be stewards of the land they farm and have a definite sense of responsibility towards the staff they employ and the charities they support in places such as Uganda and Sri Lanka, which provide education, health and clean water to those in need.

Alan and Valerie have grown a successful business by adding value to what they were already producing. They have tapped into a growing market where consumers want additive-free, farm-produced products, and they have focused on both quality and innovation as the cornerstones of their business.

Most of all, they have passion for what they do and integrity in the way they do it. And through it all they have remained true to the values of the faith that guides them.

Valerie and Alan's Advice for Other Businesses

Bring experienced professionals on board

Lots of small businesses make great products, but taking it from farmers' market level to dealing with large chains or multiples takes a lot of skill. Bring good people on board who have experience of working in larger organisations and can help you compete on a new level.

Success often comes from the things customers don't see

Having a great product is only a small part of a bigger picture. You also have to provide a great service through your IT systems, packaging, logistics and invoicing. These are all things your customers don't see, but are often the factors that differentiate you from your competitors and can lead to your ultimate success.

Your product comes first

If you are developing a five-year plan, the most important target is that your products and services should be better in five years' time than they are now. Sound financials and turnover are important, but the quality of your products must be to the fore.

CHAPTER 9

EVERY CLOUD HAS A SILVER LINING

– The Story of EMIT

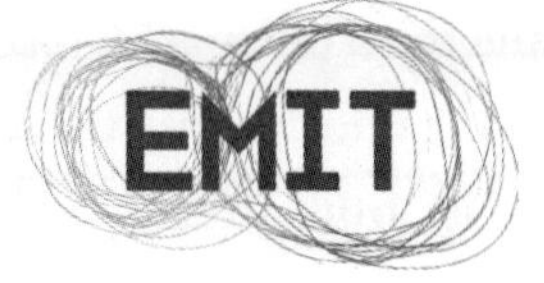

www.emitsolutions.ie

IT equipment, systems and services now underpin almost every modern business function. From sending and receiving emails to storing and protecting information, IT is at the heart of almost everything we do. But while advances in technology have resulted in many benefits for businesses, they have also brought with them additional complex challenges: what hardware to choose, which systems to opt for and how to integrate all these different elements?

Eamon Moore is one man who knows the answers to these challenges. Set up in 2003, his award-winning IT company, EMIT, now employs twenty staff and has an annual turnover of €2 million.

'We are a lead partner for both Dell and Microsoft in Ireland,' enthuses Eamon when we meet in his offices in Northwood Business Campus in Santry, on the northside of Dublin. 'Unlike most traditional IT companies, we focus strategically on the integration of IT with the key business objectives of our clients.'

Eamon goes on to explain that the business is built around four key pillars. The first of these is IT infrastructure, where the company supply, install and support everything from PCs and laptops to switches and servers. Secondly, they provide Microsoft-based cloud computing services, which enable companies to move their data from the companies' own servers to the Cloud, where it is stored securely in data centres managed 24/7 by Microsoft. The third pillar is IT security. Driven largely by an increase in hacking and security risks, the company helps clients protect their data from threats both within their businesses and external to them.

'We were the first in Ireland to launch our "Firewall as a Service" offering. This allows businesses to outsource their security to a specialist company on a monthly subscription basis. We then provide them with monthly security reports, including statistics on any potential threats across all their internal as well as their remote networks or mobile technologies,' explains Eamon.

Finally, the fourth pillar of the company, business productivity, involves providing software that offers greater operational efficiencies. These include Customer Relationship Management (CRM) systems that allow sales staff to manage leads and track customers from initial enquiry to final delivery of products or services.

'Using Excel sheets is fine for gathering information, but importing this type of data into a CRM allows businesses to interrogate it and produce all manner of useful reports and statistics. While most owners and managers of businesses still use their gut to make decisions, having intelligent data such as this can help improve the quality of their business decisions,' says Eamon.

The company's customers are predominantly SMEs, with staff numbers from fifteen up to 500. These are drawn from a variety of industries that include professional services, not-for-profit, technology, the financial sector and semi-state bodies.

More recently, too, the company has become active in other sectors such as construction, engineering and distribution and logistics.

Eamon Moore grew up in Beaumont, in Dublin's northside. Aged fifteen and still in secondary school, he got a part-time job in the IT department of CSK Software – a Dermot Desmond-supported company. Excited by what he learned there, he went on to complete a degree in computer applications at Dublin City University (DCU) in 2002. Jobs in the IT sector at the time were scarce, due largely to the fall-out from the bursting of the dot.com bubble two years previously. And, while this was bad enough, 2002 brought great personal heartbreak for the young Dubliner.

'My mother died that summer after a lengthy battle with cancer, something that hit my sister and me very hard,' explains Eamon. 'Her dying wish had been that I would pass my final exams. So the day of her funeral was a bittersweet occasion because that day I received my college results – first class honours – something that would have made her very happy indeed,' he adds.

A few weeks later Finbarr Crowley, the managing partner of the legal firm looking after his mother's affairs, rang to say that his firm were looking for IT support and asked if he would consider working two days a week for them.

'He had one condition, though, and that was that I had to become a business or sole trader rather than an employee. I didn't really understand why at first,' explains Eamon. 'It was only years later that he told me he felt I was destined to work for myself and wanted to give me a push in that direction. Using my mother's dining room table as my office, EMIT [Eamon Moore IT] Solutions was born. Within a few months, word spread to other companies and soon my diary began to fill up. I was now in business for myself.'

Over time, Eamon expanded both his client base and his team. The downturn in the economy that followed ironically helped in this regard, as more and more businesses opted to outsource their IT needs rather than hire full-time staff.

In 2012 Eamon enrolled on a course in cloud strategy, something that was to completely change his thinking about the future of the IT sector generally and his own business in particular.

'I had long held the belief that I didn't want the company to be a traditional IT business, selling hardware and break/fix contracts. But up to that point, I had been grabbing all types of business and offering far too many different services just to keep growing. I realised at that point that if I was going to be successful, I needed to develop a more focused strategy and that cloud computing needed to be at the heart of this,' says Eamon. 'That's when, after a bit of soul-searching, combined with some further research, we launched our current four-pillar strategy,' he adds.

Part of this focused strategy saw him concentrate on two key partnerships: Dell and Microsoft. Around the same time, Michael Dell himself began to take an interest in what Eamon was doing.

'He picked up on one of my blog posts, sent me a LinkedIn message and has since become a big supporter of ours,' explains Eamon proudly. 'We also had similar success with Microsoft. Having started to grow our Office 365 business quickly, Microsoft's HQ in Seattle produced a video case study on our business, which they profiled at their World Partner Conference in Orlando, something that helped us become a Microsoft

Gold partner shortly after. Having that title means that we have earned the highest standards of Microsoft's widely-recognised partnership program.'

In October 2015 the company went on to be awarded Dell's Global Social Media Partner of the Year and shortly afterwards picked up Dell's Security Award for New Partner of the Year for Ireland. Less than twelve months later they were also awarded Microsoft Global Partner of the Year for Small & Midmarket Cloud Solutions, making them only the second Irish company ever to win a Microsoft Global award.

'It's really been a joint effort from a very dedicated and loyal team,' insists Eamon. To his delight, things came full circle for him when he appointed a non-executive chairman to his board – his former mentor, Finbarr Crowley.

Eamon is now focused on scaling up the business even further. He wants to position EMIT as the partner of choice for both Microsoft and Dell in Ireland, and sees expansion coming by way of continued growth as well as through a mix of external investment and acquisition. In line with this he recently acquired the managed services business and customer base of IT service provider Softech, increasing his customer base to over 3,500 end users and adding a further €2 million in revenue to the business over the next three years. In addition, he has also recently made a number of senior appointments, including a new sales director and chief technology officer to help drive future growth.

As I leave his office, Eamon hands me his business card and points to the company's main office phone number – it is his late mother's home phone number. Today, it serves as a reminder to him of how this all started and of his mother's positive and lasting influence on his life.

Eamon's Advice for Other Businesses

Focus on your strengths

Focus on your personal strengths and what you do best in business. Part of being successful is learning when to say no to opportunities that do not take you in the direction you want to go. This can be prospective customers, new technologies or potential partnerships.

Don't be afraid to try new things

Change is everywhere. It is constant and it is good. Welcome it rather than fight against it. Those who do not adapt to changes in market conditions or customer demands run the risk of being left behind. Even if things don't work out, use these as valuable learning experiences and opportunities to do better next time.

You just can't beat experience

Surround yourself with great people, whether this is your team members, board directors, partners or mentors. There is so much to be learned from others with more experience than yourself. Being open to advice can deliver positive outcomes for your business.

CHAPTER 10

ALL FOR ONE
– The Story of One4all

www.one4all.ie

Giving gifts is a universally established practice that demonstrates appreciation and gratitude for those we care about. Often, though, we can struggle to find time to buy such gifts or we may be uncertain about what to actually buy someone. So our best intentions regularly remain just that – intentions.

It was such a scenario that led Michael Dawson to set up his own business, The Gift Voucher Shop, in 2002. Months earlier he had missed buying a gift for his mother. While he knew what he wanted to buy her, he had simply been too busy to travel across the city to complete the purchase. The experience made him realise that there was a gap in the market for quality gift vouchers that could be redeemed across a wide range of outlets. Fifteen years on, One4all gift voucher cards have become the leading brand for gift givers in Ireland, as well as having operations in the UK and Malta.

Employing seventy-five staff and with an annual turnover of more than €260 million, Michael's success clearly demonstrates what can be achieved when you have a clear vision and the relentless determination to pursue it.

'Our big picture vision is to spread happiness through

thoughtful, versatile gifting solutions,' says Michael. 'We are especially proud that our gift cards are now available online as well as in more than 18,000 outlets throughout the country, including post offices and Topaz filling stations.'

The company recently introduced an innovative feature to their online offering that allows customers to take a photograph of themselves, a friend or loved one and then upload it to create a personalised gift card, complete with their own message.

'It's a first in Europe and customers are loving the fact that these personalised cards are delivered within twenty-four hours,' he explains.

Corporate sales have also become a large part of his business, with many companies choosing gift cards instead of cash or other gifts, especially at Christmas time.

'Our cards are eligible under the Benefit in Kind tax savings scheme that allows employers to give up to €500 worth of a gift to employees. Many companies are now realising that our cards are a practical and versatile way of rewarding their staff,' he adds.

In addition to promoting their cards, the company also works directly with corporate clients to manage internal employee loyalty programmes and points-based reward schemes.

For Michael Dawson, it has been a long journey to success and one that has been hard fought. Growing up in Baldoyle in north County Dublin, Michael's first foray into the world of business came at a very early age when he ran the school sweet shop in his local primary school. When he left school he got a job as a youth worker with the Department of Education in Ballyfermot, before going on to work for Fianna Fáil as the party's national organiser. After the general election of 1989 he was appointed for a short time to the senate. But while he greatly enjoyed the experience, the pull of business was stronger. The following year, in the midst of the frenzy that gripped the country during the soccer World Cup, Italia '90, Michael spotted an opportunity to start his own business.

'Many people were complaining that they either couldn't afford to travel to Italy or couldn't get tickets for the matches, so I decided to bring the matches to Dublin – on large screens,' explains Michael. 'I had four gigantic video screens installed in the RDS exhibition and conference centre, around which we built a real Italian experience, complete with food and music. I even flew in medieval flag throwers from Florence to add to the atmosphere.'

The event proved an overwhelming success, with more than 48,000 fans turning up.

The following year, with his confidence still running high, Michael decided to try his hand at another new venture. Having seen the popularity of drive-in movies in the US, he decided to bring the concept to Ireland. That summer he invested in setting up large movie screens in Dublin's Phoenix Park, the largest enclosed public park in any capital city in Europe. Unfortunately, this time things didn't go his way. The summer turned out to be one of the wettest on record and not only did it wash away any hopes for Michael's new concept, it also eroded all the money he had made the previous year.

Bruised but undeterred, he went in search of the next big idea. This time he turned his attention to the growing lottery card sector and having extensively researched the market, developed and patented a series of musical-based lottery cards. Confident that the market for these lay in the US, he spent the next six years commuting back and forth in an effort to break into the market.

'It wasn't an easy time as I was away a lot from my late wife, Pauline, and our three young sons,' remembers Michael.

Despite his best efforts, he couldn't raise the investment he needed to make the venture work and, after only limited success, decided it was time to call it a day and return home.

'I was totally broke by then,' admits Michael. 'In order to make ends meet, we had to turn our home into a bed and breakfast.'

Even with his many setbacks, Michael was not about to give in. Before long, he had moved on to his next business idea – prepaid gift voucher cards.

'The concept for One4all gift cards was borne out of necessity. I had been tasked by my wife to get a hotel voucher for my mother as a Christmas gift. Because we lived in Malahide and the hotel was on the other side of the city, Christmas came and went without me having an opportunity to get it,' admits Michael. 'When Christmas was over, I began to wonder why, in the modern age, it wasn't possible to simply buy a voucher in my local shop or even online that could be used for such a purpose.'

All his research led him to the overwhelming conclusion that this was a killer idea. But, in spite of spending all the money he could gather at the time on promoting it, things were slow to take off.

'We knew we had a revolutionary product, but it took almost three years before we were generating enough sales to know we actually had a future – a stark lesson as to just how slow and difficult it can be to change people's buying habits,' admits Michael. 'There were other setbacks too. We launched our fundraising drive just two days before 9/11, so we ended up only raising half of what we were looking for. In hindsight, this turned out a blessing, in that it forced us to build a very lean start-up – an approach that has stood to us ever since.'

To scale up the business, Michael took the strategic decision to partner with Ireland's state-owned postal service, An Post. A highly trusted brand with an existing network of over 1,200 outlets, An Post came with the added benefit that its staff are experienced in handling money. The strategy proved so successful that An Post later became a major investor and the company's largest shareholder.

In 2004 the company launched in Malta and two years later in the UK where, in addition to selling their own branded gift cards, they now administer budget cards on behalf of the British Post Office. In 2015 their corporate sales side of the business, One4all Rewards, experienced unprecedented growth, in part due to the increase by the Minister for Finance of the threshold for corporate gifts to employees from €250 to €500.

'The business is not all about me,' insists Michael. 'We have a great team who are critical to our success, and I am incredibly proud of their achievements but also their commitment to corporate social responsibility, which has become embedded as a core part of our culture.'

As part of their desire to give back, Michael and his staff cycle to raise money for development projects in Haiti, an initiative set up by past participants in the Ernst & Young Entrepreneur of the Year Awards, in which Michael was a finalist in 2007. For the past five years, too, they have managed the Junior Entrepreneurs Programme, a national initiative started by Kerry entrepreneur Jerry Kennelly, which supports over 1,200 children in school-based enterprise education programmes throughout north County Dublin.

Michael Dawson has much of which to be proud. In

particular, he is proud that he has been able to spread happiness through gift giving, and that he has been able to create jobs in his local area. While nothing came easy for him, it was overcoming these very challenges that has enabled him to reach where he is now. You can't but feel that he has earned every success that has come his way.

Michael's Advice for Other Businesses

It takes time

However long you expect it will take to get your business up and running – double it and double it again. Then you should be okay. You have to plan for such delays while at the same time continuing to push forward relentlessly.

Adequate start-up funding

It always takes more money to launch your business than you expect and you usually make less money than you initially envisaged. If possible, and to ensure security, aim to have enough funding in the beginning to get your business to a profitable and secure position as quickly as possible.

Build management capability early on

It is important to surround yourself with good people, especially in the early days. Also, pull together an advisory board that you can use as a sounding board or as mentors. There are many experienced people out there who are willing to offer support – but you have to be prepared to ask.

CHAPTER 11

MAN ON A MISSION
– The Story of Horseware

www.horseware.com

If medals were awarded for perseverance and tenacity in business, then Louth-based entrepreneur Tom McGuiness deserves gold. As founder and managing director of Horseware Ireland, Tom has faced more than his fair share of challenges and disasters. But faith in himself and in God has given him the power to overcome.

Thirty years ago Tom started a small sideline business sewing horse blankets by hand and has since grown the company to become a world leader in equine products. Today he employs over 750 staff around the world and has annual revenues of more than €45 million. His Dundalk-based global headquarters is just one of a number of factories the company now owns across Ireland, the US, China and Cambodia. In the showroom, life-size horse mannequins are draped in beautifully engineered horse rugs designed to keep horses protected from flies and bugs as well as from exposure to the sun or excessive cold weather. There are other accessories too, including head collars, bridles, saddles and horse boots. The company also produces an extensive range of clothing and accessories for riders.

Tom's is an unusual story. He grew up in Dundalk, where his family ran a riding school. He went to agricultural college in Tyrone but felt it wasn't for him and decided instead to go to the missions. 'I had what you might call a spiritual experience,' explains Tom, 'and it changed my life.'

He spent the next eight years serving as a missionary, mostly in South America. 'I had no money and I lived only on my faith,' he says. 'I got very used to believing that things would somehow work out and that the universe would conspire to do me good. And it usually did.'

Tom's faith remains a big part of his life.

In 1979 he returned to Ireland, where he met and married Carol, an American who had come to study in the country. In time, Tom took over his family's riding school, qualified as an instructor and was happy to spend his time between running the school and competing himself. Things changed, however, when the couple's first child was born.

'A sense of responsibility suddenly hit me,' says Tom. 'I realised I had to start thinking about how I could provide financial security for my family.'

The idea for his new business came to him shortly afterwards. This happened while he was putting a rug on a horse to keep him warm. The rug was old and worn, and Tom noticed how poorly made and unfit for purpose it was. Getting into bed later that night and pulling the duvet over him, he suddenly thought – why not make horse rugs from the same material duvets are made from? For the next twelve months, he worked on perfecting a design for a horse rug that would remain in place while the horse was in motion.

Around the same time, he also stumbled upon a book about starting a business. The chapter on market research motivated him to contact a number of horse owners he knew to get feedback on his idea. The response was so overwhelmingly positive that Tom went into production.

'The first 100 rugs weren't very pretty,' admits Tom. 'But they got me started. I later bought a sewing machine and taught myself how to sew. A year and a half later, I closed the riding school and converted it into a small factory, and Horseware Products Ltd was born.'

Tom's first big break came in 1990, when he discovered hydrophilic materials, a formulation that could be applied as a coating to a horse rug and would absorb water and moisture away from the horse's body, meaning the fabric was waterproof and breathable but did not make the horse sweat.

'I was so blown away with the results that I took every penny I had and placed the biggest advert I could afford in *Horse and Hound* magazine. The response was such that I could hardly make enough rugs to keep up with demand,' says Tom.

The company grew steadily, and over the next five years Horseware dominated the horse rug market in Ireland. Keen to break into the export market, Tom contacted everyone he knew who was exporting horses. Every time these horses left Ireland, Tom made sure that they arrived to their new owners wrapped in Horseware rugs. As a result, enquires began to flood in and before long he was exporting to Sweden, Denmark, France and Germany. In order to meet production requirements, he bought a new 30,000 square-foot factory in Dundalk and a second one soon after in the US.

'We realised that if we were serious about cracking the US market, we needed to have a presence there,' Tom explains.

Things were going well for Tom and his business until the first of two major disasters struck.

'The factory in the US was flattened by a hurricane. It was full of stock that we were getting ready to ship. Everything was destroyed,' says Tom.

Less than a year later came the second disaster – the factory in Dundalk burned down. This could have spelled the end for Tom but, determined to keep going, he set up in temporary premises, working two shifts to fulfil orders.

With manufacturing costs on the rise, Tom was eventually forced to get out of manufacturing and moved production to China. But his troubles didn't end.

'The bank decided to pull the plug and told me that they would no longer support me because I was manufacturing textiles and they had no faith in the sustainability of the sector,' says Tom. 'That's when I decided to invite my senior management team to buy into the business. It turned out to be the right move and from then on, things really took off.'

He attributes the success of the company to great staff and great managers who are focused on satisfying customers.

'We have invested heavily in process and control systems and we constantly innovate. Every part of the business is like a set of links in a chain, with each one dependent on the other,' says Tom.

Most of the company's growth has been organic, but Tom has bought a number of compatible businesses and brands and diversified within the equestrian sector into areas such as footwear and supplements. Outside the horse-ware sector, he recently launched CX+ Sport, a custom sportswear company which is on track to hit revenues of over €1 million in the next twelve months.

These days, Tom has his own Horseware polo team and also loves to jump.

'I am gradually removing myself from the day-to-day running of the business so I can focus more on the strategic direction of the company as well as on new product development,' explains Tom. 'It also gives me more time to indulge my passion for riding. I recently took up endurance riding and have now qualified for the European championships as well as the world games.'

But it's not all about business. Part of his faith is a desire to give back, and Tom has set up a project to develop solar kits for homes in areas of developing countries where there is no electricity. More recently, he built a school for the poor in Cambodia.

Tom McGuiness has made an incredible journey from missionary to successful entrepreneur. Through it all, he has never lost his desire to serve others. His example goes to prove that for many entrepreneurs, business is less about making money and more about making a difference.

Tom's Advice for Other Businesses

Be shrewd as snakes and harmless as doves

Jesus only ever gave one bit of direct business advice and it has helped me to strike a balance in my business affairs over the last thirty-five years. It was given to his seventy disciples before he sent them out on their first sales trip. He said, 'Look, I am sending you out as sheep among wolves. So be as shrewd as snakes and harmless as doves.' The world of business is a dangerous place. First be smart, because if you do the dumb-dove thing first, you won't survive long.

Develop a giving attitude

Develop an attitude of giving and constantly strive to add real value to your customers and to your staff. Remember too, that it costs between five and nine times more to get a new customer than it does to keep an existing one.

Be brave – and have fun

In business as in life, you have to be willing to take risks. Business involves facing many challenges and overcoming many obstacles and that takes courage. Don't be afraid to be brave but also remember to have fun along the way.

CHAPTER 12

A MARRIAGE MADE IN HOTEL HEAVEN

– The Story of Harvey's Point

www.harveyspoint.com

Tourists who visit Ireland regularly remark on how deeply impressed they are by the natural beauty and the genuine warmth of the Irish people. Nowhere is this heard more than from visiting County Donegal. It is there, located ten minutes' drive from Donegal town, on the shores of Lough Eske and at the foot of the Blue Stack Mountains, that you will find Harvey's Point resort hotel.

A hidden oasis nestled into a backdrop of mountain, tree and lake, this hotel is certainly something special. It was voted the No. 1 hotel in Ireland by TripAdvisor from 2013 to 2017 and won the Georgina Campbell 'Hotel of the Year' 2017. Run by Deirdre McGlone and her Swiss-born husband, Marc Gysling, the hotel consists of sixty-four rooms and suites, and has a real family feel to it.

Deirdre, who brims with zest and enthusiasm, explains that customers are drawn mostly from the Irish leisure market and include couples taking a break, as well as individuals and groups who come for golf, angling, hiking and surfing. Many others simply come to unwind and de-stress.

'We also have a thriving wedding business and a growing conference trade, and we are seeing an increase in visitors from the UK, mainland Europe and the US,' says Deirdre.

Staff are friendly and engaging, the décor is soothing and the traditional turf fires create an earthy smell and a homely feel. The ballroom is large, the bar a subtle mix of trendy and classical, and the restaurant, with its open kitchen, has magnificent views of Lough Eske. And the bedrooms are surprisingly large.

Over lunch, Deirdre takes a tour of tables in the restaurant, welcoming guests who have just arrived and thanking those who are leaving – with an invitation to return soon. It's easy to see that she loves what she does. And love too, has played a major part in how she and Marc ended up owning the hotel.

Harvey's Point was originally the brainchild of Deirdre's brother-in-law, Jody Gysling. From Switzerland, he first visited Donegal in 1983, fell in love with the county and ended up buying an old cottage on twenty acres of land. Jody did up the cottage and extended it to cater for the increasing number of his Swiss friends who wanted to come to fish, walk and drink beer. So frequent were their visits that Jody had the idea of building a small guesthouse. Soon, the guesthouse had turned into a twenty-bedroom hotel. Realising that he needed help, Jody reached out to his younger brother Marc, then living in Switzerland, and invited him to come and help.

Marc, with no previous cooking experience, started out in the kitchen, scrubbing pots and helping the chef. He quickly found a hidden talent and by 1995 had taken over as head chef.

Deirdre grew up not far from the hotel. Throughout her teenage years, she worked part-time in local bars and restaurants. Having completed a course in European Studies and Languages at University College Limerick, she returned home for a summer break and was invited by Jody and Marc to help out during the busy season.

'I never imagined that Marc and I would end up owning the hotel,' explains Deirdre. But that is exactly what happened. The young couple fell in love and later married. In 1996 they bought the hotel from Jody who, along with his wife Renate, still lives close by and remains an integral part of the team.

Over the following years the couple continued to invest in the hotel, adding a further fifty-six rooms in 2005, at a cost of over €5 million. The extra rooms transformed the place into a superior hotel. Their investment was a wise move. Two years later Harvey's Point won the AA Hotel of the Year Award and the following year received the Condé Nast Johansens Award for the most excellent service in Ireland and the UK. In 2012 Deirdre was named Hotel Manager of the Year by the Irish Hospitality Institute, and the hotel received the award for Best Customer Service that same year at both the Irish Restaurant Awards and the National Hospitality Awards.

But Harvey's Point has known challenges too.

'For many years, our location in the north-west was a major problem, as tourists tended to head to the west or south-west of the country,' explains Deirdre. 'Today, however, our location, with its natural beauty, has become one of our unique selling points.'

But then Deirdre and Marc seem to have a knack for turning challenges into opportunities. In an effort to make the ballroom pay, they began offering a carvery lunch on Sundays, which now attracts hundreds of diners every week. In order to help fill midweek capacity, they introduced a Summertime Cabaret Show in 2000. Running every Wednesday evening from June through to October, this has full houses every night.

However, their ingenuity was well tested during the downturn, when they were forced to reduce wages and move to a three-day week during the quieter winter months. By 2011, with the worst behind them, they reinvested in the hotel's facilities, including refurbishing the bedrooms, developing a conference and events suite, and revamping the bar and the restaurant.

More recently, they created The Lodge @ Harvey's Point – a stand-alone building on the grounds of the hotel, with thirteen compact rooms with communal lounge areas. To drive growth, they began targeting new markets, such as well-being and yoga retreats, and special interest programmes including walking, creative writing, art and gardening. They added 'foodie weekends' where guests can enjoy the best in local and seasonal food and drink.

'In many ways, our business has grown stronger because of the downturn. We had to work harder, but it forced us to put in place tighter cost controls,' explains Deirdre.

Their efforts have paid off, with year-on-year growth. And they are not finished yet. Projects in the pipeline include twelve additional guest bedrooms overlooking the lake, renovating the banqueting suite, building a barbecue area in the old boathouse, and a new swimming pool, gym and spa area.

'It's our staff who are really the key to our success,' explains Marc. 'We have a strong sense of family here, of caring for each other, and this culture manifests itself in how our staff treat customers,' he insists.

Deirdre adds: 'Every one of the team is prepared to go that extra mile and with a smile. They have all played an integral role in the development of the business and our customer feedback continually shows that our staff are definitely our biggest asset.'

The story of Harvey's Point began as a cottage hidden in the hills of Donegal. With imagination, love and considerable investment, it evolved into a holiday home, guesthouse and then an award-winning hotel. There is something magical about this lakeshore oasis, but, like so many businesses, it is the friendliness of the staff that really makes it special.

A quick look at TripAdvisor tells its own story: *WOW, Stunning, fabulous, outstanding, blown away, absolutely brilliant* and *a little piece of heaven* are just some of the glowing recommendations. The final comment comes from another reviewer who proclaims: *There may be a new benchmark for the Irish hospitality sector in terms of both facilities and service. It's called Harvey's Point.*

Deirdre and Marc's Advice for Other Businesses

Listen to your customers

Know your customers' expectations – and exceed them. Take the time to develop strong relationships with them.

Have a business plan

You don't have to stick rigidly to a business plan that you've drawn up before launching, but it's useful to have a road map to help you focus on the key priorities.

Innovate to stay ahead

You have to continually invest in your business – and that includes your products and your people. And you also have to continually invest in your own training and development.

CHAPTER 13

HAVING THE BOTTLE FOR BUSINESS

– The Story of Celtic Pure Water

www.celticpure.ie

'Start small but think big.' That's the advice of Padraig McEneaney, founder and CEO of Celtic Pure water bottling company. Set up in 2000 as a part-time venture in the garage of Padraig's family home just outside Carrickmacross in County Monaghan, the company now produces over 100 million bottles of spring water annually, employs sixty-five staff and has an annual turnover of more than €16 million. From very humble beginnings, his customers now include large chains of multiples, forecourt and food service companies, as well as major wholesale groups throughout Ireland and the UK.

'We also manufacture for stores under their own private labels, both here and in the UK,' explains Padraig.

His modern and highly automated production facility is a case of nature meeting modern technology. The source of the water is a natural spring that has existed on the McEneaney's farm for hundreds of years. Located some 300 metres beneath the drumlin hills of rural Monaghan, the water passes through a natural limestone filtration process before being piped into the production facility. Here it is bottled in sizes ranging from 250ml up to five-litre containers. The company also has a water cooler division where it sells 19.5 litre containers for use in corporate office environments, factories and gyms.

Padraig McEneaney grew up on the small family farm. Leaving school aged just sixteen, his ambition was to take over the farm, but things didn't turn out as he had planned.

'It took me about six weeks to realise that there was neither room nor money for both my father and I on the farm,' admits Padraig.

Instead, he found a job in the local meat factory, where he started out as a general operative on the production line before quickly working his way up to become the factory's top person for boning meat.

'I was earning great money at the time but it wasn't something I wanted to do for the rest of my life,' recalls Padraig.

By 1998 he had decided that the best thing he could do was start his own business. Unsure what type of business, he began looking around for ideas and sources of inspiration. And that's when it dawned on him that the answer might lie in the natural spring well he and his family had been enjoying for years. The question was whether he would be able to turn a simple idea into a thriving business. But that is exactly what he did.

Together with his wife, Pauline, who came up with the name Celtic Pure, Padraig began filling the water from the spring into large five-litre containers in the small garage attached to their family home. Every evening the couple loaded up Padraig's van with containers of water and he and a friend headed to Navan town, in the neighbouring county of Meath, to sell these door to door.

'Navan was far enough away that if it all went wrong, no one would know us,' laughs Padraig. 'But the customers really liked what we were offering, because five-litre containers were difficult to carry home as part of the weekly shopping, and because we had fewer overheads, we were able to charge less than normal retail outlets,' he explains.

Padraig recalls how he made €250 in his first week of business. That was enough money and enough research to convince him that this might just be a viable opportunity. He asked customers if they would like water delivered to their homes each week in the same way as the milkman delivered milk. In so doing, and over time, he built up a loyal customer base as well as a business model that was now generating recurring revenue.

In 2000, and encouraged by his findings, he officially set up the company with just €10,000. 'I started small at first. That way I was able to reduce the risk if it didn't work out,' explains Padraig.

His evening excursions to Navan began to expand and he widened his reach to include other towns and villages throughout Counties Monaghan, Cavan, Louth and Meath.

'It took time and a lot of shoe leather to build the business,' explains Padraig. 'I decided early on that I was the only person who could make this happen and that ultimate success would be down to my ability to push the product, and my own faith in achieving my bigger vision. And maybe there was a certain amount of thickness or stubbornness involved as well,' he adds, laughing.

His belief and passion shone through and word of mouth soon spread, as customers, delighted with his service and keen to help him succeed, began to suggest to their friends and neighbours that they, too, should sign up to a weekly supply of Celtic Pure.

Next, Padraig began targeting local independent shops, and before long had added a growing retail element to his direct delivery business.

He continued to run the business from the family's garage until 2003, when pressure on production led him to invest in building a new, purpose-built, 30,000 square-foot factory on a nearby green field site. He even travelled to China to buy a small bottling line to enable him to begin automating the bottling, labelling and packing process.

In 2007 he loaded his transit van with packs of bottled water and headed to London, to the ExCeL Food Show. 'I worked hard to develop as many contacts with buyers as I could at the show and that helped kick-start the export side of the business.'

Again, under pressure to meet growing demand, he courageously invested several million in expanding the facility further, as well as enhancing the quality of the company's labelling and branding. Rather than import empty bottles, he invested in an expensive and highly specialised blow-moulding machine, which allowed him to manufacture his own plastic bottles.

'In that way, we had our own source of water, manufactured our own bottles, and bottled and packed everything ourselves. It put us in full control of the entire process, which was something unique among our competitors,' he adds.

In 2008 Padraig won a contract to supply the BWG Foods group. This was followed in 2011 with Aldi, then Dunnes Stores in 2014 and Lidl in 2017. In addition, he now supplies the Applegreen Group and Dublin Airport Authority, as well as major wholesaler groups and food services companies throughout Ireland and the UK. He continues to invest significantly in new bottling lines and recently bored two new wells in order to increase capacity to over 50,000 litres per hour. He also purchased an adjacent thirteen-acre site and has recently constructed a new 70,000 square-foot warehousing facility and office block at a cost of over €4 million. His next plan will see him invest a further €6 million in a state-of-the-art warehouse management system. He is also working on a range of still and sparkling flavoured water products.

'We hope these will hit the shelves in 2018 and that this will push our sales to over €20 million by 2020.'

Growing the business did not happen without challenges, and he is hugely grateful for all the support he has received from his staff and newly expanded management team, as well as from his wife and family.

For Padraig McEneaney the prospect of a career in farming was not a viable option, so he created his own opportunity using the resources available to him. From the outset, he had a vision of what he wanted to achieve. But Padraig had more than vision; he had the passion, persistence and focus to keep moving forward, in small steps, in the direction of his dreams.

Padraig's Advice for Other Businesses

Start small but have a long-term strategy

The important thing in business is to get started. Starting small is a sure way to reduce the risk if your business doesn't work out. It is also important to have a long-term strategy, so have a picture in your mind of where you want to take the business and how you are going to get there. Only then will you be in a position to share this with your staff and other stakeholders.

Put emphasis on developing and fostering good business relationships

It is important to understand the need to build trust. Stay close to your customers and don't underestimate the value of supporting local or national sporting or other organisations as a way to build brand awareness and loyalty.

Perseverance and determination

If you are going to create and build your own business, perseverance and determination are key attributes. Raising finance can be challenging in the beginning and limited cash flow can slow potential growth. However, it is important to focus on taking small steps in the direction of your bigger vision. Always remember that success takes time and effort. There are few, if any, short cuts.

CHAPTER 14

IT'S CLASSIFIED

– The Story of DoneDeal

DoneDeal

www.donedeal.ie

DoneDeal is Ireland's largest classified ad website and has, in recent years, become the de facto place for anyone looking to buy or sell goods online. Set up in 2005 by Swedish native Fred Karlsson and his County Wexford-born wife, Geraldine, the website now attracts more than 600,000 visitors every day and has over 320,000 ads for visitors to browse.

When I first visited Fred in 2014, the company was employing thirty-three staff and had an annual turnover of more than €9 million. The following year, the business was sold to international media group Schibsted, who merged it with two other leading Irish brands, Daft.ie and Adverts.ie, to create a new entity, Digital Media Ventures.

What struck me most when I visited the offices was the friendliness of the staff. Many were sitting on gym balls rather than office chairs and the modern décor looked more akin to Google or Facebook than an Irish company based in Wexford town.

'We upload about 4,500 new adverts onto the site every day across more than 270 sections, covering everything from clothing and furniture to DIY and electronics. We also sell farm animals, machinery, houses and cars,' explains Fred. 'Seventy-five per cent of all second-hand cars sold in Ireland are being advertised on our site.'

For Fred and Geraldine, the focus was always about making the process easy for users so that they could upload the advertisement themselves, together with photographs of the item they wish to sell.

'The ad goes live straight away,' says Fred. 'Anyone interested in buying the product contacts the seller directly via email or telephone and the deal is done between them. Once we've helped make the connection, we get out of the way.'

'As a computer programmer I have often wanted to work on the latest technologies, but in reality most people are not on the latest technologies, so we developed the site for the level of technology that suits most people. It didn't always excite me from a techie point of view, but it was definitely the right decision for the business.'

Fred Karlsson grew up in Sweden. His entrepreneurial streak was evident from the age of fourteen when he began designing and selling video games to classmates. In 1997 he left Lund University, where he studied computer science, business administration and HR, and moved to Ireland, where he got a job with Dublin-based IT firm Gateway, who were looking for Swedish-speaking staff. It was there he met his wife-to-be, Geraldine, a computer graduate from County Wexford.

For the next few years, the couple travelled and worked first in Australia and then in Sweden, before finally moving back to Ireland in 2004. They settled in Wexford and Geraldine found a job with the Environmental Protection Agency and Fred with the IT department of Wexford County Council.

Before leaving Sweden to return to Ireland, the couple had sold their furniture through a Swedish website similar to DoneDeal. When they arrived in Ireland and went looking to buy furniture for their new home, they were surprised to find that no similar website existed. The experience got them thinking that there had to be an opening for one.

'Up to that point, anyone in Ireland who wanted to sell unwanted items would place a small classified ad in the back of newspapers. But these weren't great in that they were limited to very few words and usually didn't include photographs so people couldn't really see what they were buying,' explains Fred. 'We came to the conclusion that if similar sites existed in most other countries, then it was only a matter of time before someone started one here, and we thought, why shouldn't that be us? After all, we had the IT experience.'

Securing the initial investment to get the business off the ground proved hard, so Fred continued to work in his council job by day and spent the evenings and weekends developing their new website. Within a year and a half, the website was making enough money to enable Fred to leave his day job and concentrate solely on the business. A year later, Geraldine left her job and joined him.

'One thing that really helped us in the early days was having a clear vision for where we wanted to take the business,' says Fred. 'We had it written on the wall at home: "To make DoneDeal Ireland's biggest classifieds website – by number of users, number of ads and number of items sold." I didn't realise it at the time, but this really helped our focus in achieving these targets.'

A typical bootstrap start-up, Fred and Geraldine ran the business from a small room in their home. With no money for marketing, they depended on word of mouth from satisfied customers who had used their site and began telling others about their experience.

The couple had their share of funny ads, such as the one for a 'Baravan' – a caravan converted into a bar.

'That advert went viral very quickly,' says Fred. 'The "Baravan" was bought by an Irish guy living in New Zealand. There had been an earthquake and many of the pubs there were damaged, so he decided to buy the "Baravan", ship it to New Zealand and open up his own pub.'

Then there was the story of the farmer who sold bales of hay on which he claimed leading model Georgia Salpa had sat during a photo shoot for a fashion magazine.

The company's first national TV and radio advertising campaign also caught the public's attention. Called 'Husband for Sale', the advert told the story of a fictitious Irish couple: wife Deborah, who puts her husband of fourteen years, Donall, up for sale on the DoneDeal website. The husband gets a surprise when the purchaser arrives to collect him. The campaign was so successful it attracted thousands of new users to the site.

Instead of having a negative effect on the company, the downturn – when it hit in 2008 – actually had a positive impact on their business.

'In 2005, when we started the business, no one was really interested in buying second-hand furniture, but that changed during the recession and it became not only acceptable but cool to buy used items such as clothes, furniture and children's toys,' explains Fred.

By 2010 the business was doing so well that Fred was shortlisted as a finalist in the Ernst & Young Entrepreneur of the Year. The following year he and Geraldine achieved their goal when they became Ireland's biggest classifieds website.

But it hasn't been all about business for this couple. Community and charity also matter to them. Every few months they would select a different charity to support, chosen by different staff members.

By 2015, when the business was sold to its new owners, DoneDeal had donated over €1 million to charity.

'It feels great to know that we not only managed to build a successful business but were also able to give back to the community,' says Fred proudly.

Both he and Geraldine have since left the company. Today, Fred remains active in business and has become an early-stage investor in a number of start-ups, among them Melosity (www.melosity.com), an online studio where musicians can collaborate with other musicians on the same track from anywhere in the world; PurpleTag (https://purpletag.ie), an online shoe retailer; and MeetingsBooker (www.meetingsbooker.com), an online booking platform for meeting and conference venues around the world.

Fred Karlsson came to Ireland in search of work and adventure. He not only found a job but a wife and business partner. Together, the couple succeeded in building a business that fast became a household name. Moreover, they created an online platform that has helped thousands of people convert unwanted goods into cash. Any would-be entrepreneur looking for inspiring role models need look no further than Fred and Geraldine Karlsson.

Fred's Advice for Other Businesses

Have a clear vision

It's important to have a clear vision, one that makes you want to jump out of bed on Monday mornings. Part of that vision requires a clear idea of the end goal. But make sure to put some numbers onto this so that it becomes real and grounded.

What not to do is equally important

As important as it is to know what to do, it is also important to know what not to do. As any business starts to grow, there will be lots and lots of opportunities, more than you can ever hope to pursue. Unless these are 100 per cent aligned with the vision and goal you have set for the business, you have to turn them down. If you don't, you will be dragged in too many different directions and run the risk of not achieving your goal.

Build your business to sell, even if you never intend to

Build your business so that it is saleable. This does not mean that you have to sell, but it is a good discipline to put in the structures that ensure a business can thrive when you are not there. Central to this is building the right team of highly talented and motivated staff. Hire well and create a company culture that empowers and supports your team.

CHAPTER 15

KING OF FAST FOOD KITCHENS
– The Story of H&K International

www.hki.com

Napoleon Hill, one of the great writers on success, wisely remarked that 'no person ever achieved worthwhile success who did not, at one time or other, find themselves with at least one foot hanging well over the brink of failure.'

Such is certainly true of David Bobbet, CEO of H&K International. I heard David's story for the first time when he and I travelled to Silicon Valley as part of a group of finalists in the Ernst & Young Entrepreneur of the Year Awards. I realised immediately that this is a story that has the capacity to inspire anyone who has ever faced a challenge in their life.

Headquartered in Dublin but with operations in thirteen different countries, H&K International manufactures stainless-steel kitchen equipment for large restaurant chains such as McDonalds, Burger King and Kentucky Fried Chicken.

'Our strength is being able to design and deliver complete fit-outs anywhere in the world, and have them up and running within weeks. This is what has enabled us to work with leading restaurant brands who are engaged in rapid worldwide expansion,' David explains. 'Our product list includes meat freezers, stainless-steel food preparation tables, warming bins, drinks systems, ventilation hoods, grills and fryers. In fact, we provide more than 7,000 different items.'

David Bobbet did not start out in the restaurant business. From Dublin, he was educated in Newbridge, County Kildare, and then studied business at Trinity College Dublin. He planned to become a chartered accountant and took up a position with leading accounting firm KPMG. But, although he worked hard, David could not pass his accountancy exams.

After failing four sets, he left KPMG and was unemployed for the following year. Finally, he did pass his exams and qualified as an accountant in 1985. He then joined H&K on what was intended to be a two-week assignment.

'I was delighted to be working again, but I never imagined that I would end up taking over the company,' says David.

H&K International had been set up in Canada in 1975 to supply kitchen equipment to restaurants throughout Canada and the US, and was later enticed by the Irish government's Industrial Development Authority (IDA) to set up in Ireland. By the time David joined the company, the business was losing so much money that he feared it might not last another six months. However, it survived.

Having recognised the ability of his new recruit, the then CEO, Brian Ranalow, began assigning the young David to areas in the business that were experiencing problems. Gradually over the next ten years, David developed a reputation as a man who knew how to get things done.

'I worked hard to both challenge and change the long-held belief within the company that we were simply an engineering business,' explains David. 'I could see greater opportunities, especially if we could become a "one-stop shop" for restaurant customers by providing integrated solutions and better management processes.'

Firstly, however, he would have to get himself into a position to influence the future direction of the business. His chance came in 1996 when he was appointed managing director for Europe. Under his innovative and ambitious management, the European business performed so well that he was appointed global chief operations officer. His defining moment came in 2002 when the owners decided to exit the business and David helped lead a management buyout that saw him become the largest shareholder and chief executive.

'I thought at the time that if I could just turn the business around, it would be like winning the lottery.'

But it wasn't going to be easy for the new CEO. Within ten days of taking control, disaster struck. McDonald's strategy changed. The company decided it wasn't going to open any more new restaurants. Because H&K specialised in fitting out new restaurants, the company lost eighty-five per cent of its entire business almost overnight.

'It was a complete shock and a watershed experience for me. It hit me particularly hard when we had to close down the manufacturing plant in Dublin and lay off ninety staff,' says David solemnly.

The experience, difficult as it was, made the new CEO more determined than ever to make a success of the business. He started to turn the company around by targeting the maintenance and remodelling of existing restaurants rather than relying only on new ones. Before long, his vision of repositioning the company as a 'one-stop shop' was in motion and the company began providing a full range of services, including kitchen design, steel fabrication, installation and project management, as well as a new spare parts and aftercare service.

'We spread our wings to new markets and developed manufacturing and service operations in thirteen countries around the world, and a sourcing company in China,' David explains. 'We built a great team and focused heavily on developing the right company culture – something that is lived from the top down. This has been a key enabler in our success. We all need mentors and I was fortunate to have a great one in Brian Ranalow, our chairman, who led the H&K management buy-out in 2002 and who has guided and supported me throughout my thirty years in the business.'

Today, the company employs 1,400 full-time and 300 contract staff in eleven countries. They also supply more than 20,000 restaurants in eighty countries, of which 15,000 are McDonald's and those remaining are made up of other well-known brands. This year the company's turnover will reach a staggering $500 million.

What have been David's proudest moments in business?

'To have been recognised by McDonald's Corporation as their Global Equipment Supplier of the Year in 2010, 2013 and 2015,' he says. 'It's also rewarding to know that the kitchens we provide serve 10 billion customers annually around the world.

'We will continue to focus on the many opportunities that exist for growth, such as supporting McDonald's move to fresh beef and chicken, and new ways for customers to order and pay. This will see the company remodel 5,000 restaurants in the US and 6,000 in Europe by 2020. We are continuing to invest heavily in technologies, including rolling out our proprietary technology that enables us to monitor the working of equipment in 800 restaurants in Australia and 1,300 in the UK. We innovate faster every year, so that we can support the roll-out of menu changes in restaurants on a global scale and under extraordinarily tight timetables.'

A strong family man, with a passion for sport, David hits

the gym most mornings. He feels this gives him the energy and clear thinking he requires to run a worldwide company.

'Business is like playing rugby,' he says. 'You have to fight for every yard gained.'

David Bobbet has certainly gained yards over the years, if not miles. Having led his company back from the brink of failure in 2002, he has gone on to build it into the global success story it is today.

His astonishing achievement goes to prove how right Napoleon Hill was after all.

David's Advice for Other Businesses

Build a great team

The key to success is to build a great team capable of working together to achieve a common goal. That goal should be to satisfy your customers' needs in the most efficient manner. As a business leader, you need to surround yourself with people who are better than you are at key aspects of the business – from innovation to customer service.

Culture supported by the correct information

A leader's role is to define the culture of the company and ensure that this is developed and maintained throughout the organisation. Key to that is keeping things simple, eliminating both personal egos and internal politics and making sure decisions are taken based on information and facts rather than theory or speculation.

Meeting the needs of your customers – continuously

Achieving long-term success is dependent on your ability to continuously meet the needs of your customers. This requires that you and your team maintain a steady focus on customers' needs while at the same time bringing forward new and innovative solutions in line with how these needs are changing and developing. Being able to implement these solutions quickly – a speedboat rather than a large tanker – will ensure you stay close to your customers and they to you.

CHAPTER 16

THE PROOF OF THE PUDDING – The Story of Clonakilty

www.clonakiltyblackpudding.ie

Ireland has a well-earned reputation as one of the world's leading food-producing countries. Among its best-known and loved brands is Clonakilty Black Pudding. In the hands of the Twomey family since the 1980s, the traditional recipe of the now famous pudding dates back several hundred years before that. Today, Clonakilty Black Pudding is owned and run by Colette Twomey in the west Cork town from which it takes its name. Employing fifty-three staff, including those working in the original butcher's shop on Clonakilty's Pearse Street, the company has an annual turnover of more than €15 million.

Colette grew up on a farm in Minane Bridge in County Cork. Her future husband, Edward Twomey, lived across the fields. After school, she studied to become a brain-scanning technician but at the age of twenty-two abandoned those plans and moved instead to Clonakilty, where she married her childhood friend. That same year Edward took over the butcher's shop from his uncle and along with the shop came the recipe for Clonakilty black pudding.

Harrington Family Butchers, as it was called in the nineteenth century, was a place for small farmhouses in the area to sell the black pudding they made as a way to supplement their modest farm incomes. One such budding entrepreneur was Johanna O'Brien of Sam's Cross, near Clonakilty. When Johanna eventually retired, she passed the precious recipe for her popular black pudding on to Mr Harrington. To this day, Clonakilty Black Pudding is made from the same mix of beef meat, dried beef blood, pinhead oatmeal from Flahavan's in Waterford, minced onions from West Cork Veg Solutions in Bandon and a secret blend of spices that Johanna used in the 1880s. The recipe had been passed down through each owner of the butcher's shop, until it was taken over by Edward.

'Edward really didn't have any interest in making the pudding and would have much preferred to concentrate on the meat side of the business,' admits Colette. 'However, seeing how much interest there was in the pudding and how far some people were prepared to travel to buy it, he decided to continue the tradition. The only sure way to protect it, though, was to keep the recipe a secret, which we have done to this day,' she adds, remaining tight-lipped.

To help with marketing, Edward hired Tomás Tuipéar, a local sign writer and designer with an interest in local history. Together they devised the logo to include both the Clonakilty name and the original Harrington's name. From there, Edward began selling the pudding to other butchers and shops locally. Colette helped out by selling the pudding at agricultural shows, Irish Countrywomen's Association events and at the annual Spring Show in the RDS, Dublin, all of which helped expand the brand throughout the country.

Their first big break came when a guesthouse owner in County Sligo served their black pudding to a man who had been staying there. The following week, Colette received a call from this man, saying that he would like to stock it in his shops. He turned out to be a director of the Quinnsworth chain of supermarkets. That was the point where the business took off.

'We never really had a master plan,' admits Colette. 'Edward's personality and his enthusiasm and passion were such that he just wanted to make sure that anyone who liked the black pudding as much as we did should be able to buy it in their local shop. We worked to make that vision a reality. In that sense, the product came first and we built the business structures behind it as it grew.'

Because they only had one van at that point, Edward and Colette were struggling to make deliveries to the many stores keen to stock their product. This problem was eased with the arrival of the supermarket chains. Not only did this result in scale for the business, but because of the supermarkets' central billing and distribution arrangements, the company only had to deliver to a single, central warehouse location, from where the supermarket chain would distribute to their individual stores.

With a route to market now clearly established, Colette and Edward turned their attention to expanding the range of products. With the help of food scientists from nearby University College Cork, the couple developed recipes for white pudding and sausages. The business grew and as a result the company decided to move production to a licensed facility in the Little Island Industrial Estate on the outskirts of Cork city.

However, in 2005, tragedy struck. Edward became ill and passed away that same year. It was a terrible time for Colette and her family. She was faced with the unenviable choice between holding onto the business or selling it. She knew everything about making and selling pudding, but nothing about running a business. She also had to consider that one day some of the couple's three children might want to take it over and she wanted to do her best to make sure they would have that option when the time came.

With that in mind, she hired a business coach, whose advice would shape not only her decision, but the future direction of the business. His advice was as direct as it was clear. 'You cannot run a business by anybody else's style. If you are going to run it, then you have to work to your own style.'

These were the very words she needed to hear. She decided to hold on to the business.

'I realised, however, that it would not be enough for the company to continue doing what we had been doing up to that point; that we would have to grow and innovate if we were to remain successful.'

In time her confidence grew. Recognising her own strengths as well as her limitations, she began to surround herself with a great team who excelled in areas she did not. Gradually the business began to grow.

Over time too, the country's eating habits began to change. Renowned chef Michael Clifford was the first to start using black pudding for meals other than breakfasts, when he added it as a starter to his menus. Before long it had become fashionable to use it as a topping on everything from toast and salads to pizzas.

In 2012, and with the help of Bord Bia, the company began supplying Tesco in the UK. From there, Colette secured further contracts to supply stores in Dubai, Hong Kong and Spain. With this larger customer base, she added additional ranges of sausages, rashers and pork to her product mix.

'We also began receiving emails on a daily basis from Irish

people who had moved to Australia, wanting to source our products there. Due to the constraints on the importation of meat products into the country, we couldn't send direct from Ireland and so partnered with a local butcher there to make our branded black pudding, white pudding and sausages in Melbourne, and deliver from there to all major Australian cities.'

Recently the company built a new manufacturing facility and visitors' centre in Clonakilty, bringing the famous black pudding home to its place of origin.

As Colette Twomey looks back over the years since she took over the running of the business, she has much to be proud of. She has taken a traditional cottage industry and transformed it into a thriving international food brand. She has embraced change. And she has done so with great personal bravery, resolve and determination. I have no doubt that her late husband, Edward, would be immensely proud of all she has achieved.

Colette's Advice for Other Businesses

Give customers what they want

The basic rule of a successful business is simple: find out what the customer wants and give it to them. Your job then is to commit to continuing to serve their needs and to do so profitably. That's the way you create a sustainable business.

Together is better

One of the key skills is to surround yourself with people who have a different knowledge and skill set than your own. Together you can make things happen much better and faster than you ever could on your own.

Believe in yourself

Believe in yourself and in your abilities. Learn to trust yourself. Set goals that stretch you and believe in your ability to achieve these goals. Success awaits you but first you have to be prepared for a lot of hard work.

CHAPTER 17

IN THE DRIVER'S SEAT
– The Story of Ardee Coach Trim

www.ardeecoachtrim.com

For those who have ever experienced unemployment, the road back can be challenging. Frank Lennon knows this well. From Ardee in County Louth, he had been unemployed for three years when, in 1989, he became manager of a small community-based business. Today he and his wife, Anne, own Ardee Coach Trim Ltd and employ fifty staff. This year they will see revenues exceed €3.5 million.

'We specialise in the fit-out and refurbishment of buses, coaches and mini-buses, including bus seats, aisle carpets, window curtains, headrest covers and seat belts,' explains Frank. 'As a "one-stop shop", we do everything from repairing and re-spraying bus exteriors to selling second-hand buses.'

Ardee Coach Trim did not start out like most businesses. It was set up as a community development project by local voluntary groups who wanted to create jobs in their community in response to rising unemployment. Soon after it began trading, Frank, who was unemployed at the time but had previously trained as a mechanic, was invited to become manager. Soon afterwards the company got their first big break when Dublin Bus became a key customer. As business grew, however, their location in the middle of Ardee town left them restricted for space.

'We simply didn't have room to grow,' explains Frank. 'That created a dilemma for the community representatives at the time. Should they expand the business and take on the additional cost of moving premises or should they wind the business up altogether?'

In 1994 Frank and his wife, Anne, stepped in with a third alternative – they would buy out the company and run it themselves. And that's what they did, going on to build an alternative facility on the outskirts of Ardee town with the help of the local Enterprise Agency. The new facility provided them with the extra space and capacity they needed and, over the following year, they doubled their turnover. Not long after, they also won their first contract to actually manufacture seats for Dublin Bus, as opposed to simply repairing existing ones.

By 2004, with business continuing to increase, they were again forced to expand.

'This was an important step as it allowed us to design a better lay-out for our workflow and create greater efficiencies in our production processes,' explains Frank.

On the day I visit the new premises a number of double-decker buses in the signature yellow and blue Dublin Bus colours are waiting to be adapted into open-top tour buses for use by Dublin City Tours. In the metal fabrication area, lengths of steel are being shaped to make the new frames for the bus seats. Next, paint in the form of dried powder is sprayed onto the surface of the steel using a special spray gun that electrostatically charges the paint particles causing them to jump onto the waiting metal frame, as if the frames had suddenly been turned into large steel magnets. Once covered, the powder-laden metal frames are moved to large ovens where they are hung freely like sides of bacon in an industrial cooker and baked at temperatures of 200°C.

'This powder coating process helps the paint form a smooth and extremely hard-wearing outer skin,' explains Frank.

In a separate area, one team of workers is striping old seats while another is busy measuring and cutting lengths of foam and fabric to re-cover them. A jeep which Frank's eldest son, Ciarán, a mechanical engineer, has remodelled for use in nearby Boliden Tara Mines, is being fitted out and will soon be used to transport workers and equipment underground. As I make my way around the site, it becomes clear that everyone here takes great pride in what they do.

But the business didn't always have it easy. For example, in 2004 a large international bus-building firm went out of business owing the company more than €180,000.

'That was a massive body-blow for us at the time,' admits Frank. 'We were forced to let go of staff in order to downsize or "right-size" the company, and for the next year and a half we had to live on an extended overdraft. However, the experience had one upside in that it forced us to knuckle down and work harder than ever before in order to rebuild our turnover.'

Frank began targeting new customers and soon started winning contracts with companies such as Ulster Bus and Wrightbus, as well as independent bus and coach operators around the country. Then, just as he and the company were back in a solid position, the economy tanked.

'The transport industry took a massive hit in the downturn, with increased costs and lack of cash flow as a result of banks not lending,' Frank says.

Because many of his customers were small independent operators, they couldn't afford to pay for new vehicles, yet the vehicles they had needed to be refurbished or replaced if they were to have a chance of continuing in business. Frank's response was innovative: a rent-to-buy scheme for bus operators who could now rent the buses until they were in a position to buy them outright.

'While it had huge implications for our cash flow, it proved a real win-win for us and our customers,' explains Frank. 'So much so that we sold over seventy buses during that time.'

Frank and Anne's biggest setback, however, was yet to come. In 2008 they lost one of their five sons to suicide. His death devastated them and their entire family.

'Oisín was just a month shy of twenty-two. He was a twin, and full of life and fun,' Frank says with pride.

In Frank's office are two large windows looking out across the factory floor. On one side is a picture of a smiling Oisín, handsome in his black-tie graduation outfit. On the left window is a large calendar that blocks Frank's view of the factory floor where Oisín took his own life. It is something that confronts Frank every day he comes to work.

'I believe that Oisín is still very much with us,' Frank says. 'I even had a conversation with him recently where I told him that I had to get back and focus on business and make sure that we kept on track.'

Frank believes in life after death. That belief, and his real and continuing connection to Oisín, is what helps him cope.

'It changes you, though,' admits Frank. 'It makes you appreciate life more, makes you value your family more and it makes you more determined to carve out a better work–life balance.'

The business is a family affair. Frank's wife, Anne, works full-time as a social worker but is a source of great strength to Frank inside and outside the business. Three of his remaining sons, Ciarán, Eoin and Cathal, work in the business while Domhnall, the fourth, attends college but helps out when not studying.

Frank faces the issue of putting in place a succession plan for when the time comes. But for now, his focus is on continuing to grow the business. He has many innovative projects he wants to pursue, such as developing a range of lightweight seats to help reduce the weight of buses and so increase their fuel efficiency.

Frank Lennon has faced, and overcome, many challenges in his life. When he was unemployed and got the opportunity to become manager of Ardee Coach Trim he grabbed it with both hands. When the opportunity came to buy out the community-based enterprise he grabbed that, too. And he has faced the greatest heartbreak imaginable for any parent – the tragic loss of a child. Through it all, Frank has demonstrated characteristics true of most successful entrepreneurs – a positive and optimistic outlook for the future and a steely determination to cope with whatever life throws at him.

Frank's Advice for Other Businesses

Always stay positive

Everybody takes hits along the way. The important thing is to carry on even in the face of challenges. If you fall, find the strength to pick yourself up and start again. Develop a positive mindset so you learn to see possibilities rather than problems.

If you can think it, you can do it

If you can envision something in your mind then you already have the capability to make it a reality. But first you have to believe in yourself, your ideas and in your own potential.

Entrepreneurs make their own luck

People often say that 'luck' has a lot to do with success – that someone was just lucky. Most of the time entrepreneurs make their own luck. They take risks – often sizable risks. They stick with it and persevere through difficult times. For most, success is not achieved in an instant or overnight but as a result of prolonged hard work and total dedication.

CHAPTER 18

HOW DOES YOUR GARDEN GROW?

– The Story of Arboretum

www.arboretum.ie

Gardening and cooking have become so popular that it is rare to turn on a television set without coming across a programme on one or the other. For many, these are just hobbies, but County Carlow-based entrepreneur Rachel Doyle has managed to find a way of combining them both into a hugely successful business. She set up Ireland's first five-star garden centre, Arboretum, in Leighlinbridge in 1976, and today employs 100 staff and generates an annual turnover of more than €9.5 million.

In 2015 she bought a second garden centre at a cost of almost €2.5 million and renamed it Arboretum Kilquade. Set on five acres of beautiful Wicklow landscape, Rachel has since invested heavily to provide the same five-star experience there that is found in her flagship Carlow store. There is a wide selection of plant offerings as well as gardening equipment, furniture, barbecues, a beautiful gift store, bookshop, fashion area and even a kitchen and home furnishings section. And just as with the Carlow store, at the heart of the centre is the beautiful Secret Garden Café. It's easy to see how the place has become such a mecca for garden lovers, with many coming for inspiration, while others come to shop, eat or simply enjoy the tranquillity of the space.

Upbeat and animated, it's clear that Rachel loves what she does. She grew up in the remote village of Clonmore on the Carlow–Wicklow border. Her father, a builder's labourer, was a talented gardener and Rachel recalls working alongside him in their garden each evening after he came home from work.

'Our garden provided fresh food for the family and in many ways we were quite self-sufficient,' she recalls.

When she finished school, Rachel got a job doing office work but began to feel unfulfilled. For a time, she tried her hand at primary teaching but her love of gardening and the outdoors wouldn't go away. So, at the age of twenty-two, she headed to An Grianan College in Termonfeckin, in County Louth, to study commercial horticulture.

'I loved it because we learned about everything from fruit and vegetables to protected crops and amenity horticulture,' she says.

Having completed her degree, Rachel returned home with the dream of starting her own horticultural business with her husband, Frank. Back then it was difficult for anyone to get a bank loan for a new business, but particularly for a young woman in what was still perceived to be a male-dominated sector. But Rachel wasn't about to give up. Her passion eventually won over her local bank manager, who agreed to loan her the £2,000 she needed to get started (this was before Ireland switched to the euro).

Still teaching part-time, she would come home from school every day and get to work in the family's garage, from where she would sell seeds and plants she had grown from small cuttings.

'Our up-and-over roller shutter garage door became my shop window,' she says. 'However, because we were miles off the main road, people had to travel off the beaten track to find me. So for that reason, we decided to rent a premises in Carlow town instead.'

The couple's decision proved a wise one and business quickly began to boom. In 1999 they bought a development site in Carlow town, which they later sold to retailer Aldi. The money from the sale enabled them to purchase a ten-acre site in Leighlinbridge, just outside the town. Rachel's dream of building her business had now begun in earnest.

'To survive and to continually distinguish ourselves from other garden centres that were beginning to pop up, we became pioneering in our attitude to the business. We introduced a number of new initiatives, such as our covered outdoor plant area where customers could come year round, irrespective of the weather conditions. This in turn enabled us to target bus tours and school groups as a way to attract new visitors,' explains Rachel. 'We also created Christmas at the Arboretum as a magical time for children and families. It became so popular that people began travelling from afar to experience the atmosphere. It also had the benefit of turning what was our second worst month in terms of turnover, December, into our second best month of the year,' she says.

To increase her visibility further, Rachel wrote a weekly gardening article in both the *Carlow Nationalist* and the *Sunday Independent* newspapers. But it was her decision to open a café in the garden centre that catapulted the businesses to a whole new level.

'Introducing food turned out to be a game changer for us. Today over thirty per cent of our turnover comes from food. Everything we sell is either cooked or baked on the premises, even the biscuits you get with your cup of tea,' says Rachel.

Written in bold on the wall of the café is, 'All of our recipes are created with one driving ambition – PASSION. Whatever we cook, it's because it's in season, because it's local and because we want to eat it ourselves.'

It's unsurprising then that Arboretum Garden Centres have gone on to win many local, national and international awards for excellence in their sector.

Rachel explains that when she first discussed the idea of buying the second site in Kilquade with Frank, his advice was simply to follow her dream.

'I have always done that, and I believe all of us can achieve whatever we want as long as we have a vision and the passion and willpower to see it through,' says Rachel.

Now, after more than forty years in business, she has decided that it's time for her two sons, Barry and Fergal, to take over the reins. She will remain actively involved but in a new role, as the company's executive chair. Meeting Rachel's sons, it's clear they have inherited their mother's love of both horticulture and business. Fergal, now chief commercial officer, studied Business and IT at the Cork Institute of Technology and joined the business in 2002, while Barry, who recently took over the role as CEO, studied horticulture at the Botanic Gardens in Dublin and gained experience as a landscape contractor before joining in 2006. Both have since become joint owners of the business along with Rachel.

Although no longer CEO, Rachel is far from bored. She recently served as president of the International Garden Centre Association, where, as part of her role, she visited eleven different countries.

'I love to travel and visit other garden centres around the world. And I am constantly on the lookout for new ideas and examples of best practice and innovation which I can bring back,' she says.

She has also been appointed to the board of Bord Bia, where she is keen to help the horticulture and associated sectors develop.

Rachel Doyle has become a legend in the garden centre world both in Ireland and internationally. She is bubbly, enthusiastic and passionate about everything she gets involved in. She also seems to have found something that eludes many people in their lives – real joy. The constant smile on her face says it all. People often remark on how hard she works, at which she simply laughs because for her it really isn't work – it's her passion. Starting out, Rachel Doyle believed that she could make her dreams come true. And she has. She now wants to see her sons have the chance to do the same. A truly remarkable woman.

Rachel's Advice for Other Businesses

Be passionate about what you do

To succeed in anything, you have to have passion. And you have to believe in yourself. With passion and belief, you can move mountains; nothing is impossible. Never give up on your dreams, as they are the source of your passion.

Write a simple business plan

This is advice I got from one of my many mentors – write down your plans. What gets written down gets done. It is also a very good way to visually and mentally clarify your goals. Moreover, it allows you to gauge your progress against your set objectives.

Location is critical

If you are in the direct sales business, you have to be convenient to where your customers are so they can visit and do business with you. Proximity alone can be powerful.

CHAPTER 19

NO ONE STARTS A BIG BUSINESS
– The Story of the Barry Group

www.barrygroup.ie

One of the great truths that exists in the world of enterprise is that no one ever starts a big business. People start small businesses that hopefully grow over time. This story is a testament to that fact.

Just over sixty years ago, James A. Barry left his job as an ice-cream salesman to supply fruit and vegetables to local shops in his native Cork. Today the Barry Group, now owned and run by his son Jim, has grown to become one of Ireland's leading wholesale and distribution companies, with 250 staff and an annual turnover of more than €265 million.

At its headquarters in Mallow, County Cork, tall buildings stretch out over acres of land, housing more than 150,000 square feet of state-of-the-art warehousing and distribution facilities.

'Our business involves taking in large containers of products such as food, drink, hardware, personal care and household items and then shipping them out in much smaller quantities to retail stores and wholesalers who, in turn, sell them on to their customers,' explains Jim. 'We also supply our own symbol groups [a term for a form of franchise in the retail sector where a company does not own or operate stores, but acts as the supplier to a group of individually owned stores, which then trade under a common banner], which include 120 Costcutter outlets, fifty Quik Pick stores and over 100 Carry Out off-license outlets, as well as a network of independent retail stores throughout the country.

'In addition, our trade division supplies directly to a wide variety of smaller wholesale businesses, catering firms and pubs, as well as a growing number of export customers in the UK, US, France, Switzerland and Cyprus.'

On the surface this looks like a straightforward business model, but to run it efficiently is a complex and labour-intensive operation that involves carrying large amounts of stock, requires significant cash-flow management and calls for rigorous controls and highly integrated technology.

Everything starts in the buying department. Here, teams of experienced negotiators are on the phones to suppliers and manufacturers sourcing products at the best possible prices.

'It's the first and most basic rule in retail; if you are not buying right, you can't sell right,' says Jim.

The company have their own marketing department and their own in-house graphic design team, who work on new packaging and point of sale material, while telesales staff inform customers of the latest deals on offer.

In the company's massive warehouse, rows of pallets seem to go on forever and their height makes you wonder how anyone could know where to find anything in what is an ocean of goodies. All is revealed when I meet the forklift drivers and teams of pickers. Each one carries a hand-held scanning device that electronically guides them to the right location. Like worker bees, they buzz around, stopping here and there to pick and pack what is needed to meet the next order.

'With more than 300,000 boxes of products passing through the warehouse every week, it's critical that we have the right stock management systems in place to ensure efficiency for our customers and correct information for ourselves,' says Jim.

For that reason, the company also has its own IT department, where a team of technology professionals are charged with maintaining, updating and integrating both the hardware and software systems that drive each of the functional areas of the business.

When Jim's father, James, drops by to say hello, I can't help but imagine how vast everything must seem to him now compared to when he first started the business. Originally from the village of Banteer in north Cork, James A. Barry spotted a gap in the market to provide local shops with fresh fruit and vegetables. Buying produce from the markets in Dublin, he arranged to have this sent by train to the local station, from where he delivered it personally to his customers.

'In the beginning, he ran the whole business from his mother's sitting room,' explains Jim.

Over time, however, James A. began to broaden his offering to include soft drinks, biscuits and other confectionery items, and by the early 1970s had opened a small Cash & Carry in Mallow town. Jim recalls that, as a child, he enjoyed spending his weekends and school holidays working in the business, so much so that after secondary school he joined full-time. Steady growth followed throughout the 1980s and by the 1990s the company had established itself as a national player in the wholesale and distribution sector.

Up to that point, stores had been largely independently owned and run. However, change was about to come. And it did – in the form of the symbol groups of branded shops.

Anticipating this new trend, the Barrys made the strategic decision to set up their own chain of branded stores called Quik Pick in 1996. Four years later, by which time Jim had taken over as managing director, they acquired the franchise rights for Ireland for the Costcutter brand. Later, in 2009, and in response to the rise in alcohol sales outside the traditional pub environment, the company diversified further by buying the Carry Out chain of off-licenses.

While it all sounds straightforward, the journey has not been without its share of ups and downs.

'The retail business is fiercely competitive and we are constantly up against big multiples and giant discounters,' admits Jim. 'This became increasingly evident during the recent downturn in the economy when a price war between the large stores, together with a lack of bank credit, saw many small stores around the country forced out of business. Because some of these were our customers, this had a knock-on effect on our business.'

In 2012 Jim had what he calls his 'Aha' moment. On a trip to Silicon Valley, California, as part of the Ernst & Young Entrepreneur of the Year Programme, he had the opportunity to visit companies like Facebook and meet with senior executives from global brands such as Apple. Reflecting on the success of these companies, he began to realise the need to improve his own leadership capability and that of his senior management team. After an honest and forensic examination of every aspect of his business, Jim drew up a shortlist of projects that he and his team felt could be pivotal to the company's success. Among these was the need to introduce leaner procedures, reduce waste and drive increased efficiencies across all areas. A greater emphasis on team-building and better communication within and between departments was also highlighted. The results were extraordinary. The company retained its existing turnover level throughout the rest of the downturn and put in place a solid foundation for future growth.

Jim also realised that his purpose as a leader was not to create more followers but to develop more leaders. To this end, he invited all the members of his management team to participate in a specially designed leadership development programme, which saw the company win 'Great Place to Work' awards, as well as being named as one of Deloitte's Best Managed Companies in 2015, 2016 and 2017. Jim himself was named 'Ireland's Most Trusted Leader' at the 2015 'Great Place to Work' awards.

'These initiatives help the team to feel valued and more engaged, which in turn leads to a higher level of customer care and service,' says Jim.

Being innovative and seeking to constantly reinvent the business is now part of the company's DNA. They recently launched their own branded products, such as their Appletree Green Cider and Brandeberg beer. And it's a strategy Jim wants to see extended to other product areas.

'We are also increasing our focus on fresh and hot food. The recent introduction of a chilled food distribution solution, in co-operation with Cuisine de France, will allow us to offer a wider range of products to our customers. And we also see the introduction of healthier food options as something we will focus on more in the future,' he adds.

Focusing on giving back has also become important to Jim. As well as helping promote enterprise education among young people, his company contributes to an array of charities and good causes.

Jim Barry is an outstanding leader and a visionary in the

world of retail, wholesale and distribution. He is intensely passionate and genuinely cares about his business, his staff, his customers and his community. I am sure that when his father, James A., looks back to sixty years ago, he could never have imagined that his small fruit and veg run would one day turn into such a huge and successful business with an annual turnover of more than a quarter of a billion euros.

It's true that no one ever starts a big business, but the right leader with the right skills can definitely help a business grow into one. Jim Barry has certainly proven that.

Jim's Advice for Other Businesses

Create a positive team environment

Invest time and resources in developing a positive culture in the workplace. When people feel supported, engaged and empowered, they will enjoy coming to work, they will perform better and, as a result, so will your overall business.

Customer service is vital – don't leave it to chance

If you and your staff don't look after your customers, your competitors certainly will. You can't leave customer service to chance. It's vital that you put in place processes that encourage, monitor and reward good customer service.

Robust cash flow is vital

Many good businesses fail to grow and some fail altogether because of a lack of good cash-flow management. Cash flow is the lifeblood of every business. Make sure you have strong and robust cash-flow systems in place while at the same time embracing a lean mindset.

CHAPTER 20

TACKLING PARKINSON'S AND MORE
– The Story of Beats Medical

www.beatsmedical.com

Physiotherapist turned digital health entrepreneur Ciara Clancy and her company, Beats Medical, have developed an app that successfully treats the symptoms of people with Parkinson's disease. Set up in late 2012, and now with offices in Dublin, London and Lisbon, the company employs eight staff and has annual revenues of over €1 million.

'Parkinson's affects around ten million people round the world. It is a neurological disorder caused by a shortage of dopamine in the brain, a chemical that helps instructions cross from one nerve cell to the next, enabling a person to control their movement,' explains Ciara. 'However, even using medication, people with Parkinson's may experience difficulties with walking, speech or hand movements. In a healthy brain, when someone starts to walk, there are signals that go off like a beat or a sound wave that goes "step, step, step". These beats vary from person to person and can even vary from day to day for the same person. But for those with Parkinson's, these signals become impaired, resulting in shortened, shuffling steps, or even freezing. Here, a person with Parkinson's can get stuck on the same spot for seconds or even minutes, unable to generate the correct signals to enable them to move.'

For over fifty years, hospitals have been using a treatment called Metronome Therapy. Tried and tested, this auditory cueing therapy helps generate the required signals to produce movement using an external sound wave that is either played out loud or delivered by way of a set of headphones. Previously, however, this treatment was only available in hospitals. What Ciara and her team have done is take this clinically proven treatment out of hospital and delivered it via an app which those with the condition can download onto their mobile phones for use in their own homes or while on the move.

'Our aim is to help those with Parkinson's feel like people rather than patients, by helping them reclaim their independence and empowering them to manage their own condition,' says Ciara.

'The person opens their phone every morning, places it in their pocket and then carries out a simple two-minute walk test, where the phone essentially assesses their walking for that day. The app then automatically generates the required beat prescription for that day via a specially designed algorithm. This gives them the correct signal to cue and control their movement and walking. The key here is that the auditory beats are tailored not only to the individual but also on an individual daily basis,' explains Ciara.

Beats Medical now has users in over forty countries worldwide and while the average age for the onset of the condition is mid-fifties, Ciara says that they have users ranging in age from twenty-four to ninety-four. Around her office are thank-you cards from many of these, including one from a user in the UK who successfully used the app to help him walk from the northern-most point to the southern-most point of the UK. Others have used it to help run marathons, climb mountains and even row the Thames.

'For many people, it can be as simple as helping them sing to their grandchildren or write a birthday card to a loved one. It is stories like these that really motivate us to do what we do,' says Ciara.

Ciara Clancy is from Skerries, County Dublin. As a teenager, she volunteered in her local physiotherapist's practice. It was there that she got to see first-hand the positive impact that treatment could have on those with Parkinson's. She was so inspired by what she had witnessed that she decided to study physiotherapy in Trinity College Dublin, where she focused her thesis on the subject of therapies for those with the condition.

'One day while working in a hospital, I noticed that a patient who was twenty minutes late for therapy had got stuck outside, frozen on the spot at the main entrance of the hospital. It dawned on me that patients were coming into the hospital for treatment for their symptoms but that these very symptoms were actually preventing some of them from getting to the hospital in the first place,' explains Ciara. 'That was a light bulb moment. I realised what people really needed was a way to access this treatment whenever they needed it and wherever they were. And I immediately realised that technology was the way to achieve this. I realised, too, that I could only impact ten or twenty people a day in a clinic setting but that, with technology, I had the potential to impact thousands across the world every day. That was what motivated me to set up Beats Medical.'

It took Ciara two years to develop the technology and two more to have it validated. Luckily, because Metronome Therapy was already well proven, validation centred on the efficacy of using an app as the delivery mechanism. Once launched, she got a lot of attention. In 2015 she won the European award at the

Cartier Women's Initiative Awards for female entrepreneurs, was a finalist in the 2016 Ernst & Young Entrepreneur of the Year Programme, and won Google's international 'Adopt a StartUp' competition – all of which helped raise the company's profile both at home and abroad. In 2017 she was selected from among more than 1,800 entrants aged between eighteen and thirty-five years to win the award for Ireland's Best Young Entrepreneur.

Conscious of her lack of business experience, Ciara set up an experienced advisory board to support her in scaling the business. She recently launched her first US-based clinical trial with Washington University, which has the top-ranked physical therapy programme in the US, a move that will serve to evaluate the long-term impact of her technology on the symptoms of Parkinson's.

She has continued to add new treatments to the app, including speech, language and occupational hand therapy. But she now wants to do even more. Ciara is currently working on taking other clinically proven treatments currently only available in hospital settings and making these available to people with neurological conditions such as strokes, multiple sclerosis, dyspraxia and cerebral palsy. Her aim is to have the same impact on these conditions as she is having on Parkinson's.

'For me, it's all about supporting individuals and families to have a better quality of life and I truly believe that non-intrusive technologies can have a powerful impact on improving the independence of millions of people around the world,' she says.

Ciara Clancy is an engaging and quietly confident young woman committed to making the world a better place. She never set out to become an entrepreneur, but came to realise that setting up her own business was the best way to deliver solutions to the problems she encountered. Combining a passion for helping others with her knowledge of physiotherapy and technology, she has found a way to bridge the gap between both. In doing so, she is already making a difference in the lives of thousands of people. Many people search for a way to make an impact on the world; Ciara Clancy has found one.

Ciara's Advice for Other Businesses

Keep the user at the centre

It's important to deliver what your users need. By keeping your users at the centre of everything you do, you ensure that they continue to benefit from your product or service. As a result, they will stay with you and become ambassadors for your business.

Think of the bigger picture

We all get caught up in day-to-day operational challenges, but it is vital that we remember to make decisions based on our overall strategy for where we want the business to be in five or ten years' time.

Keep on keeping on

Every one of us faces setbacks and knocks. What matters most is how we respond to these, how we get back up and continue to drive forward with confidence. Persistence is an essential key to achieving success in any business.

CHAPTER 21

THE WATERLESS CAR WASH

– The Story of No-H2O

www.noh2o.com

We often assume that to be successful in business, a person has to come up with a totally new idea – something never tried before. But many great businesses are built on adding a new or innovative twist to an already existing concept.

Set up in 2007, Emmet O'Brien's waterless car wash company, No-H2O, with its distinctive green and white branding, now has more than thirty franchise locations throughout Ireland, the Czech Republic and Dubai. In addition, Emmet has also successfully launched a range of eco-friendly car care products that can be found in retail stores across Ireland, the UK, UAE, Australia and New Zealand. With eight staff employed directly and more than eighty throughout his network of franchises, he is on target to achieve a turnover this year of more than €1.7 million, eighty-five per cent of which now comes from exports.

But how can a car wash be waterless?

'Unlike regular drive-through car washes that use up to 132 litres of water per wash, we don't use any water. Instead, we use a special liquid formula that not only cleans the car but also leaves the most unbelievable shine,' explains Emmet in the company's headquarters in Sandyford's Beacon South Quarter, in south County Dublin.

Applied using a microfibre cloth, the liquid contains a positive charge that, when combined with the negative charge from the cloth, causes the dirt to transfer to the cloth, leaving behind a polished finish unlike any other car wash product on the market.

The formula?

'That's a trade secret,' says Emmet with a smile.

For Emmet O'Brien, the journey to becoming an entrepreneur has been an interesting one. He grew up in Monkstown, Dublin, but later moved to the UK to pursue his dream of becoming a professional racing driver.

'I spent nine years as a professional driver for BMW and the VW Group where I got to compete in a number of World and European Touring Car Championships. It was at one of these race events where auto products were on display that I was first introduced to the idea of a waterless car wash. And I could immediately see the potential,' says Emmet.

By that point he had already come to the realisation that life as a professional racing driver could not go on indefinitely and that he would need to find or create an alternative career for himself. But he was also adamant that any such career needed to be something he had a belief in and was passionate about. This was it.

'I could see the gap in the market because of the convenience of the system but also because it was waterless and there were growing restrictions being applied all over the place on water usage,' he explains.

The following year, Emmet set up No-H2O, acquired a

licence for this new waterless car-cleaning product and went in search of his preferred site – a multi-storey car park in Dublin city.

'I thought this would be perfect because I didn't need water or drainage and I could simply set up next to where people parked their cars thereby offering the ultimate in convenience,' he says. But finding a site turned out to be more challenging than he had imagined.

'Car park owners laughed at me in the beginning. They just couldn't get their heads around the idea of washing cars without water,' explains Emmet.

Q-Park eventually offered him his first location and he gradually built up the business from there. Apart from washing cars for consumers, Emmet also began working on a B2B (business to business) model where he washed cars for car dealerships on their own forecourts without having to move them to a wash bay elsewhere. Business grew steadily and soon he opened franchise operations in other locations.

In 2014 Emmet made the strategic decision to buy out the intellectual property rights for the product globally. This put him officially in the driving seat for future growth and gave him the incentive to expand the business. Over the following two years he won the European contracts to supply the Hertz and Europcar car rental networks with car wash products. While the increased cash flow helped fund growth, it was the experience in exporting that would give him the confidence he needed to expand even further.

Emmet then decided to develop his own brand of car care products aimed at the DIY retail market, including bottles of waterless wash, car polish, wheel and glass wash, and interior and soft-top cleaning products. He signed distribution agreements with leading retail outlets in the UK, Czech Republic and Slovakia. Today his products are also available in more than 400 stores across Australia and New Zealand. In tandem with growing the retail side of the business, Emmet went on to set up his first franchise models in the UAE in 2015 and the Czech Republic in 2016.

The company has also recently launched its own car wash app, No-H_2O On Demand. Now available in Ireland and soon to be available in the Czech Republic, Dubai and Florida, he sees the app becoming the Uber of car washing.

'The app will allow customers to call a car wash on demand. Our mobile franchise operators will then arrive to the customer's location on a scooter and complete the car wash in situ. The operator won't even need to meet the customer because everything from booking to payment will be done electronically.'

It is an exciting proposition and one that also has global potential. Not one to sit back, Emmet recently returned from the USA where he met with a number of retail chains in a bid to break into the US market.

'We are in talks with two of the largest retailers in the USA and expect to have our product lines on their shelves in the near future. We're busy now sorting out our manufacturing in the US and making sure we can deliver to a potential 8,000–9,000 stores through these two retailers alone,' he says excitedly.

'The pace is definitely slower than car racing but the satisfaction I get from seeing the business grow is equally rewarding,' he adds.

Emmet O'Brien is an impressive young entrepreneur. Intelligent and focused, he has shown great skill and judgement in taking what – on the surface at least – looked like a simple business idea and, by adding elements of convenience and eco-friendliness, transforming it into a rapidly growing international success story.

Emmet's Advice for Other Businesses

Believe in yourself

You have to believe in yourself, your product and your brand. If you don't, how can you expect staff, customers or investors to believe in you? Belief has to start with you as the business owner.

Pay attention to detail

Paying attention to detail conveys the right intent and shows commitment to your customers. It makes them feel acknowledged and valued. It will also be part of what makes your business stand out from your competitors.

Official work hours don't exist

If you are really committed to being successful then you have to be willing to do whatever it takes. One of the first things you have to let go of is the idea of a nine-to-five work schedule. When you own your own business that simply doesn't exist.

CHAPTER 22

PASSION FOR PAYMENTS

– The Story of Realex and fire.com

www.fire.com

www.realexpayments.com

In 2000 entrepreneur Colm Lyon left his secure job in Ulster Bank. Armed with nothing more than a good idea, a mobile phone and a laptop, he set out to create a new online payments business, Realex Payments. When I first interviewed him in 2015, his business had offices in Dublin, London and Paris, was employing 170 people and had an annual turnover of €20 million. Shortly after that, the company was sold to US-based Global Payments for €115 million. The move saw Realex Payments become part of a much larger financial institution that is currently processing more than €30 billion worth of payments per year.

Back in 2015, Colm explained what the company did.

'Simply put, Realex Payments provides the technology that enables large and small online businesses to accept payments from their customers.'

At the time, the company had customers in over thirty different countries, among them Vodafone, Aer Lingus, Virgin Atlantic, Paddy Power, AA Insurance, notonthehighstreet.com and boohoo.com. They had also entered into partnership arrangements with a number of large international financial services firms who were distributing their services under their own brand labels. These included Global Payments, who specialise in card payment processing for customers ranging in size from owner-managed businesses to multinationals across every sector. It was this entity that would eventually buy Colm's company.

As part of the sale transaction, Colm acquired ownership of a regulated subsidiary, Fire Financial Services, now trading as fire.com. Today he is focused on growing this business with the same energy and drive as he did his previous one.

Colm Lyon grew up in Clontarf, County Dublin and it was there he got his first taste of business. While still in his early teens he – along with his five brothers – would deliver the morning newspapers to houses in the local area. Apart from the money, he made a number of important contacts, including one neighbour who would eventually become a trusted mentor and friend. His name was John Teeling, himself a well-known entrepreneur and, at the time, a lecturer in commerce in University College Dublin (UCD).

After what he jokingly calls a 'practice run' at the Leaving Certificate, Colm decided to repeat the year. With the encouragement of his new mentor, he secured the points needed to study commerce in UCD. His goal was achieved when he graduated with a Bachelor's degree in commerce as well as a Master's degree in management science.

Despite his qualifications, Colm struggled to find work, but he persevered and was eventually offered a three-month contract with Ulster Bank.

'That three months turned into fourteen years,' jokes Colm.

While he eventually became head of central IT for Ulster Bank markets, his long-held desire to start his own business never waned.

'I found myself becoming increasingly frustrated at the pace at which things were happening in the bank,' he says. 'The Internet had come along and the whole world was starting to go digital. I knew instinctively that the issue of online payments would be one that would need to be solved, and soon. I began studying the market and realised that more and more retailers were contacting the bank looking for a solution as to how to accept payments online. But the banks didn't have one. The need to create a gateway to link retailers to the banks just made perfect sense to me.'

Mid-2000, Colm decided it was time to strike out on his own. He left the bank and, along with a friend he had met in UCD, set up Realex Payments. His friend subsequently left to work as an academic in the US, and Colm was joined by a former colleague from the bank, Owen O'Byrne. Together, they set about designing and developing the first version of their new online payments system. By March the following year, they had secured their first customer, directski.com. By the end of the year over twenty businesses had signed up. The pair knew they were on their way.

However, raising money to fund the growth of the business proved even more challenging than winning their first customer. Firstly, a venture capital firm almost invested. Then a high net worth business angel (also known as an 'informal private investor', who invests capital in companies during their early stage of development, as well as contributing their know-how and experience) came close to putting up money, but in both cases the deal never got across the line.

Frustrated but more determined than ever, Colm turned to his suppliers and asked if they might consider providing their services free, initially, in order to help him get the business established. To his surprise, most agreed. It is something he has never forgotten.

'Today, people call this a "lean" approach. For us it was as basic as survival,' says Colm. 'When you have no money and you can't raise it, you have to learn to ask for help and we did.'

At the end of 2001 the business did raise €320,000 by way of BES funding (the Business Expansion Scheme is a tax relief investment scheme). It would turn out to be the only capital the company would ever need to raise.

Talking to Colm Lyon, what strikes me is how much of a strategic thinker he is. He talks freely about strategy, about company culture, about building capability and about the need for core values.

'Up to that point we weren't growing at the rate we knew we were capable of,' he says. 'Many companies get to the €2–3 million mark quite quickly, but struggle to push beyond that. That's when you need to focus more on strategy. Entrepreneurial drive gets you started but as you begin to grow and scale, you have to start developing processes for managing your business and your people. In essence you have to become a better leader.'

The following year, he set up 'The Realex Academy', an in-house staff development programme whereby each new staff member is trained in the company's core values of passion, innovation, security, delivery and service. Colm also brought his focus on strategy to life in the company's physical environment, using a series of whiteboard spaces in the shape of tall, circular-walled structures that he called 'ring forts'. It is here that teams hold their short stand-up meetings every morning and where they go to brainstorm on possible solutions to challenges they encounter.

'The idea is that everyone is encouraged to leave their judgement outside. They are encouraged to envisage where we might be tomorrow, rather than be constrained by where we are today,' explains Colm.

When Realex Payments was sold in 2015, Colm chose to hang on to a subsidiary of the business, Fire Financial Services and spun it out as a separate entity.

'Fire provides businesses and personal customers with digital accounts which can be opened quickly online or via a mobile app. Customers can open multiple accounts in sterling and euro, enabling bank transfers to and from any bank account in the UK or Eurozone,' explains Colm. 'We have recently signed up with MasterCard as a principal member and now offer a Fire debit card. It is a compelling proposition and right on the edge of developments in Fintech [financial technology],' he adds.

And the market thinks so too, with over 1,000 businesses already using the platform.

In January 2016 Colm was awarded the 'Industry Achievement of the Year' award at the Cards and Payments Awards in London – essentially, the Oscars of the payments sector. Today, in addition to Fire, he is an investor in other early stage Irish businesses: Pundit Arena, a sports media platform that provides aspiring journalists and fans with an opportunity to showcase their work; VT Networks, which provides an affordable and energy-efficient network for sensors and devices that make up the Internet of Things (IoT); and LikeWhere, a personalised destination experience app for airlines and travel brands.

Like most successful entrepreneurs, Colm Lyon wants to make a difference. He wants to change the way we pay for goods and services and to improve this process for the customer, the retailer and for banks. Full of energy, exploding with ideas and bubbling with passion, Colm Lyon exudes every trait you might imagine in a successful entrepreneur.

Colm's Advice for Other Businesses

Listen

First, listen to yourself. What is it that you really want? Why are you starting your business? Listen to others. Seek to build teams based on shared values. Above all, don't be afraid to develop a big vision for the future. And then go after it with everything you have.

Persist

Stick with your vision and your plan. By all means pivot if you need to but do not make that an excuse for not focusing. Do not let failure get in the way. Instead, see it as a step on your longer journey to success.

Engage

Engage with everyone you can. Talk to prospects, partners and staff. Constantly circulate throughout your network and collaborate in order to better understand the problem you are trying to solve.

CHAPTER 23

STEELY DETERMINATION
– The Story of Kiernan Structural Steel

www.kssl.ie
www.kiernansteel.co.uk

In 1989 Frank Kiernan and his wife Dolores were both made redundant: he from a steel erection company, she from her accounting job in a different construction business. When their attempts at finding alternative employment failed, the couple were left facing a bleak future. Like so many of their friends during that period, they considered emigrating, but with four young children they felt leaving Ireland was not an option for them. Instead, with no more than a few pounds and a handful of tools, they set up their own business, Kiernan Structural Steel.

What started out as a way to create jobs for themselves and provide for their family has today grown into a hugely successful business, with 110 staff and an annual turnover of more than €25 million. Kiernan's steel and cladding products, which are made at the firm's production facility outside Longford town, have been used in the construction of everything from pharmaceutical plants and food processing factories to office blocks, data centres, schools, hospitals, sports stadiums and even bridges.

'We have worked on building projects for many top Irish and

international firms, including Google and Intel; pharmaceutical companies such as Élan, Abbott, Baxter, and Merck Sharp & Dohme; food firms such as Diageo, Kerry Group and Glanbia, and leading retail brands such as Tesco, Dunnes, Musgraves, Lidl, Aldi and Pallas,' says Frank proudly.

Inside their expansive factory, large industrial machines cut raw steel beams into required lengths in what is largely an automated process. These are then brought to the drilling area where large drilling machines bore their way through the heavy metal to create bolt-holes. In the shot-blasting area, the steel is machine cleaned and polished. Each beam weighs many tonnes and so has to be moved around the factory by way of large overhead gantry cranes. A group of welders weld the beams together, and these steel trusses are then spray-painted, quality-checked and moved to loading bays for onward delivery. There is an almost robotic rhythm to the factory, where everything moves like clockwork.

But things didn't always run so smoothly for Frank and Dolores.

Frank, who is originally from County Longford, served his time as an apprentice welder with Steel Fabricators in Longford town, before going to work as a foreman with a Dublin firm, where he worked on large projects such as Moneypoint and Shannonbridge power stations.

Dolores grew up in County Leitrim, about ten miles away from where the business is currently located. She had spent most of her early work life in the accounts departments of various firms, including ICI in Dublin and GEM Construction in Longford.

'Our business may be large now, but it had very humble beginnings,' says Frank modestly. 'When we started out, we were in an old, two-bay hay shed at the rear of our home where our first few jobs consisted of making small sheds for local farmers.'

The couple got up early every morning. Their first job of each day was to draw out whatever shed was about to be made. They did this by hand, on the tarmac yard at the back of the house, using chalk. Around 8 a.m. a team of part-time staff joined them.

Things were going slowly for the couple in the beginning, but in the early 1990s they received a welcome boost when the government introduced grants for farmers wanting to build new sheds. To cope with increased demand, the couple built new premises and hired their first full-time employees. With this extra capacity and the experience they gained from working on smaller projects, they began to target the wider construction sector, initially winning business from local building firms, as well as factories such as C&D Foods in Edgeworthstown and Hanley's in nearby Rooskey.

'The early days were tough going,' says Frank. 'Getting access to bank finance was a real challenge, so we had to rely heavily on good credit terms from our suppliers to get jobs done. We also had to make the profit from one job fund the cost of the next – it was that tight,' explains Frank.

In 1996 the couple bought the first of their automated sawing and drilling CNC machines at a cost of over £300,000. Although a huge investment at the time, it proved a wise move, one that dramatically increased productivity and enabled them to undertake even larger projects.

'Soon afterwards, we landed our first pharma job with Élan Pharmaceuticals in Athlone, which propelled us to an even higher level,' says Frank.

However, by 2007 they began feeling the pain of the collapse of the construction sector, with their turnover falling to as low as €3.5 million in 2010.

'It was a tough time for us,' admits Frank. 'Margins on the few projects we did have were cut to the bone and we were forced to greatly reduce staff numbers, with the remaining staff taking pay cuts to help us survive,' he adds.

There was one positive outcome, however, in that the company decided to turn their attention towards the export market for the first time and, with the help of London-based Irish builders and developers, were able to secure their first contracts in the UK. Other projects soon followed, such as with the Sisk Group for Primark in Hanover, Germany.

In 2012 they won two major contracts: with Diageo for the new Guinness Brewhouse at St James's Gate in Dublin and for a new power station at Great Island in County Wexford. A steady flow of projects followed, including the Intel plant in Leixlip, a new distribution hub for Pallas Foods in Ashbourne and the new Global Technology Innovation Centre for Kerry Group in Naas. More recently, they have gone on to complete work for Alexion Pharmaceuticals, BMS BioPharma company, and a number of data centres, as well as the Kia Oval Cricket ground in London.

In 2014 Frank and Dolores built a new 45,000 square-foot facility with a state-of-the-art paint shop and a post-fabrication shot blaster, enabling them to compete on even larger projects. Their sons have also joined the couple in the business – John, a structural engineer now looks after quality control, while Frank Jnr works as a contract manager overseeing the on-site element of the business.

Despite being a family-owned and family-run company,

Frank insists all staff have a say in how the company is run. 'Highly skilled and mostly local, many have been working with us for up to twenty years,' he says.

As for the future?

'We are focused on growing our market share here in Ireland and continuing to expand our foothold in the export market and in the UK construction sector in particular,' says Frank.

The story of Kiernan Structural Steel is an example of how one couple managed to turn what could have been a bleak future into a hugely successful one, through initiative, hard work and perseverance. Both tell me that they will never forget the help and support they received along the way from staff, customers, suppliers and neighbours.

On the wall in the reception of the factory is an aerial photograph of the old hay shed where the business first began. Next to it is another aerial photograph, of the factory and yard as they are today, covering an area of more than six acres. The contrast is a powerful reminder of just how far this hard-working couple have come.

Frank and Dolores's Advice for Other Businesses

It takes 100 per cent effort

Don't get into business unless you're willing to work extremely hard and give it 100 per cent. Running your own business is demanding but there is a great sense of accomplishment and achievement when it eventually comes together.

Honesty is the best policy

Be honest and honourable in your dealings with staff, suppliers and customers. Treat others as you would like to be treated yourself. Make your word your bond. This will result in a happy workforce, good relations with suppliers and repeat business from your customers.

Adapt to your environment

Be ready to adapt to changes in the world around you. Nothing in business stays the same for long. This is the challenge – and equally the opportunity. Don't be afraid to take on jobs that stretch you. That's how we grow and develop.

CHAPTER 24

FROM SPARE BEDROOM TO PARCEL MOTEL

– The Story of Nightline

www.nightline.ie

In 1992, when friends John Tuohy and Dave Field set up a courier business in the spare bedroom of John's house, they had no idea just how successful their business would become. Today, their Nightline Group employs over 1,000 direct and indirect staff and, with a turnover of more than €60 million, has grown to become the largest independent parcel and freight delivery firm in Ireland. Their now distinctive white and green vans can readily be seen as they weave their way up, down and across the country delivering more than 1.2 million parcels every month.

'The secret of our success comes down to our simple promise,' says John, the company's CEO, 'that we will get our customers' letter, document, parcel or package to its destination, anywhere on the planet, on time and on budget. Today we have over 1,300 regular clients across almost every conceivable business sector – from major retail brands and multinational tech giants to large engineering companies and small start-up businesses,' he adds.

Due to the expense of owning and running company vehicles, more and more businesses are choosing to use professional courier services such as Nightline to deliver goods. With no upfront capital costs, no driver overheads, no repairs or down time and a guarantee of on-time deliveries, it is easy to see why.

'Our business is now made up of five separate divisions,' explains John. '"Nightline Delivers" is our core service where we will pick up or deliver a package anywhere on the island of Ireland. "Nightline International" delivers packages anywhere in the world through a combination of our own depots and international affiliated partners. "Nightline Logistics" offers a supply chain management system to companies, with secure storage and a complete pick-pack-and-delivery service. And we also work in conjunction with international mail companies through our Eirpost division, where we offer businesses fast, secure and affordable global mail services.'

For businesses and consumers alike, Nightline has become widely known for their innovative 'Parcel Motel' division. Conveniently located on fuel forecourts and shopping centres across the country, consumers are now able to have their packages delivered to their nearest Parcel Motel, from which they can be retrieved in their own time using a secure access code provided by the company.

'Much of the success of this initiative lies in the fact that more consumers are now shopping on-line,' says John. 'Many of our customers in Ireland were ordering products from UK websites and finding these would not deliver to an address outside the UK. By providing our Nightline address in Belfast, in Northern Ireland, a customer can have their items delivered there where our vans collect them daily, and then deliver them to the customer's nearest Parcel Motel here in the South.'

It's an initiative that has proved hugely successful, with over 300,000 users having already signed up.

Their success today is a far cry from where the pair first started. John Tuohy and Dave Field are both from Artane in Dublin. In fact, they grew up only a few doors away from each other. John left school early and, having tried his hand at different roles, he eventually got a job as a driver with a local courier firm. Dave too, had become a driver and both eventually found themselves working for the same multinational courier business. By then, John had completed a Start Your Own Business course with the plan of one day starting his own company.

'I loved the course. For me it was the first time I had ever heard about things like cash flow and marketing. And while I didn't go on to start my own business straight away, the seeds were sown,' says John.

Dave too had secretly harboured the idea of setting up a business if the opportunity ever presented itself. And such an opportunity came in 1992, when both were offered redundancy. They decided this was the chance they had been waiting for and decided to combine their resources and set up a new courier business together.

'We invested €10,000 each and started with just two vans and one mobile phone between us,' recalls John with a laugh. The pair soon outgrew John's spare bedroom and began renting a small warehouse. Like most start-ups, they did their best to give the impression of being bigger than they were. In the morning, they would don their suits and ties to meet potential customers. By the afternoon they were back in their uniforms sorting parcels in the warehouse and then by evening time they were busy in the office preparing invoices and doing accounts.

'We did the chasing up of monies owed to us ourselves which really helped us stay on top of our cash flow in the early years,' explains John. 'So much so that we never needed outside investment and have been able to reply on a combination of reinvestment of profits and bank debt to support our growth ever since.'

As they began to win business, the pair decided to move into a serviced office building over a meat factory near the airport. Two weeks after moving in, the building burned down. Undeterred, the pair started again with the support of the building's owner, who helped them locate alternative premises. A year later they hired their first employee, Caroline. That, too, became an important milestone in John's life, as he and Caroline later married.

By the early 1990s, John and Dave found a high value niche working with some of Ireland's largest manufacturing firms.

'When a machine broke down, we ensured the spare parts would be delivered to the factory quickly. Companies needed parts delivered and installed within hours, rather than days or weeks, as any delay in production meant significant lost revenue,' explains John.

The pair quickly developed a reputation for providing a trusted and responsive delivery service. It was a reputation they would have to rely on later, when Ireland's growing cost-base forced many manufacturing companies to move their operations to lower-cost countries.

John and Dave decided to target other businesses that needed to deliver high-value products to their customers, such as mobile phones, games consoles and fashion garments. In doing so, the pair successfully navigated their way through a challenge that could otherwise have damaged the business.

In 2004 the company won a contract with a major consumer electronics firm that required them to open a base in Northern Ireland. Since then, they have developed this into a substantial business in its own right, employing over 100 people.

With business growing and volumes increasing, the company moved into their current premises, a 100,000 square-foot facility on Jamestown Road, Finglas, in Dublin, which better equipped them to compete directly with larger multinational courier firms. At this point, the pair began to look more seriously at their positioning in the marketplace, including assessing the company's branding. Having conducted professional research into market recognition of their brand, they were shocked to discover a low level of brand-awareness among business customers when compared with their competitors. Disappointed, they commissioned a new brand identity.

'Until then, our investment had been in new equipment. However, as soon as we began to invest in advertising and marketing, business began to increase,' explains John. 'For the first time, I had come to fully appreciate the power of marketing.'

Nightline's business has more than doubled since that time and John believes that their re-branding exercise played a significant role in this growth. As it grew, the pair remained very hands-on in the business.

'We have succeeded by playing to our individual and combined strengths,' explains John. 'I looked after the areas of strategy and planning for the business, while Dave focused more on operations and customer relations. We also stayed close to our customers and have continuously sought to develop strategies to respond to the changing demands in the market.'

In May 2017 their hard work paid off when Nightline was bought by US logistics giant UPS for a significant but undisclosed sum.

If it is true that most of the regrets in our lives are caused, not by the things we do but by the things we leave undone, then John Tuohy and Dave Field need have no such regrets. They both set out with the intention of one day starting their own business. And that's exactly what they did.

John and Dave's Advice for Other Businesses

Just go for it!

If you have an idea, and the drive to make it happen, you don't want to look back and regret that you didn't do something about it.

Aim high

Aspire to excellence in business. Do your best to constantly maintain those standards. If you do, that attitude will rub off on clients and colleagues.

Be prepared

Being dynamic is important, but it is nothing without a well-thought-out strategy. Showing that you have considered all options before acting gains respect from those who might not necessarily share your opinions.

CHAPTER 25

FROM REDUNDANCY TO ROTISSERIE
– The Story of Poulet Bonne Femme

www.pouletbonnefemme.com

In 2008 Sara Mitchell and her husband, Gavin McCarthy, both found themselves out of work. With a newborn baby and few job prospects in sight, this enterprising couple spent what little savings they had starting a business roasting free-range meats. Today, Poulet Bonne Femme employs forty-five staff and has an annual turnover of more than €1.7 million. Theirs is a story of great determination and even greater resilience.

'We are Ireland's first free-range rotisserie meats business,' explains Sara. 'We sell meats straight from the spit, including chicken, ham, pork, beef and lamb. These are sold whole to take away, in sandwiches or with salads and sides. What's unique about a rotisserie is that the meat can continuously baste in its own juices while the fat drips off, making it tender, succulent and convenient, but with a home-cooked feel.'

Business is booming for the hard-working couple, but this was never a path they had envisaged for themselves. Sara grew up in Monkstown in Dublin and studied marketing and French in Portobello College, Rathmines. Her first job was with a tech start-up. From there she moved to London, where she worked in marketing and events with drinks giant Budweiser. In 2005 she returned to Dublin and got a job in sales and marketing with a property company. Two years later, in June 2007, she married Gavin. Previously an estate agent with Hooke and MacDonald, he had by then taken up a role with property developer Bernard McNamara. The future looked bright. The following August, they welcomed their first child, Sam, into the world and Sara gave up work to look after their young son.

Things looked like they couldn't get any better – until, that is, they began to fall apart. Because of the recession Gavin lost his job and couldn't find another because the property market had tanked. The couple considered emigrating to Canada but neither wanted to leave Ireland. The only option left to them was to try to set up their own business.

'We brainstormed lots of ideas but the rotisserie was the one we kept coming back to. We remembered enjoying chicken off the spit on holidays in Spain and we thought it might go well in Ireland. We invested the small amount of redundancy Gavin had received, plus all the savings we had – which wasn't much – into buying a food grade trailer and the best rotisserie machine we could afford. My mother came up with the name, based on a recipe from the south of France,' explains Sara.

Shortly afterwards, in May 2009, the pair took a small stall at the farmers market in Leopardstown. They were now officially in business.

'Some people thought we were mad to try and sell free-range chicken at a time when the country was in the midst of its worst downturn,' says Sara. 'But we've never supported the idea of caged birds so for us, it had to be free-range. Even though more expensive, the meat also tastes so much better.'

Starting a new business brought challenges, including learning about food preparation and how to survive on tight cash flows. But the greatest challenge for them both was getting used to the reality of working in a trailer, selling chickens to friends and former work colleagues.

'It was life changing. But we genuinely grew to love it,' says Sara. 'In the beginning, there was often just the two of us in the trailer with Sam in a buggy. Those were the days before we could afford childcare,' she says, smiling.

Before long the pair had invested in a second trailer and were working harder than ever.

'We signed up, at huge expense, for a stand at the Oxygen music festival in Laois and went down with a fridge-van full of chickens expecting to sell tonnes of picnic boxes. But we soon realised we had judged the crowd wrong,' admits Sara. 'Having bought so much stock, we were faced with disaster. We eventually improvised and cut up French bread sticks, filled them with chicken and sold them as chicken rolls for a fiver. Customers then started arriving in their droves. We just about broke even, but the experience became the catalyst for creating our now award-winning range of Poulet Bonne Femme sandwiches.'

But they weren't out of the woods just yet. During the heavy snow of late 2010 farmers' markets were cancelled and Sara and Gavin had nowhere to sell their meats.

'We had no option but to try and do something. So we rang all the customers we knew and offered to deliver cooked chicken to their homes,' explains Sara. 'I can still remember loading our two boys, Sam and Marc, into the car and driving all around Dublin. It was the only way we could make ends meet at the time,' she admits.

The experience, though painful, helped them realise that they needed a dedicated premises. Eventually they found one, in Monkstown. They were ready to push the button on it when they heard the news that Avoca were opening up just down the road, with their own rotisserie section.

'We were gutted,' admits Sara. 'We even thought of abandoning the whole idea. Then my father advised us to just pick up the phone and ring Simon Pratt, the CEO, and offer to go in and run the rotisserie for him. To our delight, Simon accepted and that was really the beginning of Poulet Bonne Femme.'

The company now has outlets in five Avoca stores – Monkstown, Rathcoole, Suffolk Street, Kilmacanogue and their most recent and largest store yet, in Dunboyne.

These are run on a 'concession' basis, where Avoca supply the space and Poulet Bonne Femme provide their own equipment and staff. Instead of rent, Avoca receive a percentage of turnover.

Last year, Sara and Gavin also opened a new central production unit and are now producing their own branded fridge products.

'We recently signed a five-year deal with Aramark which has allowed us to open an outlet in Dundrum Town Centre, with a second one due to open shortly in University College Dublin.

'We see opportunities to open more stores in Ireland, as well as in the UK. And we'd love to open our own branded store at some time in the future,' adds Sara.

In addition, they are developing their corporate delivery service, delivering free-range cooked meats to offices across Dublin.

'We have come to believe that Gavin losing his job was the best thing that could have happened to us. In the past we had two lives – one work and the other family. Today, they blend into one. I think that this was meant to be,' says Sara.

Sara's Advice for Other Businesses

Hard work and dedication solve most problems

If you want to run your own business, you have to be willing to put in the hard work. Everything takes effort and you have to be willing to take full responsibility for everything you are doing. If it's going to work, it's up to you to make it happen.

Keep going even at the worst times

There will be times when you will feel like giving up. But these are the times you need to persevere. Very often the problems we think may end our business are the ones that can bring the best opportunities for success.

Get advice from experienced mentors

Surround yourself with people who know what they are doing. For example, I joined the 'Going for Growth' programme which is an Enterprise Ireland-supported, women only enterprise programme and it turned out to be one of the best things I ever did. (Enterprise Ireland is the Irish government agency that supports indigenous businesses.) The advice and guidance I received from other highly experienced female business owners was invaluable and changed my outlook on growing Poulet Bonne Femme. It gave me the skills and the time to think more strategically and to work *on* the business rather than working *in* it.

CHAPTER 26

WE CAN SEE YOU
– The Story of Netwatch

netwatch

www.netwatchsystem.com

David Walsh and Niall Kelly set up security monitoring company Netwatch in 2003 when a mutual friend was attacked after he went to check on a commercial premise that was being broken into. Today, from their high-tech hub just outside Carlow town, their company monitors more than 3,200 homes and business premises across four separate continents. With 195 employees and annual revenues of more than €22 million per year, their business continues to go from strength to strength.

From their initial base in Carlow, they now have offices in Birmingham in the UK as well as Pittsburgh, Chicago, Boston and New York in the US. Approximately ninety per cent of their customers come from the commercial sector, including everything from factories and offices to GAA clubs and a growing number of churches. The remaining ten per cent are residential owners, including many high profile figures from the worlds of business, music and sport, as well as leading industrialists in places like Johannesburg in South Africa and wealthy oil barons in Dallas, Texas. They are even reported to be looking after members of the British royal family.

'Using the most advanced camera technology and intelligence software, we are able to identify intruders attempting to break into a premises. Using two-way communication software, we can speak directly to them, shouting specific warnings such as, "You in the red jacket, you are being watched by security cameras, please leave this premises immediately",' explains David.

It has been an interesting journey for friends David and Niall. David Walsh grew up in Castleisland, County Kerry, where he and his seven siblings and their parents and grandmother lived in a small cottage.

'Those years shaped my attitude to life – in that my parents were incredibly positive people who made us all grow up believing we were the luckiest family in the world,' explains David.

David went to University College Dublin, where he studied agricultural science, before taking up a sales and business development role with KEENAN, a leading manufacturer of agricultural machinery and feeding systems based in Carlow. It was there that he met his future business partner. From Carlow, Niall Kelly had studied electronic engineering at Carlow Institute of Technology and had previously worked as general manager of a golf course construction company before joining the electronics department at KEENAN.

'The idea to start a business often comes from the personal experiences of its founders and that was definitely true in our case,' explains David. 'A friend of ours was working in a local company and was the designated keyholder for the premises. One night he raced out to the site to turn off what he thought was a faulty alarm but, unfortunately for him, there was a real burglary taking place and he was immediately set upon by the intruders. Shocked by what had happened, Niall and I began discussing how there had to be a better way to protect a company's premises as well as safeguarding first responders.'

During their search for solutions, they made contact with an Australian company who manufactured video transmission equipment, predominantly for the military. Having visited the company, they decided the best solution would be to combine two-way audio with video surveillance.

'It was a real breakthrough moment,' explains David. 'Rather than arriving after the event, we could now create a new business where we could actually capture security breaches as they occurred and more importantly, prevent them from happening at all.'

In 2003 the pair returned from Australia. Excited by their new idea and armed with their new technology, they immediately handed in their notice and Netwatch was born.

First though, there was the usual challenge faced by all budding entrepreneurs – how to fund their new venture?

'Raising finance is always an issue for start-ups,' explains David. 'And like many entrepreneurs starting out, we didn't have a lot of money, so we ended up having to remortgage our homes to raise the required capital.'

8 February 2003 is a date that is carved in David's memory – that's because it's the day the company's first customer went live.

'It was a factory and warehouse which had been broken into a few months earlier,' he recalls. 'And they are still a customer today,' he adds proudly.

By 2007, and with support from the government's enterprise agency, Enterprise Ireland, David and Niall set up their own research and development facility, where they went on to develop high-end video processing software that enabled them to detect the subtle differences between real breaches and false alarms caused by weather, trees or animals.

'This was important because it meant our team could react more quickly as we were only dealing with real events,' says David.

Most companies experience pivotal moments through their life and Netwatch's first pivot came in 2008 when David and Niall decided to turn their business model completely on its head. They decided they would install their surveillance equipment free of charge and that the customer would instead pay for their service on a daily or monthly basis. It was a bold and radical decision.

The move, however, proved an overwhelming success. Apart from the initial strain on their cash flow, the strategy gave them something most companies yearn for – a source of recurring revenue. It also made it easier for them to convince customers to sign up because they were no longer being presented with a hefty up-front bill for equipment. Another added advantage was that it made it more difficult for other firms to compete.

Companies regularly get presented with opportunities that are hard to say no to and Netwatch was no different.

'At one point we were offered the opportunity to take on the contract to monitor thousands of traditional, non-camera-based home alarms but we passed on it,' explains David. 'It wasn't that we didn't need the additional income. We did. But we had staked our claim on our desire to be the number one company in the world in video surveillance and we knew that this opportunity, good as it was, would lead us off-path.'

Their decision proved correct.

When the recession hit in 2008, David and Niall decided that rather than worry about things they could not control, they would instead focus their energies only on the things they could.

'We put our heads down and deliberately didn't listen to all the negativity. We invested in increasing the capacity of our communications hub, doubled our marketing spend and focused on developing an international customer base,' explains David.

This approach soon led them to launch in the UK, largely on the back of requests from Irish companies operating there. In 2012 they launched in the US – a move that would lead to exponential growth for the business. They chose to add former Boston police commissioner Kathleen O'Toole to their board, which helped them secure important early wins, including the Massachusetts Institute of Technology (MIT). The move proved so successful that now seventy per cent of their total turnover comes from the US.

'We recently raised an investment of almost €20 million to support our expansion plans there and I expect to be spending even more time there over the next few years as that's really where the growth is coming from,' says David.

David is adamant that much of Netwatch's success is down to their staff and to the customer-centred culture that exists within the company.

'In our business, customers chose us because of our technology but they stay with us because of our people,' he insists.

The story of Netwatch is an inspiring one. What started out as an idea to tackle a local problem has grown into an international business that is making a positive impact on companies and individuals around the world. One can only be impressed by how these two men, from their Carlow base, have become such deserving leaders in a truly global market.

David and Niall's Advice for Other Businesses

Learn from your setbacks

Accept that you will experience knocks and setbacks. These are part of the journey of every business. The secret is to learn from these and move on without allowing them to dilute your enthusiasm or your ambition for the future.

Being focused is vital

Some companies try to be everything to everybody. However, in our experience, the narrower the focus the greater the opportunity to become an expert in your chosen market.

Have confidence in yourself and your ideas

We all need to believe in what we are doing and in our ability to achieve success in our chosen field. We also need to have confidence that, as Irish businesses, we can play as well as anyone else on the world stage.

CHAPTER 27

INNOVATE OR DIE
– The Story of Blueface

www.blueface.com

The story of David and Goliath may be simple, but it serves as a constant reminder of how courage and conviction can enable us to take on bigger, more powerful opponents, and win.

It takes great courage to become an entrepreneur and even greater courage to start a business in a sector dominated by large incumbents with deep pockets. But that is exactly what Alan Foy, CEO of Blueface, and his colleagues did when they decided to enter the hugely competitive telecommunications market. Today they employ more than fifty staff between their headquarters in the IFSC, Dublin and their offices in the UK and Italy.

The company began by providing landline and mobile phone services to SME and home-office customers but have since moved to include many large enterprise customers and global carriers among their growing customer base.

'Our VoIP, or Voice over Internet Protocol platform, converts traditional landline voice services into digital signals which are sent, at high speed, over the broadband connection, allowing us to deliver more savings than any other provider in the market,' explains Alan. 'Our mobile services are provided thanks to our virtual mobile operator relationship on the Three network.'

It's a compelling proposition and one which has helped businesses save up to as much as forty per cent on their telephone costs. While Alan is shy about sharing the company's turnover, he is happy to confirm that revenues have increased twenty-five per cent year on year. And while still relatively small, Blueface has become something of a disrupter within the sector.

'Unlike other telecom operators, we don't charge line rental fees nor do we require customers to spend money on expensive equipment,' Alan explains. 'Our "Follow Me" functionality enables customers to be contacted on their business phone number, which can follow them to their mobile or another landline even while they are away.'

And at a time when more workers are mobile or home-based, it's easy to see how such increased flexibility is attractive.

There is a natural humility about Alan Foy. Yet he seems to have found a comfortable balance between that humility and the ambitious entrepreneurial spirit that clearly drives him. He grew up in Glasnevin, Dublin, and studied business at Trinity College, where he won business student of the year. It was during his time in college that his entrepreneurial career began. His first business involved organising airport services, transport and accommodation for VIPs visiting Ireland. It was an exciting time for the eighteen-year-old budding businessman, who got to meet and greet some of the world's most famous music and entertainment legends.

'After college I worked in wealth management for NCB Stockbrokers (now Investec) where I learned two great lessons. The first is that building a strong team is key to the success of any business and, second, that a business is only a real business if it is not dependent solely on you to run it,' explains Alan. 'Both of these lessons have continued to shape my thinking ever since,' he adds.

In 2008, driven by the desire to be in business for himself, he took the courageous step of leaving NCB and setting up a new company, Venture Wave. This was essentially an investment vehicle, which he used to assess potential opportunities worth investing in. All the while, he kept his eye open for a business opportunity that would entice him to get involved on a full-time basis. His plans received a boost when Lord Iveagh of the Guinness family agreed to become a co-investor.

Having assessed many proposals from companies seeking investment, the pair settled on one that ticked all their boxes. It was in the communication technology sector, was innovative and had huge potential to scale up both in Ireland and beyond. The company was called Blueface.

'The company had been set up in 2004 by two technology engineers,' explains Alan. 'However, for the next five years, they did what many start-ups do, they focused most of their energies and resources on developing the features and functionality of the service rather than seeking to capitalise on the sales and business development aspect of their business. They had also primarily focused on the residential sector rather than the SME or enterprise market.'

Towards the end of 2009, Alan and Venture Wave completed a management buy-in to the company where they became the largest shareholder in the business. Alan became the company's new CEO. He soon realised that to compete with the bigger telecom firms in the industry, he needed to drive up revenues, and that the quickest and most sustainable way to achieve this was by focusing more on business customers.

'It was a total pivot for the business at the time,' admits Alan. 'But the strategy worked and today over ninety per cent of the company's revenue comes from business customers including sole traders, small and medium-sized businesses, enterprise clients, multinationals, banks, insurance companies and colleges.'

Many smaller businesses use the company's services as a way to project an image and profile that makes them appear larger than they actually are – for example, getting a New York or Silicon Valley number even though the company is based in Dublin or Cork. For clients such as banks and other institutions, whose calls are recorded for quality and other purposes, these can now be easily and securely stored on the company's cloud platform.

Alan understands the importance of driving customer satisfaction in the business and it shows, with eighty-five per cent of all new business coming from referrals. He has also managed to develop a recurring revenue business model, which means that rather than starting from scratch each year with an empty sales book, his focus is on servicing, retaining and growing a quality customer base that yields consistent monthly income.

Has it been hard competing with the big Telco providers?

'Yes,' admits Alan. 'We have to constantly compete with their massive marketing budgets. To do that we draw on our unique strengths, such as the fact that we are smaller and, therefore, much more nimble and flexible in how we respond to customers and to the needs of the market. While we focus on offering the lowest prices in the sector, we also harness the strength of our technology to offer distinct advantages and functionality designed to disrupt the marketplace. In today's fast-moving, competitive business environment, you have to innovate or die.'

'We want to build an Irish company that can scale internationally. Initially, we set out to fine-tune the model here in Ireland, tie down the pricing and continue to improve the functionality of the service but always with the idea of expanding from there.'

In 2012 the company entered the UK and Northern Ireland markets and has experienced steady growth there. It also bought a business in Italy and rebadged it as Blueface Italy. Further investment of €1.5 million in research and development has enabled it to offer a best-in-class cloud communications software platform. Such developments have seen the company move up the value chain to where it now supports many large enterprise customers and global carriers.

In 2016, ambitious for growth, the company was planning a stock market flotation, but abandoned the idea when cultural and integration difficulties emerged with the two potential acquisitions they had identified.

Later that year Blueface received an approach from a large US firm, which wanted to buy the company. The company declined the offer, choosing instead to focus on building a business that could one day become a global Irish brand up there with CRH and Ryanair. Having met with a number of private equity investors, it raised €10 million in March 2017 to fund its global expansion.

'Having already deployed our platform in seven countries, including Ireland, the UK, Italy, France, Germany, Spain and the US, and ready to hire a further eighty staff, we are now well positioned to be a global provider of cloud communications with a proprietary, differentiated software platform that can operate in the SaaS [software as a service, where you pay a monthly subscription rather than having to pay up-front capital costs] universe, with its key asset being an ambitious team that won't settle for second best,' says Alan.

In January 2018 Blueface merged with Star2Star Communications, a US-based hybrid cloud computing communications company, and the combined entity is now valued at approximately $500 million.

Answering the call to become an entrepreneur, Alan Foy chose the telecommunications space where he saw opportunities to be disruptive. Strategically, he shifted his company's focus towards business customers and with a clear focus on customer service has converted satisfied customers into brand ambassadors. His determination to scale the business saw him successfully enter a number of new markets while building a dynamic workforce capable of managing the company's continued growth. In 2017 he was chosen as a finalist in the Ernst & Young Entrepreneur of the Year Awards.

Just as in the story of David and Goliath, Alan Foy has shown that one should not be discouraged simply by the fact that opponents or competitors are larger or better resourced. What counts most is courage and the conviction not to be afraid to take on the challenge in the first place.

Alan's Advice for Other Businesses

Find a good business partner

Find a business partner who is compatible with you. Try to choose someone who has complementary competencies and skills. It is helpful to have someone who can travel on the entrepreneurial journey with you and who can help modulate the many highs and lows.

Build a team of talented people

No one ever builds a company on their own. Your job as business leader is to find the right team, inspire them with your passion and energy, and then get out of their way.

Expand your comfort zone

To succeed, you have to jump out of your comfort zone. What you want lives on the other side of your comfort zone. Don't put off what you can do today – action is the cornerstone of entrepreneurship.

CHAPTER 28

SMALL WHEELS, BIG FUTURE

– The Story of LittleBig Bikes

littlebig

www.littlebigbikes.com

Getting your first bicycle as a child is one of those milestones most of us never forget. However, for parents, deciding on what type of bicycle to buy their child can be more complex than expected. There is the question of height. Tyre thickness. Stabilisers. Not to mention the fact that you might be asked whether or not you want pedals.

My wife, Trish, and I were asked this question when buying a bike for our then three-and-a-half-year-old son, Bobby. My response was to jump to my son's defence: 'Without pedals?' I replied. 'Of course he'll want pedals. Our little man will be well able for a normal bike.'

However, once the shop owner showed us what a balance bike was, we were intrigued. When he told us that it was part of the LittleBig Bikes range of children's bicycles and had been designed by a young man who had previously worked in his shop, we became even more intrigued.

Curious to learn more, I went in search of the young man whose innovative bikes were taking the market by storm. Set up in 2014, LittleBig Bikes is the brainchild of Simon Evans. A passionate amateur cyclist, his business may still be relatively small, with two staff and an annual turnover of just over half a million euros. However, given the love he has for what he does, together with the quality of his designs, he seems destined for great success.

'The LittleBig bike is a unique three-in-one bike that adapts to a growing child's needs,' explains Simon as he shows me around his production facility and showroom in Wicklow town. 'Starting as a pedal-less balance bike, the young rider propels him or herself forward by pushing off the ground with their feet. By gliding along without stabilisers, kids quickly develop their co-ordination and motor skills.'

What is unique about Simon's design is that, instead of having to buy a new bike as your child grows, all you do is rotate the rear of the bike's frame, turning it into a bigger balance bike with a higher saddle and longer handlebar reach. Then, once your child is ready for the next stage, you add a separate pedal and crank attachment, instantly converting it into a full pedal bike. Because your child has already learned how to balance, using pedals is much easier than if he or she was transitioning from stabilisers. A simple but ingenious design, this allows the bike to be used by children all the way from the age of two up to seven.

'We focus almost exclusively on selling online, which has made it possible for us to sell to customers from all over the world,' explains Simon. 'Approximately forty per cent of our business comes from the UK, forty per cent from the US, ten per cent from Ireland and the remaining ten per cent from places ranging from Canada and Egypt to the UAE, Korea and even Japan.'

As we speak, Simon is putting the finishing touches to an order that came in online the previous night – from Dallas, Texas. Sometimes, he can't believe the level of interest his new bikes are generating.

Originally from Greystones, County Wicklow, Simon Evans got hooked on cycling at an early age. Having received a degree in civil, structural and environmental engineering from Trinity College Dublin, he moved to Cambridge in the UK, where he worked for the next three years as a structural engineer on historic buildings, including the Royal Observatory, Greenwich, and the Royal College of Arts.

In 2008 he decided it was time to leave his job to fulfil his lifelong ambition of cycling around the world. Together with his long-time friend, Fearghal O'Nuallain, he spent the next eighteen months cycling up to sixteen hours a day and covering more than 30,000km through some of the highest, driest and most remote places on earth. In doing so, they became the first Irish people to successfully circumnavigate the globe by bicycle – raising over €25,000 for the charity Aware in the process. However, coming home to Ireland in 2010 would prove every bit as challenging as the cycle ride he had just completed.

'Because of the slowdown in the building sector it was impossible to get engineering work,' admits Simon. 'Not wanting to emigrate, I took up a temporary job in a local bicycle shop as a mechanic while I weighed up my options. While there, I saw first-hand the many shortcomings of the current crop of kid's bikes. Most were heavy, cumbersome and generally of poor quality. Because kids grow so quickly, many parents, for cost reasons, often go for cheaper options or buy bikes that are way too big so their kids can grow into it – something that is not good for either a child's balance or their confidence. During my time there, I came across balance bikes for the first time – a relatively recent introduction to Ireland – and saw how easy and intuitive they were for kids to ride. Standing next to a row of bikes one day, I literally had a light bulb moment where I thought, kids keep growing, so why not make a bike that can grow with them?'

Simon spent the next two years tweaking his designs and finalising prototypes before eventually finding a manufacturer that could produce the bikes to the quality he wanted, while keeping the price affordable for parents.

'The parts come in from China, but we assemble everything here. That way we control the quality of every bike we sell, while also giving customers the added reassurance that everything has been fully checked by us before being shipped,' says Simon.

LittleBig Bikes has received many awards for its unique designs, including an acclaimed international Red Dot Award for outstanding design alongside global brands such as Ferrari and McLaren.

'We also recently received the "Best in Class" award from Two Wheeling Tots, the most comprehensive review website for kids' bikes,' explains Simon proudly. 'We are launching bike customisation options where customers can choose wheel and frame colours. We're also launching new German and French versions of our website to help expand into these EU markets. My aim now is to continue to build the brand internationally, grow sales and ensure that our customers and their children are 100 per cent happy with what we offer. If we can do that, we'll ensure that we make a name for the LittleBig bike as the best, most adaptable children's bike on the market,' he adds.

With a patent pending on his designs that will give him protection in 128 countries around the world, the long journey to success looks like it's just beginning for the young Wicklow man. But then, Simon Evans has already proved that he is a man that can stay the course when it comes to long journeys.

Simon's Advice for Other Businesses

Use your personality

Try to reflect your own personality within your brand rather than relying solely on a logo or corporate image. In the same way that people sometimes love to shop at a local farmers' market rather than a supermarket chain, many people love to support unique small businesses that have a real face. Make yourself part of your business's story.

Keep a tight eye on your cash flow

It is vital that you have enough money in the bank. If you are a small business, you should check both your bank account and your online payments system every day to make sure you know what you have and what will be lodged over the coming week. In that way you can ensure that your income matches your outgoings and avoid unwelcome and unexpected difficulties.

Keep things simple and lean

Try not to over-complicate your business. If you can manage to keep it simple as well as lean, you will be able to adapt to changes or challenges more quickly. This will give you a significant advantage over other larger and more established companies who may find it more difficult than you to respond to changing market conditions and trends.

CHAPTER 29

LOSING A JOB BUT FINDING A VOCATION

– The Story of Wallace Myers International

www.wallacemyers.ie

Ken Harbourne lost his job in 2010 when the recruitment business in which he worked closed down. In response, he decided to set up his own recruitment company. With nothing more than the €15,000 he received as part of his redundancy settlement, he has now succeeded in growing Wallace Myers International to a team of thirty-five staff and a turnover of more than €5.5 million – all in less than six years.

'We are busy all year round because we cover a broad range of office-based professional roles that are increasingly in demand, from accounting and finance to legal, HR and sales as well as marketing, technology, business support and administration. And we have a separate division dedicated specifically to finding staff and managers for the retail sector,' explains Ken.

Ninety per cent of the company's existing customers are based in Ireland and include large multinational firms, high growth start-ups, as well as Irish firms that are trading internationally. Wallace Myers also places candidates in countries where Ken's Irish customers have overseas operations. As part of his ambitious plan to internationalise the business, he has recently opened an office in Prague, where he already employs four staff.

But his journey has not been easy. Ken Harbourne grew up

in Beaumont, on Dublin's northside, where his father worked as managing director of Peugeot Ireland. Business and a strong work ethic were principles he was exposed to from an early age. Like many future entrepreneurs, Ken had a variety of part-time jobs during his teenage years, from working in bars to helping out in a local printing factory. After school, he did a degree in marketing at the Marketing Institute in Dun Laoghaire, while putting in thirty hours a week as a manager with Dunnes Stores.

In 1999 Ken landed a job with Calibre Recruitment, largely on the results of a personality profile assessment that identified his ideal job as recruitment consultant. The role turned out to correctly match both his interests and his aptitudes.

'The owner of the company was very direct with me: "Generate €10,000 a month or we'll fire you." That was certainly a strong motivator,' says Ken.

He was handed a phone and a copy of the *Yellow Pages* and told to get to work. The new recruiter took to his role quickly. He got out his list of Dunnes Stores suppliers where he had previously worked and set to work ringing them to see if they had any vacancies. After two months in the job, he had succeeded in breaking the company's sales record and within six months was generating seventy per cent of the company's revenue. And this was despite the fact that there were over thirty other recruitment consultants working in the business at the time.

After a year, Ken was ready for a new challenge and headed to Sydney, Australia, where he also worked in recruitment, placing Irish and UK candidates in banking roles in the city. When he returned home to Ireland, he was offered a job managing the Irish operations of Robert Hall International, the world's oldest and most profitable recruitment company.

At the time, the company had only two employees in Ireland and was losing over €200,000 a year. In less than four years under Ken's guidance the company was employing thirty-five staff and making over €600,000 net profit per year.

'In 2010, with the recession kicking in, Robert Hall decided to pull out of several European countries, including Ireland. The news came without warning and after nearly seven years with the company, the team and I were made redundant. The office closed down one hour later,' says Ken. 'I remember calling my wife who was in tears on the phone. We had a Celtic Tiger mortgage at the time and our first child on the way. We just couldn't believe this was happening.'

With commitments to meet and few other options available to him at the time, Ken decided to set up his own company and two days later Wallace Myers International was born.

'In picking a name for the business, I looked up the ten most popular surnames in the US and the ten most popular surnames in the UK and found two that worked well together. And I added International at the end,' he explains.

With every cent of his €15,000 redundancy package now invested in the business, Ken set about renting a small office in Dublin. Having secured his recruitment agency license, he was now in business for himself.

'It was a scary time. When you're a start-up and unproven, it's a big challenge to attract top companies as clients as well as top performing candidates,' admits Ken. 'However, I soon found out that when your back is to the wall, you'll find a way to make it work. I had to,' he says emphatically.

Ken set about building a brand that would stand out from his competitors. Drawing on his seventeen years' experience, he developed a world-class operating model based on being ethical and acting in people's best interests. He was also adamant about taking a long-term perspective by putting the client's interests ahead of securing short-term fees.

'These principles, together with the quality of our staff, have proven key to the company's success,' says Ken. 'In our industry, you are only as good as the staff member or consultant that represents you and that's where we win.'

Ken plans to open at least three more European offices over the next five years, and to grow annual revenues to €40 million over the same time frame. He has not forgotten the challenges he faced along the way and continues to give back to the community through his support for Jobcare – a local non-profit initiative that assists professionally skilled individuals and graduates who are struggling to find work.

'It's funny to think that, had I not been made redundant, I might still be working for my old employer now,' he adds with a smile.

What Ken Harbourne has managed to achieve – and in such a short timescale, too – is remarkable. His route to becoming an entrepreneur was born out of adversity and necessity, which are themselves strong motivating forces. And despite having gotten this far so quickly, he looks like someone who is only getting warmed up.

Ken's Advice for Other Businesses

Choose your professional advisors carefully

Choose accountants and solicitors who are experienced and preferably on recommendation. You should also insist that they are honest and forthright with you and that they become proactive when offering advice as opposed to just doing their basic jobs.

Be an expert in your sector

Only set up a business if you are a subject matter expert in that sector and you know from proven experience that you are better at it than your competitors. Starting any business is challenging but starting one in a totally new area can be full of pitfalls.

Lead by example

To be successful, always stay hands-on and lead by example. Don't get so caught up in general administration and back office stuff that you lose sight of the most important aspect of the business – the customer and your need to consistently deliver great service to them.

CHAPTER 30

HUG YOUR CUSTOMER
– The Story of Louis Copeland & Sons

LOUIS COPELAND
AND SONS

www.louiscopeland.com

Louis Copeland is by far Ireland's best-known tailor and men's clothing retailer. His mission is to provide Ireland's men with the highest quality garments as well as an unrivalled level of customer service. Now in their fourth generation, the Copeland name has been synonymous with quality tailoring for the last 100 years.

Renowned for having dressed everyone from movie stars and presidents to top businessmen and sporting heroes, I first met Louis in 2009 when I went to buy a suit for the first series of the TV programme *Dragons' Den.* I was struck by his ability to connect, and it quickly became clear that here was a man who not only understood his trade but also the principles of good business. Both are in his blood.

Copeland's was started by Louis' grandfather, Hyman Kaplan, a Jewish trouser-maker who moved to Ireland from Lithuania in 1912.

'My grandfather changed his name to Copeland and later passed on the business to my father, also named Louis. Who in turn passed it to my brother Adrian and I.' Louis himself started working in the business when he was only twelve. 'After school and at weekends, I would help with everything from sweeping the floor to tidying up around the shop,' explains Louis. At the age of fourteen, he left school to attend tailoring college, then served out his apprenticeship in a factory on Thomas Street that specialised in men's suits.

'I was about seventeen years old when I officially joined the family business,' Louis says. 'My father had his own workshop, where he was designing and manufacturing the suits that were sold in the shop.'

It was there, under the watchful eye of his father, that Louis honed his now famous skills as a tailor. Since then, he and his brother Adrian have grown the business to include seven stores. Six of these are located in Dublin: Capel Street (where Louis is mostly based), Pembroke Street (where Adrian spends most of his time), Wicklow Street, Custom House Quay and two in Dundrum (one of which is a Gant branded store). The seventh store is situated in Galway. It's an impressive achievement that now generates more than €14 million in annual turnover and has created over seventy jobs.

'The business itself has also evolved over the years from when we only sold made-to-measure suits. Today, you can buy a wide range of ready-made designer suits off the peg,' explains Louis. 'To survive in business, you have to be willing to continuously change. If you are not moving forward then you are, in effect, moving backwards because everybody else around you is moving forward.'

Pictures adorn the walls of his store of some of those who have been fitted out by Louis, including Tom Jones, Jedward, Pierce Brosnan and sporting legends from the worlds of golf, snooker, horse racing and boxing. There are even letters of thanks from former American presidents Ronald Reagan and Bill Clinton.

So what about the perception that Louis Copeland's is

only for high-profile celebrities or mega-successful business people?

'We have dressed many celebrities over the years and we are grateful that they have become great ambassadors for the business. But the bulk of our business is from members of the general public who come to us for quality wear as well as for special occasions such as weddings,' says Louis.

What's the secret to surviving in the business for so long?

'That's simple. It's because we put the customer first. We treat people the way we would like to be treated,' says Louis. 'You have to hug your customers,' he adds with a warm smile. He then explains that he is referring to the title of a well-known book by author and American businessman Jack Mitchell on how to personalise sales to achieve outstanding results.

'Of course he doesn't mean literally hugging your customers,' Louis goes on. 'What he means is including personal touches that build lasting relationships and customer loyalty, such as remembering a customer's name, their work interests or hobbies or simply offering them a cup of coffee while they wait for garments to be altered.'

In the wrong hands such a philosophy could come across as phony, but not in the case of Louis and his staff – they have a genuine and authentic interest in their customers.

Louis tells me that he doesn't have an office. 'My office is on the shop floor,' he says.

Does he model himself on anyone?

'Yes, I want to do for menswear what Feargal Quinn from Superquinn did for the supermarket sector,' he answers, 'and customer service is right at the heart of that.'

I am anxious to understand how he replicates the integrity of his customer service model across all seven stores.

'We are blessed to have great staff,' he says. 'Many started as messenger boys with us and have worked their way up in the business. But it's also important to hug your team as well as your customers. It's well understood in business that staff tend to mirror the attitudes and leadership style of their bosses, so we try to set high and consistent standards.'

At 7 a.m. every Saturday Louis has an hour-and-a-half meeting with all staff in the Capel Street branch, where they review the previous week and plan for the week ahead. At 7 a.m. every Tuesday he and Adrian meet with the managers of all seven stores for a two-hour meeting to look at how each store is performing.

'We typically set two or three goals and focus on them for the week. You have to be continuously trying new things,' explains Louis.

Louis himself is a member of the highly regarded International Menswear Group, an international body made up of the best menswear retailers from each country. It is there he gets many of his new ideas for the business.

'We meet each year for a week,' explains Louis. 'We share marketing ideas and strategies that are working for us. We even regularly swap staff for periods so they get exposed to new insights and learning from around the world.'

However, like all businesses, his journey has not between without challenges.

'The recent downturn in the economy saw turnover fall by as much as forty per cent in some stores,' he admits. To counteract this, Louis worked closely with his suppliers to negotiate better prices that he, in turn, was able to pass on to his customers. In 2013 he introduced his own Louis Copeland suit label, followed by his Louis Copeland shirt collection, which provide greater choice and more affordable options for customers.

On the marketing front, he invested heavily in launching his now twice-yearly brochure, shot in locations ranging from Glendalough to Barcelona and Marrakech. He even brought in a new 'Made to Measure' service, allowing customers to choose everything about their suit, from fit to fabric and lining, and even personalised embroidering.

Louis remains positive about the future. Although he expects that, like all business owners, he will have to get up a little earlier and work a little harder. He already works seven days a week, including four hours on Sunday. 'But it's not really work when you enjoy what you do,' he tells me. 'I get my adrenalin from meeting people and making sure they have a happy experience with us.' He also hits the gym every morning at 6.30 a.m. before heading to the shop. 'It's very important to be fit and healthy if you are to have enough energy to excel in business.'

Louis Copeland is an inspirational entrepreneur. Having taken over from their father, he and his brother Adrian have successfully grown the business into an iconic brand. No doubt, when the time comes, they will pass it on to their sons who also work in the business and are also called Louis and Adrian. In the meantime, Louis will continue to deliver the exemplary level of customer service that has become the hallmark of his brand.

When I leave the store, I don't actually get a physical hug from him, but I do get a firm handshake, a clap on the back and the customary Louis Copeland smile.

Louis' Advice for Other Businesses

Hug your customer

Cultivate a genuine interest among all your staff about the need to build personal relationships. Look after your customers well and treat them as you would like to be treated.

Hug your people

It is important to hire the right staff, who will care about your business and your customers. But it is also important that you invest time in training them so they can grow and develop.

Keep moving forward

Continuously look to the future and to the challenges faced by your customers. Therein lie your opportunities.

CHAPTER 31

ONE PER CENT BETTER IN 100 DIFFERENT WAYS
– The Story of Kelly's Resort Hotel

www.kellys.ie

There are few Irish businesses whose reputation for customer service and loyalty can match that of Kelly's Resort. Located alongside five miles of beautiful sandy beach, Kelly's in Rosslare, County Wexford, is a popular destination for both Irish and overseas visitors.

This family business was set up in 1895, originally as a small tearoom, by the present owner Bill Kelly's great-grandparents. Today, it is a modern holiday resort with 120 guest rooms, a staff of 225 and an annual turnover of more than €14 million. The success of Kelly's could easily be attributed to its stunning location and its expansive and modern facilities, but the real secret to its longevity lies elsewhere. The friendly and engaging nature of the hotel's staff is what is immediately apparent; more surprising, however, is the rapport that exists among the resort's guests.

'It's part of the magic that happens here,' explains Bill. 'And it's definitely why some people have been coming back here every year for the last thirty years.'

There are individuals and couples strolling through the

grounds, while others sit quietly reading or engaged in intimate conversations with one another. Children and adults of all ages move through the resort making use of the indoor swimming pools, tennis courts, fitness centre, playroom and jogging track, while others busy themselves with everything from badminton and bowls to croquet. There are also several restaurants and bars, and an award-winning sea spa with a seawater vitality pool and thermal suite.

Bill is quick to acknowledge the work done by his parents and grandparents in developing and enhancing the facilities. 'My job has been to build on what they started,' he says modestly. 'And location is important; we are blessed to sit along a beautiful beach, less than two hours from Dublin and Cork.'

Since taking over, Bill has continued to invest heavily, adding new facilities such as the 15,000 square-foot spa and treatment rooms, which were added in 2006 at a cost of €7 million. Continuous refurbishing and upgrading of rooms is also a necessary part of keeping them attractive and inviting. Recently, too, a new kitchen and laundry were added at a further cost of €1.5 million.

'But the most important thing in any hotel is to look after your customers. We can create the best physical product but it's really the staff that give warmth and personality to the place and that bring people back,' Bill stresses.

And it works. About eighty per cent of those visiting the hotel come almost religiously every year – often for the same dates and with their entire families. Bill regularly welcomes couples with children whom he remembers serving when they themselves were only children.

'It begins to make you feel old,' he laughs, adding, 'guests make great friends here, through playing golf, having a drink or through their children getting to know other children. People will also regularly book their annual holidays to coincide with other families they know.

'My aim is to have people come here as customers but leave as ambassadors,' he tells me.

With occupancy levels currently running at over ninety-two per cent year-to-date, it's an approach that seems to be working. This is an extraordinary achievement for a non-city-centre hotel.

Bill constantly reminds new staff of the fact that it is not he who pays their wages, but the customers. 'Once staff understand that, it changes the way they think and act,' he says.

His management style is relaxed but focused. Neither he nor his management team spend much time in their offices. Instead, his office is on the floor, alongside staff.

'If they are under pressure, restaurant staff can call on me or any manager to help clear a table or get drinks for a customer,' says Bill. 'That way, everyone understands that the focus is always on making sure the customer has a good experience.'

Bill strives for what he calls 'Moments of Truth' or 'Wow Moments', where staff noticeably go out of their way to help customers. 'It can be as simple as a staff member taking a customer to where the toilets are, rather than just giving them directions,' he explains.

He believes that it is these individual contacts – thousands of them each day – that make all the difference. 'If each staff member can create one or two "Wow Moments" every day, imagine the impact that can have on the overall business,' he says.

Bill and his French-born wife, Isabelle, took over the running of Kelly's in 1987. He met Isabelle – daughter of a leading wine-maker from the Châteauneuf-du-Pape region of France

– in Switzerland when they were both training in hotel management in Lausanne.

After college Bill spent a number of years working in hotels in Florida, Taiwan and Paris, before returning to take over the family business. His father, also Bill, had died ten years earlier, at the age of fifty. 'My mother, Breda, did an amazing job of running the hotel after that,' he tells me proudly. 'With seven children to take care of, it can't have been easy.'

The recent recession was a challenging time for the business but a combined strategy of reinvesting in the resort's facilities, as well as reducing operating costs, helped see it through. To counteract the downturn and help keep turnover up, Bill introduced incentives such as early bird menus in the resort's restaurants.

'We could have let staff go but that would have impacted on the level of customer experience, and as a result, the long-term sustainability of the business,' he says.

Instead, Bill brought his staff together and explained that no one was going to lose their jobs. Nor were they going to have their wages cut. However, in order to continue to meet the demands of a changing market place, he asked them to commit to greater flexibility and even greater customer service.

In addition, he looked for innovative ways of attracting new customers, such as teaming up with well-known figures in the worlds of fitness, cooking, gardening and painting in order to provide fun, creative activity breaks throughout the year. These proved so popular that he continued them once the business environment improved.

Bill now has help running the business, since his daughter, Laura, joined. 'It's great to welcome a fifth generation of Kellys into the business,' he says proudly.

And as if running a busy hotel and resort wasn't enough to keep him busy, Bill recently opened Kelly's Café, a 120 seater café near Wexford town, as well as a small deli and coffee shop, Kelly's Deli, near the beach in Rosslare.

In his spare time, Bill plays golf and tennis and generally keeps fit. He undertook his first triathlon in his early forties and ran his first marathon at the age of forty-five. 'Being physically fit helps me stay energised and focused,' he says.

There is no doubt that Kelly's Resort is a special place. The location, on a stretch of golden sandy beach, provides an instant feeling of relaxation. So too does the resort's long list of amenities and facilities. But Bill Kelly is right. It's the people that make the difference. The real magic of this place is its staff. For they and Bill have long since realised that customer service is not a department tucked away in an office somewhere; customer service is every staff member's job.

It comes as no surprise then that those who have stayed here rejoice in telling others how great Kelly's is; it's because, they too, have become proud ambassadors.

Bill's Advice for Other Businesses

Recognise the lifetime value of your customers

Success is not measured by the amount of business or bookings at any one point but by the amount of repeat business you receive over time. To succeed long term, you have to understand the lifetime value of every customer.

A different way to look at competition

Successful companies are not always 100 per cent better in every way than their competitors. Instead, they are often just one per cent better, but in a 100 different ways. Decide on what ways you want to be better and make these your points of differentiation.

It's staff who make the difference

Staff, more than anything else in your business, will give it its personality. As owners and managers we can get the physical product right, but only staff can create the experience that brings people back again and again.

CHAPTER 32

FROM PSYCHOLOGIST TO GLOBAL ENTREPRENEUR – The Story of RigneyDolphin and RelateCare

www.rigneydolphin.ie
www.relatecare.com

It is always fascinating to discover what prompts entrepreneurs to swap the safety of paid employment for the precarious world of self-employment. Many, it turns out, can trace their decision to a specific moment when they consciously decided to stop dreaming about being an entrepreneur and actually become one.

Frank Dolphin is one such entrepreneur. His career path took him from clinical psychologist and university lecturer to a successful international business builder – all because of a throwaway remark from a university student. Together with his wife, Adrienne, Frank has founded two companies: RigneyDolphin in 1990 and RelateCare in 2013, which between them employ 570 staff and generate more than €20 million in annual revenues.

'Our two businesses are related yet different,' explains Frank from his companies' headquarters in the IDA Business Park in Waterford city. 'RigneyDolphin provides business process outsourcing solutions [the modern name for what used to be termed a call centre] to large-scale organisations in the public and private sectors. This means we look after everything from sales, customer service and support helplines, to admin and back office-type functions on behalf of our clients.'

Now one of the largest such service providers in the country, the company works across sectors as diverse as utilities and healthcare, as well as financial services, telecommunications and automotive. Among their many customers are BMW, Audi, Vodafone, SSE Airtricity, the Health Service Executive (HSE) and An Post.

The second business, which the couple co-founded with business partner Conor Byrne, specialises in international healthcare outsourcing and consultancy. 'Put simply, we work with large hospital groups in the US, where we look after scheduling appointments and follow-up calls with patients after they are discharged,' says Frank.

'The US has a different system to Ireland, in that hospitals get fined if a patient has to be readmitted. To reduce the likelihood of this happening, resources are targeted at making sure they stick to their recovery programme. Our job is to contact them a few days after they are discharged, to remind them of the need – for example – to take their meds, change the dressing on their wounds or follow the post-operative exercises they have been given by doctors or physiotherapists.'

The company also provides a 'Nurse on Call' service where patients who phone a hospital to speak to a nurse get through to one of the RelateCare US-registered nurses based in the company's centres in either Waterford or Cleveland, Ohio.

'In the US, patients generally choose to go directly to their hospital, rather than be referred by their local doctor, as is mostly the case here,' explains Frank. 'Therefore, for hospitals, it's not just about making sure procedures are carried out correctly –

it's about ensuring that the whole customer experience is a positive one; otherwise patients will vote with their feet and go elsewhere – ultimately impacting the hospital's bottom line.'

At home, Frank and his team work with the HSE, providing support services for those wishing to give up smoking. More recently, they have begun working in other regions, such as Abu Dhabi in the UAE.

Frank's journey into business is an interesting one. Having grown up in Birr, County Offaly, he graduated from University College Dublin with a PhD in psychology. It was there he met his future wife, Adrienne – a computer science student from Carndonagh, County Donegal. Frank's first job was as a clinical research psychologist with Dublin's Temple Street Hospital, where he worked with young children with speech disorders. Later he lectured in psychology in Trinity College before moving to Waterford Institute of Technology where he set up the institute's psychology department.

'We all have light-bulb moments and I had mine while teaching organisational psychology to a class of undergraduates. A debate ensued about the importance of leadership in our society. I remember saying how important I thought leadership was, and how we all needed to step forward if we wanted to make our impact in the world. One student stopped me in my tracks when he asked, "Well if it's so important to be a leader, then why are you talking to us about it rather than actually becoming one?" I had no answer,' says Frank.

Reflecting on the question, he realised it was time to heed the voice that had long been in his head and start his own business.

'Thankfully, Adrienne was hugely supportive, even though it meant me leaving my permanent, pensionable job – not easy considering we had two young children and another on the way,' he says.

He began by offering training, psychometric testing and employee profiling to companies who were recruiting. This led him to recognise the growing trend towards outsourced services and contract staff. Shortly afterwards he set up RigneyDolphin, a small call centre, named for his own and his mother's surnames.

'It was scary but once we landed our first client, Vodafone, we began to feel more confident. We are still working with them today,' says Frank.

He is quick to admit that he did not have a well-thought-out plan in the beginning and instead took opportunities as they came along.

'The banks considered a psychologist trying to make it in business a very high risk,' says Frank. 'And because there wasn't much cash around in the early 1990s, we had to start the business in our front room. Eventually we decided to re-mortgage our home to fund the business properly. There were many sleepless nights in those early years,' he admits.

Frank went on to build a strong customer base, particularly among telecoms companies. However, he was nervous about becoming overly reliant on one sector and so began to explore other areas. Based on his previous experience in health, it made sense to investigate opportunities in that space.

Then came a chance meeting at an Enterprise Ireland event in Dublin with the CEO of Cleveland Clinic in Ohio, who needed someone to help restructure the clinic's call centre. With over 43,000 staff, Cleveland Clinic was among the top hospital groups in the US. This would prove the perfect opportunity for Frank to diversify not only from his over-reliance on the telecoms sector but also from his over-reliance on the Irish market. Building on that experience, he continues to roll the service out to other leading hospital groups across the US.

'We live in a fast-changing world,' Franks explains. 'To remain successful, we continue to embrace new technologies such as cloud, that allows our customers to communicate with us via email, web chat, SMS and social media. To use the common parlance, we're now multi-channel and multi-modal.'

He recognises the value of his team in both businesses. 'Their closeness and loyalty has been key to our ongoing growth and development,' he stresses.

Not one to sit still, Frank and Adrienne recently set up a third company, this time with two existing employees. Intriniti is a software development business providing bespoke management tools for call centres and high volume telephony-based businesses.

Frank's desire to give back has seen him serve as chairman of the HSE, Temple Street Children's Hospital and the Review Group for the New Children's Hospital and the Dublin Midland Hospital Group.

Frank Dolphin may not have started out with a grandiose strategic plan but his journey from psychologist and lecturer to successful entrepreneur is inspiring. If he were to meet his former student now, he would surely say thank you for the motivation that simple question generated. Frank has not only become a successful business owner, but the sort of leader he lectured about all those years ago.

Frank's Advice for Other Businesses

Diversity spreads risk

Seek to diversify your product or service offering, as well as your markets and geography. This spreads risk and reduces over-dependence on any one sector or market.

Have fun

'All work and no play ...' You have to enjoy what you are doing, otherwise you will never sustain the effort required to succeed. When the fun goes out of it, reinvent, refocus and renew.

Trust your gut

Good advisors are important, but at the end of the day you have to trust your gut. It's what got you to where you are now. Others can help and advise but ultimately you have to believe in what you are doing. Learn to develop confidence in your own judgement.

CHAPTER 33

FROM HOME-MAKING TO DEAL-MAKING

– The Story of J. J. O'Toole

J J O'Toole Ltd
YOUR PACKAGING PARTNER SINCE 1914

www.jjotoole.ie

Businesses tend to operate in a complex and ever-changing environment, which means longevity is a fair indication of how good they are at what they do. J. J. O'Toole Ltd is clearly doing something right. Set up in 1914 and based in Raheen in County Limerick, it is Ireland's oldest packaging supplier.

The company's CEO, Vicki O'Toole, is a confident and articulate businesswoman. She took over the business in 2010 following the death of her husband, Fergus, grandson of the original founder. It has been a long and challenging journey for the once full-time mother and homemaker, one that she never set out to undertake. A combination of tragedy and necessity left her with few options but to rise to the challenge. Today, she leads a dynamic and award-winning business that employs twenty-five staff and has an annual turnover of more than €10 million.

'My late husband Fergus' grandfather, J. J., started the business over 100 years ago, supplying paper and stationery to businesses in the Limerick area. Since then we have gone on to concentrate on packaging solutions,' explains Vicki. 'I think that what has sustained our success has been our focus on providing customers with products of exceptional quality, delivered with excellent service while maintaining honesty and integrity in all our dealings,' she says.

The company's product list includes everything from exquisite high-end luxury packaging, to more basic grip-seal bags, bubble wrap, deli containers and butcher bags.

'Our "one-stop solution" approach has been key to us winning business from many of Ireland and the UK's leading firms, across retail, food and general industry,' says Vicki.

Among the colourful display of bags, packaging and wrapping papers is work she has produced for well-known brands such as Brown Thomas, Avoca, Newbridge Silverware, Kilkenny Group, Meadows and Byrne, Musgrave's, Dunnes Stores and Lloyds Pharmacy. But the business also has a strong export component, with around twenty per cent of its work now coming from leading high-street brands in the UK, such as Selfridges & Co. and Fenwick on Bond Street in London.

'While we do a lot of work for these blue chip-type companies, we also supply everyone from butchers and delicatessens to restaurants, independent boutiques, golf clubs, schools, online businesses and lots more,' says Vicki.

Vicki O'Toole's journey has been an interesting one. She grew up in County Limerick, where from a young age she was exposed to the world of business. Her father ran a hugely successful company called McMahon Builders Providers, with branches all across the country. She studied law for a year in University College Cork, but decided that academia wasn't for her. After a year au pairing in Paris, she returned home to work in the family's business. In 1985 she met and married Fergus O'Toole. At the time Fergus was managing director of the company that had been set up by his grandfather and previously run by his father. When the couple had the first of their five children, Vicki became a full-time mother, although she would help Fergus in the business during busy periods or to cover staff who were sick or on leave. Then, in 2001 and out of the blue, Fergus became ill.

'It was the first sign of his depression we had seen,' explains Vicki. 'The following year he got worse, compounded by the effects on the business of the new plastic bag tax. At the time, eighty per cent of the company's turnover came from supplying plastic bags to the retail sector. This change in legislation meant, however, that retailers now had to charge customers for every plastic bag they used. This meant that many retailers simply stopped using plastic bags. The result was that the company's total turnover dropped by forty per cent overnight.'

Fergus' depression worsened and Vicki found herself more and more involved in the day-to-day running of the business.

'It was tough. Our youngest child was only a year old,' she recalls. 'At first, I didn't know where to begin. Every day became a school day for me – and still is,' she adds.

By 2005 Vicki had taken over as managing director of the business. Gradually she began to introduce changes, including an in-house graphic design service, as well as outsourcing production to paper manufacturers across Europe and the Far East in order to better compete. Her increased attention to detail and her renewed focus on customer service saw the company develop a reputation as a leader in the premier luxury packing space and soon she began winning major new contracts with brands such as Brown Thomas and Selfridges & Co. in the UK. As the number of customers grew, so did Vicki's confidence and self-belief.

She then wrote to Simon Pratt, MD of the Avoca group of stores.

'I told him I really wanted to work with Avoca,' explains Vicki. 'I got to meet with the company and have been supplying them ever since. As with all our customers, my job is to get to know everything about their brand so we can create packaging that best reflects their business.'

In 2010 everything changed for Vicki. That year, Fergus tragically died.

'I wanted to sell the business,' says Vicki. 'I couldn't see what else to do. And only for my brother, I may well have. He convinced me to wait a while until I could think more clearly. It began to dawn on me that I had five children, the youngest of whom was nine, and, above everything else, I still had to provide for them,' she says.

Worried about running the business and looking after her family, she decided to give it three months to see if she could juggle both. With the support of her staff, and great kindness and patience shown by customers and colleagues, Vicki got through this initial period. And from there, things gradually began to get easier.

'I used to hate it when people told me things would get easier, but they did,' she says. 'As a woman stepping in to the shoes of three generations of men, I also had to face the challenge of gaining acceptance and respect from some colleagues and business associates.'

Determination and perseverance saw her through and she has continued to grow the business, adding new clients such as Shannon Airport, Diesel, Francis Brennan, Dunnes Stores, Toymaster, Zest and Max Benjamin. In 2016 the company was awarded the entire luxury-packaging contract with Selfridges & Co.

'To be chosen by the best department store in the world is fantastic,' Vicki says proudly.

With revenues growing and new enquiries coming in every day, she is increasingly confident about the future of the business.

'The combination of a more positive overture in the economy generally, together with a greater awareness of our brand among retailers and other clients, is helping to drive this growth,' she explains.

Does she ever wonder what Fergus would think about her success? Or what his grandfather J. J. would think of a woman at the helm?

'I do often wonder,' she replies. 'I think they'd be happy … at least, I hope so.'

Vicky's Advice for Other Businesses

Undertake a feasibility study

For new businesses, it is always a good idea to conduct a feasibility study into the viability of your idea as well as the size and requirements of your target market. Equally, for existing businesses, it is always worth spending time planning your next move in order to help anticipate challenges and predict positive outcomes.

Success comes from combining passion and hard work

There is no substitute for having a passion for what you do. If you enjoy your work you will be more likely to stick at it. Similarly, few, if any, business owners get rich without putting in effort and hard work. There are few short cuts, and it's usually effort that pays dividends.

Ignore the naysayers

The world is full of people who will try to tell you that you can't succeed. Be positive and believe in yourself and your ideas. It's not about proving naysayers wrong but about not allowing them to distract you from your goals or undermine your confidence.

CHAPTER 34

PATIENT PERSPECTIVE

– The Story of Oneview Healthcare

Oneview

www.oneviewhealthcare.com

The healthcare sector is regularly in the news and very often for the wrong reasons. From long waiting lists and chronic bed shortages to patients on trollies, the demand for more and better services in our hospitals continues. Add to this the constant pressure on doctors and nursing staff as a result of staff shortages and budgetary constraints, and the challenges in our healthcare systems begin to look almost insurmountable. However, if you have ever spent time in a hospital, you will no doubt have seen first-hand how inefficient many current practices are and how these could be improved through fresh thinking and innovative approaches.

It was during one such spell in hospital that entrepreneur Mark McCloskey decided that, rather than complain about the health service, he would develop a system to help improve it. Set up in 2008, and currently operating in hospitals across Ireland, Australia, the US and Middle East, Oneview Healthcare now employs 170 staff and has annual revenues of over €9 million.

'Oneview is a software-based platform that is literally revolutionising the healthcare system,' explains Mark, whose company's global headquarters are in Blackrock, County Dublin. 'Initially, our idea was to provide a comprehensive system of communication and entertainment at the patient's bedside that would include everything from phone, email, Skype and social media to TV on-demand, movies, streaming services and gaming for children. However, we quickly expanded that concept and today our technology integrates with a hospital's own information system to provide doctors, nurses and other healthcare professionals with a single point of access to information such as a patient's medical records as well as their drug administration and treatment profiles.'

Doctors can now attend a patient's bedside and instantly call up x-rays on devices including a TV screen, tablet or smart phone. Integrated into the nurse call system, patients can select whether they want medical attention or are simply looking for a drink of water, in which case their request is directed to a care assistant leaving the nurse free to concentrate on medical matters. In addition, pre-admissions and post-discharge features allow patients to better plan their arrival as well as allowing clinical staff to monitor whether a patient is taking their prescribed medication or changing their bandages once they have been discharged.

In only eight years the company has grown to become a global success and will soon be live in six of the top fifteen acute hospitals in the US, fifty-seven hospitals in the Middle East and the two largest hospital groups in Australia, which have a combined total of 33,000 beds.

Mark McCloskey grew up in Ballally, Sandyford. After school he emigrated to the UK, where he spent five years in a variety of roles before deciding to return to Ireland. In 1988 Mark took a job selling advertisements for the *Golden Pages*. His reputation as their best-performing sales executive led to him receiving an offer of a sales role with Esat Telecom (now BT Ireland), which was expanding at the time. When the company was later sold to BT, he was approached by the founder of Easycash, Mark Roden, to help him set up his new business installing ATMs in non-bank locations around the country. This business was later sold to Royal Bank of Scotland, where Mark remained for a further two years.

'The idea for Oneview Healthcare came about when I was in hospital recovering from knee surgery,' explains Mark. 'I was in a room with three other patients and one guy kept hoarding the remote for the TV, meaning we all had to watch whatever he wanted. While the care was great, many of the hospital processes seemed inefficient, such as staff constantly asking me the same questions. Not long after being discharged, I was travelling on an aeroplane when I began to wonder how it was that I was having a much better experience with the individual in-flight entertainment system, 30,000 feet up in the air, than I had had in my hospital room. Before the plane had landed, the basic idea for Oneview Healthcare had been formed,' he says. 'But because I was neither a healthcare nor software expert, I turned to a few friends who worked in the healthcare sector and spent hours listening to their pain points or those areas where they were experiencing challenges. Based on their feedback, I recruited two software developers and together we built our new software platform.'

Mark and his wife, Niamh, then took the courageous decision to invest all of their life savings in the project, as well as re-mortgaging their family home. While the economic downturn made it a challenging time for any new business, Mark never lost heart nor did his commitment to his idea ever waver. He reached out to Enterprise Ireland and with their support began to identify those markets, globally, where spend on healthcare was still continuing.

'We identified three key regions: the United States, the Middle East and Australia, and after numerous trade visits to these regions, eventually found a number of innovative hospitals that saw the merits of what we were offering,' explains Mark. 'Although entertainment provided the initial foundation for Oneview, we quickly began to develop a solution that could demonstrate compelling benefits for hospitals around greater efficiencies and improved access to medical data, as well as providing better clinical outcomes for patients.'

In the run up to the Christmas holidays in 2012, and just before landing their very first customer, Mark and Niamh were forced to sell both their cars to pay staff wages. But their determination and sacrifices paid off shortly afterwards when they landed three major contracts in the US and Australia. With the need for funds now urgent, Mark had a chance meeting with James Fitter (an experienced corporate financier and now CEO of the company), who helped raise over €30 million for the roll-out of services to these new customers. They were now safely on their way.

'On St Patrick's Day in 2016 we became the first Irish company ever to trade on the Australian Securities Exchange – raising $62.4 million in the process,' explains Mark proudly. 'The investment has allowed us build a world-class team and an experienced advisory board.'

Looking to the future, Mark is upbeat about what he sees as the global potential of the business.

'We are focused on continued growth and are looking at new markets such as Asia, where we will soon open an office. We also see huge potential in the assisted living and senior living markets, and have recently signed contracts in this sector in both the US and Australia.'

The company also recently announced an exciting partnership with Intel, which will see both companies collaborate to deliver patient-engagement experiences beyond hospitals and into elder and community care environments using technologies that include mobile computing, sensing, data collecting, wearables and security tools.

It would now appear that the sky is the limit for Oneview.

Mark McCloskey is both an inspiring entrepreneur and a visionary. Having identified a need in the market based on his own experience, he went on to develop a world-class product and company. Like most successful entrepreneurs, he hasn't been afraid to take risks or to dream big. Hearing his story serves as a reminder that success often comes from being prepared to risk more than others think is safe and to dream more than other people think is practical.

Mark's Advice for Other Businesses

Don't be afraid to hire people smarter than yourself

Some people make the mistake of wanting to be the smartest person in their company. To be successful you need to hire the best people and be willing to learn from them. Hiring people who are smarter than you in their disciplines will fast track your success.

Remove the word 'distraction' from your vocabulary

Learn to be laser-focused on your goals and be prepared to give your heart and soul to what you are doing. Avoid being distracted by too many opportunities; seize only those that take you in the direction you want to go.

Study your competition

Keep a close eye on your competition. Study what they are doing and where you can achieve a competitive advantage over them. In a crowded marketplace, you want your customers to be happier than those of your competitors, so that they become your best sales force.

CHAPTER 35

THE COOLEST BUSINESSWOMAN IN IRELAND

– The Story of Polar Ice

PolarIce ltd

www.polarice.ie

For movie buffs and theatre enthusiasts, dry ice is known as the source of a fog-like vapour used to enhance dramatic impact. However, the uses of dry ice go way beyond the entertainment industry and it is now widely used as an important coolant in the transport and storage of all manner of perishable food and high-value pharmaceutical products.

One woman who knows plenty about dry ice is Laois-based Alison Ritchie, managing director of Ireland's leading manufacturer of dry ice, Polar Ice – a company that she helped set up in 1996 along with her father and his two brothers. Based in Portarlington, the company employs seventeen staff and has an annual turnover of over €2 million.

'Dry ice is a form of solid or frozen carbon dioxide (CO_2),' explains Alison. This CO_2 is delivered to the company's purpose-built facility in liquid form in pressurised tankers from where it is then pumped into 100 tonne on-site storage tanks. As part of the manufacturing process, this liquid is injected into a number of heavy-duty machines where the temperature drops to a staggering -78°C, causing it to solidify into a snow-like consistency. This is then further extruded through three separate pieces of equipment to form either large dry ice blocks, slices of ice or small granular pellets of ice.

'Unlike normal ice, dry ice never melts,' says Alison. 'Instead, it converts directly into a white fog-like gas, through a process known as sublimation, making it the perfect material to use in movie or theatre scenes. While we have supplied dry ice to many special effects companies, including those involved in the making of *Game of Thrones*, this represents only about two per cent of our business,' she adds. 'For the most part, our dry ice is used as a refrigerant in the shipping and storage of products that need to be kept frozen.'

Among the company's many customers is Aer Lingus, who use dry ice in their on-board catering storage units. Pharmaceutical firms too, such as Pfizer, use it in their containers when shipping high-value drugs that must be stored at continuous temperatures of below -20°C. Dry ice is also widely used in hospitals and laboratories for the storage of samples, and by the Irish Blood Transfusion Service for the transportation of vital plasma products. In the food sector, meat processors regularly use it when shipping large volumes of vacuum-packed meats on their long journeys to export markets.

I can't help but wonder: how did this young woman from Portarlington end up setting up a dry ice business of all things?

'It was during the glorious summer of 1995. I was fifteen at the time and still in secondary school,' explains Alison. 'I had gone to visit a friend who had just gotten a job in a company that made ice cubes. When my dad, Colm, came to collect me, we ended up being given a tour of the factory. At one point, he spotted a chest of dry ice that had been specially imported for a customer. Having never seen it before, he began to quiz the owner about this and about the business in general. As it turned out, the owner of the company was looking to exit the business and, having discovered that there was no one else making dry ice in Ireland, my dad decided to buy the company with a view to concentrating on manufacturing dry ice, rather than regular ice cubes.'

The business cost £45,000. So Colm, who worked as a prison officer at the time, approached two of his brothers: Enda, who worked for the Electricity Supply Board and Brendan, a garda, and each agreed to chip in £15,000. While what they bought amounted to only a couple of wet ice-making machines, some office furniture, a typewriter and a small pick-up van, at least they now had their own business from which they could grow.

'I didn't have much more than pocket money to contribute at the time,' laughs Alison. 'But I was promised twenty-five per cent of the business if I committed to work in it part-time at weekends and during school holidays and if I went on to study business in college,' she adds.

And that's what she did. She completed a degree in business studies in DCU while still working part-time in the company. In 2002, with her degree finished, she joined the business full-time and, true to their word, her father and her uncles gave her the twenty-five per cent equity stake they had promised. She was now a full-blown business partner and entrepreneur.

'Turning it into a sustainable dry ice business was not without its challenges,' explains Alison. 'By far the biggest of these was trying to raise the €2 million we needed to buy the specialised manufacturing plant. We invested all the savings we had, re-mortgaged what we could and set up a BES scheme to raise the rest. We eventually managed to gather up €1.5 million. At that point, we had already paid the deposit for the equipment but it was sitting in the US and couldn't be shipped because we were short the last €500,000. It was a scary time and the whole project was on the verge of collapsing,' she admits, wincing at the thought. 'That was until a friend introduced me to a business angel investor. After hearing my pitch and our dilemma, he took out his cheque book, looked me straight in the eye and said to me, "I'm not investing in your business, I'm investing in you", and handed me a cheque for €500,000.'

With the final investment bagged, Alison was able to get her equipment shipped and was soon the only manufacturer of dry ice in Ireland. Over time, Colm, Enda and Brendan retired from their full-time jobs and became more active in the company. From there, business began to grow.

Keen to find new uses for dry ice, Alison set up a separate non-abrasive cleaning business, Polar IceTech, which used tiny pellets of dry ice the size of rice grains to clean valuable plant and equipment, such as medical devices and power generation plant turbines. Not only did she create a further channel for her dry ice product, she also managed to turn this into a profitable business, which she later sold to a former employee.

Keen to continue her own professional development, Alison returned to college part-time and, in 2011, qualified as an accountant. In 2013, anxious to expand the business even further, she invested another €500,000 in upgrading the facility to food grade standard, which enabled the company to supply dry ice to the country's leading food producers and meat processors as a way of maintaining low temperatures during the transportation of their produce – something that resulted in overall growth of sixty-three per cent in the past three years alone.

'I also joined "Going for Growth", the Enterprise Ireland-supported women's enterprise development programme, which turned out to be an inspiration and a real game changer for me,' admits Alison. 'I found myself surrounded by like-minded women who had been through similar challenges and were not afraid to go after growth in their businesses.'

In recent months there have been changes in the ownership of the business, with Alison's father and uncles retiring, and her brother, Robert, joining her as a shareholder.

'While we've worked together for eighteen years and even though it's all business as usual, it still feels like a new start and we're both bursting with ideas and drive,' she explains.

Alison Ritchie may have a warm smile and an amiable personality, but behind her charm is a shrewd entrepreneur who possesses a steely determination to succeed.

'For me now, it's no longer about settling for good but more about going for great,' she adds with a confident smile.

Alison's Advice for Other Businesses

Find or build a support team

Surround yourself with good people. Join with like-minded business people in programmes such as 'Going for Growth', 'ACORNS' or 'SMáCHT'. They will help support and inspire you. Find a good mentor or coach also – someone who will help keep you focused during both the ups and the downs.

Respond to what your customers value

Be very clear on what your customers actually want and what they value. Be adaptable when dealing with customers and be open to learning from them. While it is important to focus on winning new business, never forget to hold onto and look after the customers you already have.

Create a business that works without you

The best businesses are those that can function effectively without you being there all the time. Aim to build a team, a structure and processes that can work without your constant involvement and supervision. That way, you can carve out time to focus on new strategies and new opportunities for growth.

CHAPTER 36

SILICON VALLEY FOR COWS
– The Story of Dairymaster

www.dairymaster.ie

Every day around the world, millions of people begin their day by pouring fresh milk into their coffee or over their favourite breakfast cereal. The milk is of course produced by cows, but there are many others who play an important role in its journey from farm to kitchen fridge.

One such company is Dairymaster. Tucked away in the quiet countryside outside Causeway, County Kerry, this award-winning company produces some of the most innovative and high-tech milking machines, milking parlours and farm equipment used throughout the world. Now employing over 350 staff, the business was set up in 1968 by local man Ned Harty. Today it is run by his son, Edmond.

Despite their success, both men remain modest and unassuming.

'We love this industry and our objective is to make dairy farming more profitable, enjoyable and sustainable for farmers everywhere. We want to be the best in the world at what we do,' says Edmond. 'Unlike many modern companies, we have also chosen to locate our research and development, as well as our manufacturing, in one single facility here in Kerry.'

Multiple tall buildings stretch across the company's eleven-acre site, each one full of machines, computer equipment and staff. Decked out in blue uniforms, the staff resemble an army immersed in activities from traditional manufacturing and software development to the latest in 3D design and intricate electronic engineering.

'Seventy per cent of everything the company produces is exported to Europe, the USA, Russia, Japan and more. Our target customers span small dairy farmers, right up to one farmer who milks 6,000 cows on a single farm in Texas,' says Edmond.

Dairymaster don't just make ordinary milking machines. Theirs incorporate the latest in high-tech applications, such as their Swiftflo Commander – essentially an iPad for cows. The next generation in touchpad technology, this has become the new brain of the milking parlour, controlling everything from milking and feeding systems to collecting information about each animal's health. Their automatic cleaners are so futuristic that they can even be programmed to clean the farmyard while the farmer sits down to his or her breakfast.

Reproduction on dairy farms has also become a key component of the company's work and their award-winning *MooMonitor+* fertility device is now one of their best-publicised innovations internationally. Fitted comfortably around the neck of the cow, this device combines the technologies of cloud computing, wearable sensing (sensors that are worn by animals or humans) and big data to monitor the cow's reproductive cycle. It is so technically advanced that it can tell when the cow is 'in heat' or when it is most opportune to receive a visit from a friendly bull or the modern AI (artificial insemination) equivalent. This information is then relayed to the farmer via text message. If the farmer fails to spot this text, the system is so well designed that its *Voice Assist* function will connect to the sound system in the milking parlour once that cow arrives for her next milking and will announce to the farmer which of his or her cows are in heat.

'In farming, time is money and yield is everything,' says Edmond. 'Most cows come in heat between the hours of 8 p.m. and 6 a.m., when, typically, the farmer is asleep or the herd is not being monitored. If you miss this window of opportunity, you delay the cow getting into calf and every time that happens, it costs the farmer, on average, €230.'

Helping to change the face of agriculture, this *MooMonitor+* has won numerous awards, including the Innovation Award at the World Dairy Expo in the USA.

The company have also developed other leading products, such as their milk tanks and cooling systems that text the farmer if there is a sudden drop in temperature, or to remind him or her that the tank requires washing before the next milking is undertaken.

'A milk tank on a farm is like a safe in a bank,' explains Edmond. 'A dairy farmer gets paid for what's in that tank, so keeping it in tip-top condition is of paramount importance and that's where our mobile technology comes in.'

The business has come a long way since it was first set up by Edmond's father. Ned Harty was the younger son of a local farmer. The tradition in Ireland at the time was that the farm was passed on to the eldest son and so Ned realised he would have to find some other career path. However, farming was all he knew and so, in 1968, he went into business, firstly selling, and later manufacturing, milking machines.

'Things were very hard at the beginning and for a long time there were more supper times than there were suppers,' remembers Ned. 'But I persevered and over time the business grew.'

Having worked in the business at weekends and during school holidays, Edmond went on to do a degree in mechanical engineering in University College Limerick, before joining the business full-time in 1998. While there, he continued to pursue his PhD before taking over as the company's CEO in 2012.

Under Ned, the company was committed to continuous and never-ending improvement, but it was Ed's passion for innovation and, in particular, software development that finally joined the dots between traditional farming methods, mechanical milking systems, manufacturing processes and emerging technologies.

'I have always been fascinated with how things work and how they can be done better and faster. When it came to dairying, I began to focus on how, as a company, we could make farming life and business life easier and more sustainable for farmers, while at the same time driving up their profits. This has now become deeply embedded in our company culture and ethos,' says Edmond.

Edmond is held in such high regard that he is regularly invited to present at international conferences on the subjects of farming and animal reproduction. He has even been invited to speak at the Web Summit about the company's award-winning *MooMonitor+* technology. BBC World also filmed a documentary on the company, which was beamed into 350 million homes and where they branded Dairymaster as Ireland's Silicon Valley for cows.

So strong is Edmond's ongoing commitment to helping transform dairy farming that he has been heavily involved in setting up a new dairy innovation centre in University College

Dublin, where he was recently appointed adjunct full professor in the School of Biosystems and Food Engineering at the university's College of Engineering and Architecture.

'My work as CEO at Dairymaster has given me a global perspective on technologies, markets and the future of the dairy sector, and I am very excited about sharing this with students.'

With more than ninety patents pending for his innovations, Edmond Harty has won many accolades, among them the overall winner of the Ernst & Young Entrepreneur of the Year 2012 and the AgriBusiness Leader of the Year Awards in 2015.

Dairymaster has come a long way, and Edmond's stewardship at the helm of the company has been nothing short of remarkable. Building on the successful company his father began, Edmond has succeeded in growing Dairymaster into an international brand that is helping to modernise a global dairy industry.

Edmond's Advice for Other Businesses

Focus on your customer

To be successful in business, focus on the needs of your customer. This involves listening to them and understanding the challenges they have and what they are trying to accomplish. Your job then becomes how to use your skills and those of your team to develop solutions that best address these needs.

Innovation is key

Use innovation as a key to do things better. Innovation is like the icing on a cake. It makes what you have to offer more attractive than your competitors. Innovation allows you to bring new solutions and new products to the market that make people want to do business with you based on your expertise.

Build a great team

No one can ever grow a business on their own. Business is a team sport that requires a variety of skills and a blended mix of experience. Working together as a team enables you to achieve much more while also having others with whom to share the burden.

CHAPTER 37

INNOVATION AND DISRUPTION

– The Story of Kent Stainless

www.kentstainless.com

Ann O'Brien is managing director of Kent Stainless. Set up in 1982 by her father Pat, the company has grown to become a world leader in the design and manufacture of stainless-steel products. Employing 106 staff between their 80,000 square-foot plant in Wexford and their offices in the UK, Holland and Qatar, the company has an annual turnover of more than €13 million. The secret to their success lies in the company's commitment to continuous innovation.

'The business was set up by my father after he was made redundant from his engineering job,' explains Ann. 'He started out doing general steel fabrication work but soon realised he needed to develop his own range of products in order to differentiate his business from others who were doing similar work.'

Success did not come overnight but was instead built gradually. Today, the company can boast an impressive list of Irish and international customers, among them stadia such as Croke Park, the Aviva and Wembley; airport and transport projects such as the Luas and Terminal 2 in Dublin, and others in Hong Kong and Jamaica; and pharmaceutical firms Abbots and Pfizer in Ireland, Wyeth in the Philippines, Novartis in the UK, Johnson & Johnson in Belgium and GSK in Nairobi.

'In 1990, we diversified and began designing and manufacturing stainless-steel drainage products, such as gullies and manholes. At the time, the company was targeting businesses involved in milk and beef processing as well as those in the drinks industry,' explains Ann. 'From there, we extended our focus to include the pharmaceutical sector and began targeting the area around Cork, which was, at the time, fast becoming one of the leading pharmaceutical centres in the world. Once we got in the door of these companies, we were able to look around and see what other products they needed. Then we'd start manufacturing these as well.'

From there, the company added hospitals, prisons, hotels and swimming pools to their expanding customer base and business grew steadily.

2001 saw the emergence of a new design phenomenon in the construction sector – streetscapes. Kent Stainless responded by developing a range of stainless-steel street furniture, including outdoor seating, litter bins, bollards and cycle racks. Business was going well but by 2007, as the crash in the construction sector was about to hit, the company realised it needed to look beyond the Irish market if it was to survive. Keen to break into the UK market, they took a contract to supply stainless-steel manhole covers and drainage products for a streetscape job in London.

'We knew we would lose money on the job. But we had to do something proactive to break into this market,' explains Ann.

It was a tactic that would pay off handsomely. As luck would have it, an architect working with Norman Foster & Partners, design architects on many large and prestigious projects throughout the UK, noticed their work.

'His office was next to the site we were working on in the Battersea area and one day, walking along the street, he looked down and spotted our stainless-steel manhole covers,' explains Ann. 'At the time, he was working on the new Wembley Stadium building so he contacted the company, and shortly afterwards we won the contract to provide hundreds of decorative traffic bollards, cycle racks and drainage covers for the stadium.'

The contract was worth more than €250,000 to the company. Even more importantly, it launched them into the UK market, where they have thrived ever since.

One of the most innovative products the company has developed to date is their range of anti-terrorist bollards for use in large sporting arenas.

'These bollards also double as large shrub and flower beds and are heavily reinforced and anchored into the ground so as not to give way in the event that they are rammed by terrorists or vandals,' explains Ann. 'We have also designed anti-terrorist litter bins which do not fragment in the event of an explosion from a bomb being placed in them.'

In 2008 the company signed the largest ever contract to be awarded in the UK and Ireland for stainless-steel furniture – for the new light rail system for Dublin, the Luas. This included a range of passenger shelters, outdoor seating and bins. In addition, they partnered with a Clare-based electronics display company, Data Display, to design and manufacture a range of digital display signs for the Luas network. The total contract was worth €5.8 million to the company.

In 2011 they went on to complete a contract for the Terminal 2 building at Dublin Airport, where they supplied everything from railings and litter bins to flag poles, security camera poles and recessed manhole covers. They also designed a unique range of pavement studs, embedded in the area around the terminal, which help assist those with visual impairment to safely navigate the pedestrian crossings. These studs were so well received that their design has since been adopted by the Transport for London agency.

'We began looking at the possibility of doing business in the Middle East in 2011,' Ann says. 'We started in Qatar where, because of the heat, it is not hygienic to leave rubbish in bins for normal collection. Instead the contents of these bins get automatically vacuumed into a series of underground tunnels and delivered to a collection point that is often miles away. We thought this might be a good place to start, so Shane Curtin, our sales and marketing director, along with technical director Michael Hurley, took an initial trip to chase an order for manhole covers for these tunnels, worth about €150,000,' she adds.

The trip proved to be a turning point for the company. Instead of coming back with an order for €150,000, the two men brought home a contract worth €5.2 million.

'This put the company into a tailspin over whether we could even meet the required six-month deadline,' confesses Ann.

But Ann and her team got to work and delivered the project on time and within budget. The following year, the company received further contracts from the Middle East, this time worth €7.6 million.

Ann stresses that while the negative side of emigration cannot be underestimated, Kent Stainless has experienced an unexpected positive aspect of the recent exodus from Ireland. 'Many architects and engineers who had in the past worked on infrastructural projects in Ireland that we had also been involved in are now working in the Middle East,' explains Ann.

'They remember the quality of the work we carried out and are now bringing us in on projects there.'

Ann joined Kent Stainless straight after school and worked her way up. At night, she studied human resource management in the National College of Ireland and in 2007 took over as managing director of the company. She believes the success of any company comes from focusing on getting great people first, and then great customers.

'Anyone can weld two bits of steel together,' she tells me. 'But what we are selling is thirty years of experience and technical know-how, as well as outstanding quality in both design and materials.'

Like most entrepreneurs, she has great praise for her staff and is keen to stress that 'No one person runs the company. It's a mix of great staff, a strong management team and a wonderful board.'

Ann O'Brien has built an exceptional business around great people, great products and great customers. She has focused on developing new and innovative products. And she has been brave enough to lead her company into new markets and new territories. Above all, she has taken risks, pushing herself and her company beyond their comfort zone. Therein lies a valuable lesson. Isn't it there – in that space beyond our comfort zones – where all our future successes lie?

Ann's Advice for Other Businesses

Break the norms

The norms of your industry are there to be broken. Be a positive disrupter if you want to achieve supernormal growth. To be really successful in your industry, you have to position your company as experts in your field.

Build your staff and your brand

Your staff and your brand are your greatest assets. Encourage staff to take action, even if it means failing from time to time. Failure brings learning and feedback. If your staff never fail, then they are not innovating enough. Protect your brand by maintaining the values it stands for.

Innovate or face death

Research and development are critical to the success of any company. Don't be afraid to ask for help when it comes to developing new innovative solutions. Innovation and new product development are what keep all of us relevant in a changing market.

CHAPTER 38

WHEN BUSINESS REALLY IS CHILD'S PLAY
– The Story of Jam Media

www.jammedia.com

For the parents of young children, TV shows, books, toys and games are not only valuable ways of keeping children occupied, but also opportunities for them to learn new concepts, develop imagination and expand vocabulary. One company leading the way in children's entertainment is Dublin-based JAM Media. Set up in 2002 by John Rice, Alan Shannon and Mark Cumberton, the company currently has offices in Dublin and Belfast, employs 160 staff and has an annual turnover of more than €9 million.

'In simple terms, we create, develop, finance and distribute children's TV and digital entertainment. Our focus is on delivering high-quality, innovative and story-driven brands with humour at their heart,' explains John, the company's CEO.

Aimed at children aged three to eleven, the company have licensed or distributed content to broadcasters in more than 120 territories, including RTÉ, BBC, Nickelodeon, France TV and ABC Australia.

One of the company's best-known shows is *Roy*, a fly-on-the wall style 'mockumentary' telling the story of an eleven-year-old cartoon boy who lives in Ballyfermot in Dublin and has a 'real' family and friends. It involves a mix of animation characters and professional actors.

'We made this originally through the Irish Film Board and it has already enjoyed four series on CBBC, as well as being distributed to over thirty other countries. We've also produced a spin-off series, *Little Roy*, featuring Roy as a five-year-old, which has already been pre-sold to eighteen territories,' says John.

Other success stories include *Baby Jake*, based on the adventures of a nine-month-old baby boy and his five-year-old brother, and *Tilly and Friends,* the story of a five-year-old girl and her gang of imaginary friends.

'At its core, our work involves creating immersive story-telling content based around engaging characters,' says John.

The response to the company's work has led them to amass a cabinet full of awards, including Irish Film & Television Academy awards, British Academy of Film and Television Arts awards and a Royal Television Society Award.

What's the secret to creating such award-winning content?

'It all starts with a light-bulb moment. That can happen anywhere, so you have to be prepared to write it down – whether on a napkin, beer mat or your mobile phone,' explains John. 'From there the idea gets developed into an initial script and then a short animation trailer which details the relationship between the various characters in the show.

'Next it's on to art direction and the development of distinct imagery for each character and the overall set.'

For each new production, John and his team develop what is referred to in the industry as 'the bible'. This is the comprehensive proposal they will present to potential broadcasters of the show. It provides an overview of the series, so that commissioning editors have a good understanding of exactly how the programme hangs together.

Once ready, John and his team take this bible and a short trailer to film and TV festivals and conferences all over the world in the hope of getting a commission. Among these is the annual Marché Internationale de Programmes Communications (MIPCOM) conference in Cannes. Attended by representatives from television studios and broadcasters across the globe, this is the marketplace for those who buy and sell new programmes and formats for international distribution.

'Being based in Ireland and the UK has been a big help to us,' says John. 'With the combined government subsidies from the Irish Film Board and support from Northern Ireland Screen, we can go out to the market with up to forty per cent of the funding already in place. This is something that really helps provide comfort to potential broadcasters that the show is actually likely to get made.'

Getting a series produced is not a speedy process. Once commissioned, it can take between eighteen months to two years to complete. To survive in an industry like this, you have to love what you do. And John clearly does.

John Rice grew up in Abbeydorney, County Kerry. He remembers as a child being captivated by cartoons. His interest in business was also evident at a very early age when he sold digital watches to his school classmates and set up sweet stalls at local community events.

'I suppose like many young entrepreneurs, I was always looking at innovative ways to supplement my pocket money,' he says with a laugh.

After school, John studied animation at Ballyfermot Senior College, before heading to the US where he got a job with 20th

Century Fox. After four years there, working mostly in feature movies, he moved to MTV in New York where his work shifted to focus more on TV. In 2000 he returned to Ireland to do a Master's degree in multimedia studies at Trinity College, where he met classmates Alan Shannon and Mark Cumberton. Two years later the trio set up their own media company, using the first letter of each of their names to create JAM Media.

'We quickly realised that technology was changing the industry and that by using software rather than traditional approaches it was now possible to create broadcast-quality content for almost half of what it would have cost in the past,' explains John.

While preparing for his daughter Rebecca's second birthday party, John came up with the idea of doing a small animation to send out as an invitation. Cutting out an image of Rebecca's head, he swapped this for the head of one of the characters in the animation.

The response from other parents was amazing, with many asking him to do the same for their children.

On the back of this, John and his colleagues then developed software that would allow TV broadcasters to invite children to submit pictures of themselves, which could then be integrated into programmes, thereby helping to personalise TV content. The feedback from broadcasters was so overwhelmingly positive that later that year they took a single episode of this content to MIPCOM in Cannes and before the week was out had bagged a deal with a US broadcaster. From there, their content eventually ended up being distributed to over 120 territories and translated into forty-five different languages. More importantly, they were now firmly established as players in the industry.

Nickelodeon later collaborated with them to produce a preschool series about a determined little bird, *Becca's Bunch*. Aired worldwide on Nickelodeon channels, the series has since been pre-sold to terrestrial broadcasters in France, Germany, Australia and the UK, and will also be produced in book format.

'We are very aware that the way children consume content is changing all the time. To succeed, we have to be where children's eyeballs are,' says John. 'Many families are also now turning away from traditional cable and subscription channels and are choosing Netflix, Amazon and Hulu, so we were delighted when we recently secured a deal with Amazon for a mixed media series about a little girl who develops a special relationship with the Loch Ness Monster. Called *Jessy and Nessy*, this is due to be streamed on all 200 Amazon Prime territories in the near future.'

John loves working in the media and animation industry. Every day is different and he gets to tell compelling stories that light up children's eyes. With digital content playing a much larger role in the future, he sees huge potential to expand into developing games and apps as well as licensing his characters to book publishers and toy companies.

Positive and upbeat by nature, John Rice laughs readily. He doesn't like to boast about his successes, which are many. Perhaps the greatest of these is the way he has managed to find a way to combine his two great loves: creating children's entertainment content with running his own business. With the company's turnover projected to grow to over €20 million over the next three years, he has much to look forward to.

His life could easily be summed up by a piece of advice we have all heard, but have not all managed to put into action: find a job you love and you'll never have to work a day in your life. John Rice clearly has.

John's Advice for Other Businesses

Belief and optimism

In business, as in life, you cannot afford to let negativity set in. By setting up your own business, you are already taking a road less travelled and you have to have full belief in yourself and your product – even if sometimes this can look like blind optimism to others.

Expect setbacks

Be prepared for setbacks and disappointments. They are a standard part of running any business. What is critical is that you learn from each setback or mistake and resolve to keep moving forward. See these as obstacles and roadblocks, rather than the end of the road.

Expand your network

Find or build a strong network. Business is about relationships and that means continuously focusing on expanding and deepening your reach. Your reputation is built on perception. Winning repeat business or referrals depends on managing these relationships.

CHAPTER 39

PROVIDING LUXURY TRAVEL TO THE STARS

– The Story of Adams & Butler

ADAMS & BUTLER

HALLMARK OF LUXURY TRAVEL

www.adamsandbutler.com (Ireland and UK)
www.africanluxury.com (Africa)
www.privateluxurytravel.com (Global)

One of the best strategies for any company looking to differentiate themselves in a crowded market place is to attempt to carve out a niche in their specific sector. This allows them to stand out from their competitors while becoming experts in their selected business area. One company which has successfully navigated such a course is Dublin-based high-end travel firm, Adams & Butler, run by Irish woman Siobhan Byrne Learat and her Kenyan-born husband, Kasao. Adams & Butler organises high-end customised travel for the super-rich and those looking for unique cultural experiences worldwide. Set up in 2003, the company employs twelve full-time staff and this year will see their turnover reach €5 million.

'We have now become the go-to contact for those looking for a unique, luxury experience in Ireland, the UK and Africa,' explains Siobhan. 'Almost all of our clients are from outside Ireland, primarily from the US, Mexico, Brazil, Australia,

Canada, Latin America, Russia and the Middle East. We do also have a handful of Irish clients but these are mostly based abroad.'

Siobhan and Kasao's clients have so far included the likes of Michael Jackson, Taylor Swift, Kim Kardashian and Kanye West, Nicholas Cage, Harrison Ford, Richard Haas, Senator Paul Ryan, several governors and ex-presidents, and numerous CEOs from top blue chip companies.

'We do everything, from booking the finest boutique and five-star hotels to the more discreet castles and private stately mansions, villas and safari camps,' says Siobhan.

Earlier this year, the company broke their own record for the most expensive itinerary booked – a family from Palm Beach, Florida who spent €270,000 for a ten-day itinerary.

I ask Siobhan for details of some of the more unusual trips they have arranged.

'We organised a trip to a castle in Ireland for an Arab prince who wanted to propose to his then girlfriend. We arranged for them to spend the day doing falconry and at the end, when the falcon returned to the woman's arm, it had with it a small package in which was a diamond engagement ring and a note asking her to marry him,' says Siobhan. 'On another occasion, we flew a couple over the Cliffs of Moher in a helicopter and landed them on a nearby beach. Later that evening, we had dinner set up in a cave complete with a violinist who serenaded them throughout. We also organised a trip to Ireland for the then treasury secretary of the US, who had always wanted to stay in an Irish castle. Afterwards, what he talked most about wasn't the time spent in the castle; it was getting a lift on a tractor with a local oyster farmer who took him on a tour of his farm. We also arranged the ultimate private safari for a Russian oligarch, who had set his sights on staying in a particular ranch in Kenya. The challenge at the time was that the place was owned by a financier family living in New York. It took us six months to track them down but we persevered and eventually it all worked out brilliantly. In most cases, our clients are cash rich but time poor, so we need to take care of things for them,' she explains.

Siobhan recalls being asked by a very famous Irish actor based in LA to find him a house to rent on Vico Road in Dalkey. None were available, so Siobhan spent days going from door to door asking if anyone knew where she could get a house to rent. One woman, who owned an apartment in London, agreed to move there for two weeks to free up her home for the actor.

'She didn't even charge him as she was so delighted he had stayed in her home,' says Siobhan.

Before setting up her own business, Siobhan enjoyed a varied career. She grew up in Dublin's Mount Merrion, where both her parents and her sister were accountants. She recalls vividly helping out in her sister's business during her teenage years – something that has benefited her ever since. After finishing her leaving cert at the age of sixteen, she got her first full-time job, only to become pregnant unexpectedly. She later returned to full-time education, completing a degree in Spanish and Arabic in University College Dublin, followed by postgraduate degrees in both business and Arabic and Middle Eastern history. For eleven years, she worked in sales, marketing, HR and finance with the Killiney Court Hotel, before joining a property company that managed a number of tourism-based properties. Then in 2003, having completed a part-time MBA (Masters in Business Administration) in the Smurfit Business

School, she set up Adams & Butler, a concept based on the exact business plan she had prepared as part of her MBA thesis.

'The first four years were tough financially. We were busy but not profitable,' admits Siobhan. 'Finding the right staff was challenging. This is a stressful business because our clients can be very demanding, and can literally change their itineraries on a daily basis. However, we have now built a team who are extremely committed to making our clients happy, no matter how strange their requests.'

Every business has a turning point and 2006 was the year things took off for Siobhan. That year she won the contract to look after pop singer Michael Jackson and his family on his extended visit to Ireland. She arranged for him to stay firstly in Luggala Estate in Wicklow and later Grouse Lodge in Westmeath.

'That really put us on the map. From then on we became the go-to company for anyone bringing celebrities to Ireland,' says Siobhan.

Two years later Siobhan met her husband, Kasao Learat, while on a visit to the safari camp in Kenya where Kasao was the assistant manager. An Elder in the Samburu tribe (relations of the famous Maasai), Kasao had trained as a park ranger in South Africa and had been made an honorary life warden of the Kenyan Wildlife Service for his work in stamping out illegal poaching.

'He wanted to make sure I knew what I was signing up for, so he made me camp in the bush, climb mountains and stay in his family's manyatta, or hutted enclosure, in Resim, where Kasao's family still live a semi-nomadic life, moving every few months,' Siobhan explains.

Today the couple arrange unique safari adventures in Kenya

where they team up with *National Geographic* documentary maker Dr Reinhard Radke, who teaches their clients how to take breathtaking wildlife photos and videos. Staying in private camps throughout Kenya, clients also get to spend a night in the bush with Kasao's tribe.

Keen to give back, the couple have set up a charity, the Nalepo Educational Fund, where they support over 100 children in school in Kenya. Because the area suffers from severe drought, many school-going children must walk miles to collect water every day and so the couple are planning to launch a crowd-funding campaign to finance the construction of a water hole for local families.

What about plans for the future?

'We have built such a successful inbound business into Ireland and the UK that we recently received enquires from parties interested in buying this side of the business. But we haven't found the right fit yet,' says Siobhan. 'I want now to focus on the outbound side of the business, where I see a growing market for wealthy middle-class Irish travellers looking for something unique abroad, a segment which is currently being catered for by UK operators,' she adds.

'Last year, we were delighted to be made Travel + Leisure A-Lister Travel Agents,' says Siobhan. 'This is the first time an Irish person has received the accolade. It was one of my dreams come true and a signal to the industry worldwide about the quality of what we provide,' she adds proudly.

Siobhan and Kasao's Advice for Other Businesses

Dare to be different

Do not be afraid to aim high, to think internationally and globally. Look out for opportunities, as they are everywhere. When you encounter them, act immediately. They won't wait for you. Aim for world class and best in practice. Set high standards for yourself and your team.

Keep an eye on finances

Your finances are the lifeblood of your company. You should know your business model inside out and especially the critical points where you are making or losing money. While it is important to have an experienced accountant, you cannot afford to be hands-off when it comes to finances.

Relationships are key to success

In business it is important to develop and maintain honest relationships based on integrity and trust. This is true in the case of customers, key suppliers, staff and major stakeholders. Focus on networking as a way to continuously expand your circle of contacts.

CHAPTER 40

THE FUTURE LOOKS BRIGHT

– The Story of Brite:Bill

www.britebill.com

If you have ever received a bill from your mobile phone provider or utility company that you didn't fully understand, then you are not alone. In fact, according to Alan Coleman, co-founder and CEO of Brite:Bill, some forty per cent of people who receive such bills end up calling their provider to seek clarification on some aspect of their bills.

Set up in 2010, along with co-founder Jim Hannon, the company employs 200 staff and has an annual turnover of over €20 million. Fifty of the company's staff are based in Dublin while the remainder are spread across their offices in London, Madrid, Toronto, Kansas and San Francisco.

'We develop software that helps our client companies improve their billing communications with their customers,' Alan tells me. 'Bills have traditionally been seen as static, cold notifications or demands for payments. However, using our specifically designed software, and operating across all platforms of communication including printed bills, online and mobile, companies can now transform the way they present and manage their billing so as to make these communications with their customers more positive, engaging and customer centric.'

The company uses the latest in analytics-based technology to create bills that are easy for customers to understand and which they will pay without the need to call the service providers' helpline or customer contact centre.

'In the US, it costs a company $10 every time a customer calls their helpline, so it makes absolute sense that if this type of needless activity could be prevented, it would be more convenient for customers and make good business sense for the service providers,' explains Alan, adding that a large US telco firm with whom he hopes to start working shortly, spends over a half a billion dollars ($500m) every year answering queries about their bills.

'Our software will help drive that down,' he insists.

The company has now built up an impressive list of national customers. Most are well-known names in the telecom sector such as Eir, UPC (Virgin) and Vodafone. However, ninety per cent of revenues come from exports to such large international clients as Tele2 in the Netherlands, T-Mobile in Germany, Rogers in Canada and Sprint in the US.

'Currently, there are more than twenty-five million individual bills, worth in excess of $5 billion, processed every month around the world on the Brite:Bill platform,' explains Alan proudly. 'Our software can design these bills so that they explain to the customers anything that is non-standard or out of the ordinary for them. The idea is to get this information in front of the customer before they become frustrated and put in a call to the service provider's contact centre,' he explains.

For example, a customer might have signed up for a new mobile phone package at €39.99 per month, but when they receive their first bill, they discover to their frustration and annoyance that the bill is for €59.99. Instead of having to ring the contact centre for an explanation, the Brite:Bill platform will pick up the variance and explain to the customer that, because they signed up in the middle of a month, the bill actually relates to a six-week period rather than a month and reassures the customer that their bill will return to the standard monthly fee, as agreed, in their next bill.

Alan also highlights how customers often struggle with the fact that some companies use different names for the products they sell compared to what actually appears on the bills their customers receive.

'Such inconsistency can lead to confusion among customers,' he explains. 'For example, if a person orders a family fibre package from their phone and broadband provider but later receives a bill that refers to a charge for a 50MB broadband and landline offering, they struggle to connect whether this is what they actually ordered because the provider has not made mention of either family or fibre in their communication. The tendency is again for the customer to ring the company's helpline for clarification leading to added frustration on the part of the customer and added cost for the service company.'

It's certainly been an exciting journey for the young Dublin man from Howth. After all, Alan Coleman never set out to become an entrepreneur.

'I didn't grow up in a business household nor did I sell the customary sandwiches to classmates for pocket money,' he says with a laugh. 'I studied computer science in University College Dublin but was terrible at the subject and only managed to scrape through.'

He found his niche when he moved on to complete a Master's in business in the Michael Smurfit Graduate Business School. Technically conversant from his degree, the application of technology in a business context would form the foundation for his next career steps as well as the eventual establishment of his own business.

His first job was with Morgan Stanley, the investment bank in London, where he helped traders get the most out of the technology they were using. Returning to Dublin in 1999, he joined a start-up called Macalla Software, which specialised in connecting mobile phone companies to banks for the purposes of allowing customers to automatically top up their phone credit.

'The four years I spent there were very exciting and formative for me,' explains Alan. 'I grew to love the freedom and the entrepreneurial aspects that working in a small company brings and began, for the first time ever, to consider setting up my own business,' he adds.

However, the downturn in the economy following 9/11 led him to seek greater job security and he joined Accenture, where he worked for the next seven years helping customers achieve better deals from their hardware and software suppliers.

'During my time there I was always exploring new ideas that might allow me to start my own business and Brite:Bill was the one that stuck,' explains Alan. 'It was the classic case of thinking about a problem that, in my opinion, needed to be fixed and coming up with potential solutions.'

He was travelling a lot at the time and found paying bills difficult. This led to the idea of creating a type of dashboard application that would allow people to better manage their bills. However, the more he studied the area, the more he realised that the real problem was actually around understanding bills.

'Those I spoke to expressed how they would often get annoyed with the service provider as a result of a getting a bill they couldn't make sense of and might even switch service provider altogether as a result,' explains Alan. 'From the service providers' position, this was resulting in customer "churn" – all due to their poor or ineffective billing communications.'

Having looked at a variety of business sectors, Alan focused his attention on the mobile phone market. It seemed to be the perfect fit from the outset. Having won business initially from Eircom (now Eir), he went on to secure contracts with Vodafone and UPC (Virgin Media). His big breakthrough came when he landed Tele2 in Holland and Rogers in Canada.

'Every company looks for that moment of scale and that was ours,' enthuses Alan. 'From there we were able to land Sprint, the fourth largest mobile network operator in the US, and we have continued to grow rapidly ever since.'

In September 2016 Alan Coleman sold Brite:Bill to Nasdaq-listed Amdocs (DOX) in a deal that was valued at €80 million.

'The transaction was a fantastic outcome for both the founders and investors who in six short years created, scaled and exited the business from a total equity investment of €5 million,' explains Alan, who remains on as the company's CEO.

Today the company continues on its strong growth trajectory and has added customers such as Comcast and AT&T. Even though now part of the Amdocs organisation, it remains a standalone brand that is benefiting from the additional sales reach and scale that such a large organisation brings.

'This has really supercharged our growth in the North American market and has also opened up new opportunities for us in both Latin America and the Asia Pacific regions,' Alan adds enthusiastically.

Alan Coleman never set out to become an entrepreneur. However, by focusing on developing a solution to a universal problem, he has become an exceptionally successful one.

Alan's Advice for Other Businesses

The best way to learn is on the job

Running a business is like learning to surf – you can read and study as much as you like about it while sitting on the beach, but it's only from actually surfing and getting hit by the big waves that you will become proficient.

A.B.C. – (always be closing)

Sales and business development is the lifeblood of every company. In business you must always be closing a sale. If you are not selling you will not have the monies to sustain and grow your business.

Hire others who put you to shame

Just like in sport, you have to pick the right team. This involves surrounding yourself with people who put you to shame because of their talent. This is especially true if you are a small company trying to take on much larger ones.

CHAPTER 41

FAMILY, FABRIC AND FURNITURE
– The Story of Finline

FINLINE FURNITURE
Handmade Irish Sofas and Chairs

www.finlinefurniture.ie

Chances are that if you have ever visited any of Ireland's finest hotels you will have sat on one of Finline Furniture's range of luxurious sofas. Located in Emo, County Laois, Finline was set up in 1979 by Kieran Finane. Today the business is run by Kieran and his two sons, Ciaran and Kilian. Together they design and manufacture a wide range of sofas for the retail market as well as under contract for leading hotels through Ireland. These include Killarney Park in County Kerry, Inchydoney Hotel and Hayfield Manor in County Cork, the Heritage Hotel at Killenard in County Laois and Ballynahinch Castle Hotel in Connemara.

'We were also specially commissioned to make the furniture for the Lough Erne Resort in County Fermanagh for the G8 Summit back in 2013,' says Kieran proudly.

In addition to their direct sales model, the company also wholesales a wide range of sofas and chairs through independent furniture retailers throughout Ireland and the UK under the brand name Heritage House. They have also shipped sofas and chairs for use in embassies and government residences in over twenty countries, including India, Egypt, Nigeria, Malaysia and Morocco.

It is in their Portlaoise facility that all the magic happens. There the sofas are built, starting with the frame. Some of these are made in the factory itself, while others are sourced from a local frame maker, depending on how busy the staff are.

'This is an important step because the frame is what gives the sofa its shape, strength and robustness,' says Kieran. 'Because we make everything to order, we can offer customers an input into how they want their sofas or chairs to look.'

Once the frame is finished, it's on to the cutting and sewing of the fabric.

'Maintaining symmetry is an important part of this process,' explains Ciaran. 'Some manufacturers cut their fabric as it comes off the roll but that can mean the pattern on one cushion is completely different to another. Our cutters have years of experience in matching, and while this means we use more fabric, our customers get a better-looking finished sofa or chair.'

Having selected and cut the fabric, their teams of seasoned upholsterers stretch and tack this to create finished pieces.

With over 2,000 possible fabrics to choose from, customers are certainly spoilt for choice.

'To a degree, we are in the fashion business,' says Kieran.

Father and sons travel regularly to fabric trade shows in Turkey, Italy, Brussels, London and Germany. Where possible, they source fabrics directly from the mills in these countries, many of which have become exclusive to Finline.

Kieran Finane grew up in County Laois. After finishing school he worked in a local agricultural co-op, before moving to Dublin to begin a lengthy career in sales, first with Heatons Hardware and then with Vita Cortex, where he sold foam to furniture makers. It was there that he first spotted a gap in the market for high-quality sofas and chairs.

In 1979 he took the courageous decision to leave his job to start his own furniture manufacturing business. Even though he and his family were still living in Dublin at the time, Kieran decided to locate his new business in his native county of Laois, believing that this would provide a more central location from which to supply the national market.

Before he could begin production, however, he needed to build a new workshop at a cost of over £100,000. At the time his entire family savings amounted to just £9,000. He made the brave decision to invest all of this in the business with a view to borrowing the rest. Having initially received a positive response from the bank, Kieran gave the go-ahead to a building contractor to start putting up the steel structure while he waited for final loan approval. When word finally came from the bank, his application had been turned down.

Kieran was devastated. Still fully committed, he decided to finish as much of the building as he could with what money he had. Not long after, the bank manager was driving past when he spotted the steel structure. Impressed by Kieran's commitment to press ahead, he approved the loan and Kieran was able to complete his new factory.

'It was certainly a big risk at the time, especially because we had a young family,' admits Kieran. 'But in hindsight, had I not done it that way, we might not be here today.'

He began by supplying retail furniture shops around the country but quickly realised that this was a very competitive market and that he would need to differentiate himself in some way from his many competitors. His answer was to offer retailers bespoke designs which they couldn't get elsewhere, as well as faster delivery times for finished products. His persistence and ingenuity finally paid off and orders began to flood in. While welcome, this meant long hours and hard work.

'I would often sleep in the factory at night, rather than use up the time travelling back to Dublin,' recalls Kieran. 'I would spread cushions on the floor and wrap a few bits of fabric around me.'

The following morning, he would go to the local hotel to shave and freshen up before staff or customers arrived.

His wife, Bridget, who passed away only recently, also played an important role in the success of the company.

'Bridget worked for AIB most of her life but also looked after the bookkeeping side of the business. She would often work until 2 a.m., doing accounts or getting invoices out, at the same time as raising four children,' he remembers fondly.

By 2007 the company had grown its annual turnover to over €6 million and was employing fifty staff. Then the downturn hit. Many retail shops began sourcing cheaper products from the Far East or Eastern Europe and high quality products such as those made by Finline were slowly squeezed out of the market.

'As a result, by 2010, our turnover had nose-dived to €2.5 million and staff numbers had fallen to thirty. And instead of full-time employment with lots of overtime, staff went to a three-day week for five months of the year,' explains Ciaran.

This new reality forced Finline to rethink their business strategy. In 2011, in an effort to counteract their over-reliance on the wholesale market, they opened a dedicated showroom in part of their factory in Emo and began selling directly to the public. This turned out to be such a success that they opened a second showroom on the Long Mile Road in Dublin in 2013, and a third in Douglas in Cork in 2015.

'Today, our direct retail business accounts for over fifty per cent of total sales,' says Ciaran.

Recently they visited China with a view to selling their furniture there and have already shipped a number of containers. They have also shipped fifteen containers of furniture to Abu Dhabi to furnish 150 houses being built by an Irish developer there.

'Thankfully, the business has turned the corner and we are once again experiencing significant growth. The hotel sector, too, is again beginning to invest in refurbishing and upgrading their premises,' explains Kieran. 'The future for the company now looks bright.'

Kieran Finane has much to be proud off. Like most successful entrepreneurs, he has never been afraid of hard work. Together with his sons, they have shown flexibility in adapting to the ever-changing furniture market. Their commitment to quality and customer service has proved instrumental in maintaining a loyal customer base. As Kieran reflects back over the years, he, like so many entrepreneurs, realises that none of this would have been possible had he not first taken the risk of leaving his job; solid proof that success in life often comes from having the courage to simply begin.

Kieran's Advice for Other Businesses

Hard work

There is no substitute for hard work. Short cuts seldom exist when it comes to success.

Common sense

Common sense, though not always very common, is an essential part of success. It helps you avoid making foolish mistakes, stay close to your customer and keep your feet firmly on the ground.

Staff

You cannot grow a business without great staff. The key is to hire well. Once you've found good staff, you need to continually invest in building team spirit and loyalty. Without the right team you will never be able to scale your business.

CHAPTER 42

SEVEN GENERATIONS AND GOING STRONG – The Story of Flahavan's

www.flahavans.com

Flahavan's porridge oats have long been a favourite among Irish consumers. In business for over 230 years, and through seven generations, the company's reputation is stronger today than ever, with more than two million servings consumed each week around the world. This is a story about a family's love for their business and their ongoing commitment to remaining relevant in an ever-changing marketplace.

Now run by John Flahavan, and located in the village of Kilmacthomas, County Waterford, the business was set up in 1785 by John's great-great-great-grandfather, Thomas Dunne. Today it employs seventy-plus staff and has an annual turnover of more than €20 million.

'The business was started on this very site and we have been milling oats in one form or another here ever since,' explains John.

When John took over the business in 2000, the company's traditional Progress Oatlets represented ninety-five per cent of total turnover, with a handful of smaller niche lines making up the balance. Now, alongside their Progress Oatlets, Flahavan's produce a wide variety of lines including their Jumbo Oats, Pinhead Oatmeal and Quick Oats convenience range, as well as muesli, granola and flapjacks.

'Today we make a total of forty-five different lines,' explains John. 'Seventy-five per cent of these are sold into the Irish market, with twenty-five per cent being exported to sixteen different countries including the UK, US, South Korea, Russia, India and Spain.'

The mill itself is an impressive structure, towering seven stories high, and uses gravity to help with the production process. The oats are sourced from local farmers, predominantly within a sixty-mile radius, many of whom have been supplying the mill for generations. Once delivered, they are dried to reduce their moisture content and to ensure they are safe to store. Later, these are transferred to the mill, where they are kilned or roasted to deliver the unique Flahavan's flavour.

Before going through the production process, the oats are put through a comprehensive automated cleaning process that removes any traces of soil or weeds. A series of high-speed rotary shellers remove the outer shells of the grain, which are then segregated and brought to the boiler house where they will be burned to generate the steam needed in the production process itself. The remaining oat flakes are then either rolled to become jumbo flakes and packed as a product in their own right, or chopped into smaller pieces to become pinhead oats, which are then steamed and rolled into the company's famous porridge oats.

Although still a traditional family-run business, much has changed since John took over.

'My father and uncle ran the business when I was young. Immediately after completing a degree in business and accounting in what is now Dublin Institute of Technology, I joined the business full-time in 1972 and have been here ever since,' says John.

Starting out in finance and sales, John eventually took over the business in 2000, having bought out the other family members who were involved at the time.

'The first significant change was our decision to get out of the agri side of the business,' explains John. 'Up to that point, we had been producing animal feedstuff, which made up almost fifty per cent of our turnover. Deciding to cut off half of our revenue was scary at the time but it allowed us to concentrate on the consumer side of the business where we saw the greatest potential. Since then our turnover has grown five-fold,' he adds.

In 2003 the company began producing a range of organic oats to fill what they thought would only be a small niche market. This soon grew to become an important part of their business and today theirs is the largest brand of organic oats sold in both the Irish and UK markets.

'Our decision to build a flapjack and granola plant in 2015 also helped introduce a new cohort of consumers to our brand,' explains John.

In 2017 Flahavan's also received a valuable boost to their profile when they took part in RTÉ's *Operation Transformation* TV programme, where they gave away more than three million servings of porridge free in one day. This not only raised further awareness of their brand but also helped reinforce their message around the role porridge plays in living healthier and longer.

John is immensely proud too of the company's commitment to sustainability, with on-site wind and water turbines now generating electricity that goes to make up as much as sixty per cent of the total energy used by the company.

'Even the oat husk shells that are burned to produce the steam needed for the drying and roasting process have led to a reduction of over 400,000 litres of diesel per year – something that is good for the business's bottom line as well as for the environment,' says John.

The company's commitment to sustainability has also seen them scoop a number of awards, including the 2017 Sustainable Energy Achievement Award.

Most of the seventy-plus staff who work there are from the local area.

'We are lucky to have a very dedicated and experienced workforce with very low levels of employee turnover,' says John. 'Everyone takes pride in what they do, and every day, at our morning tea-break, we taste that day's oat production together.'

What's next for Flahavan's?

'The one thing I have learned over the last forty-five years is that you're either moving forward or backwards; but you can never afford to stand still,' says John. 'Our objective is to continue to build our brand, grow the export side of the business and drive innovation through new product development. We have recently introduced a new UK sachet product, a Quick Oats variety as well as an Overnight Oats product and a new Red Berry Granola. We also see huge potential to expand the organic side of the business, something that is good for the consumer, for us and for the farmers we work with.'

John's wife, Mary, is a keen baker and has played a significant role in helping with recipes and product development over the years. Three of their children have also recently joined the family business: James works in international exports, Annie is in finance and Ellen in marketing.

'They are now the seventh generation of Flahavans to work

in the business and it will be a privilege to be able to pass it on to them. I really see myself more as a custodian of this business rather than its owner. My job now is to pass it on to the next generation in better shape than when I took it over,' says John.

John's Advice for Other Businesses

Prove your market first

It is always prudent to carry out research and test the market in a small way first, before investing heavily in a big launch. Get the product right and then make sure there is a demand for it before rolling it out more widely.

Balance optimism with realism

Entrepreneurs tend to be optimistic by nature. In my experience, though, launching new products into the market usually takes twice as long and costs twice as much as you first expected; being aware of this can help prevent unwanted surprises.

Leave a bit for the other fellow

My late father, who used to buy cattle for the farm, would often quote these wise words: 'If you are always trying to buy too cheap and then only wanting to sell at the very top of the market, you might well miss the market.' Take a turn but leave some profit in the deal for the next person.

CHAPTER 43

ALL YOUR EGGS IN THE ONE BASKET
– The Story of O'Egg

www.oegg.ie

In the past, the production of eggs was seen as supplementary to a farm's main source of income. Today, it has developed into a sophisticated and highly regulated industry in its own right.

One couple who know the egg industry better than most is husband-and-wife team Margaret and Leo Farrelly. In 1987 they set up their business, O'Egg, with just 150 hens. Now they produce fifty million eggs per year at their modern grading and packing facility in Clonarn near Mullagh in County Cavan, making them the largest dedicated producer of free-range eggs in the country. With thirty staff and an annual turnover of more than €6.5 million, their once small farm enterprise has morphed into a national success story.

'We are excited to be celebrating more than thirty years in the egg business,' explain Margaret and Leo.

'We focus on the production of free-range eggs and, for us, our chickens come first. That's why the quality of our eggs is so good,' insists Margaret.

'There are basically four types of eggs on the market,' she

explains. 'Cage or battery eggs, where hens are kept in cage-like conditions. Barn eggs, which are produced by hens kept indoors in a barn or hen house but not confined to tiny cages. Free-range eggs, such as we specialise in, come from birds that have the freedom to roam between outdoor pastures and indoors. And finally, organic eggs, which refers to free-range eggs produced to organic standards.'

At O'Egg, each hen house opens onto a pasture of green grass where hens are free to spend most of their day outdoors, with the added security of being able to return to the houses at night to drink fresh spring water and feed on natural grains and cereals.

'The distinctive flavour of our eggs can be attributed to the happiness of the hens,' says Leo.

In addition to producing free-range eggs, the company set up a production facility in Cootehill in County Cavan in 2012, where they produce a range of pasteurised liquid egg in bottles for home cooking as well as for commercial sauce makers, ice-cream manufacturers and bakeries.

'Given its high protein content, this has also become popular among gym users as well as being used as a mixture in cocktail bars,' adds Margaret.

The company's products can now also be found in leading retail stores such as Tesco, Dunnes and SuperValu, as well as Avoca outlets and numerous craft butchers' shops. To keep up with demand, the company also sources eggs from other producers throughout Counties Cavan, Monaghan, Longford and Meath. Collected twice weekly, these are brought in trays to the packing facility where they are graded into small, medium, large and extra-large sizes. Having been quality checked, each egg is then date stamped and each box is given an electronic batch number and bar code for traceability purposes.

'All this from the most humble of beginnings,' explains Margaret modestly.

Leo Farrelly grew up on the farm where the business is now located. Having taken over the place following the death of his father, Leo soon realised it was never going to provide him with a sustainable living, let alone support a family. Margaret, from nearby Billis, was the daughter of the local blacksmith. Her first part-time job, at the age of twelve, was collecting eggs at a nearby broiler farm. Having finished school she moved to Dublin, where she worked in banking with AIB for the next thirteen years.

'Leo and I met at a dance in the White Horse Hotel in Cootehill. That night changed everything,' recalls Margaret with a laugh. When they later married, she left Dublin and moved to Mullagh.

'Our decision to get into egg production in the first place came out of the need to supplement our family's income,' admits Margaret. 'It started when we answered an advert in the local *Anglo Celt* newspaper from a company looking for farmers to produce eggs for them. Soon afterwards, we converted an old shed on the farm into our first hen house and took possession of our very first 150 hens.'

Within six months, the couple had grown their flock to over 500 hens. Within twelve months they had obtained their own grading licence from the Department of Agriculture, enabling them to produce and sell, firstly to local shops and eventually into the Dublin market. When Musgraves introduced central distribution and their own branded free-range eggs, O'Egg was selected as a supplier.

'We are grateful that they believed in us from the very beginning and really helped support our growth,' acknowledges Margaret.

Central to the company's ongoing expansion has been their commitment to continuous investment. In 2000 they invested in a state-of-the-art grader, the first of its kind in Western Europe, and more recently invested over €1 million in the first modern egg breaker and pasteurisation system in the country.

'Innovation has been important,' says Margaret. 'In the 2000s we developed our own range of omega-enriched eggs – something that has become a big hit with consumers. The idea of producing pasteurised liquid egg came about as a result of us looking for alternative uses for our surplus eggs during off-peak times. To address the issue, we linked up with the University of Ulster, Coleraine, through InterTradeIreland's FUSION programme (the programme provides financial support to growth companies to partner with a third-level institution with specialised sectorial expertise), which eventually led to us setting up our pasteurising facility.'

The couple also recently purchased a site with the long-term plan of developing this into an innovation centre where they hope to co-locate their two existing factories. They have also embarked on a rebranding exercise based on consumer feedback.

'We realised that we had the best story in the industry but were failing to communicate our message effectively,' explains Leo. 'We decided to engage a design company to consult with customers and consumers whose overwhelming feedback suggested that we needed a strong personality as part of our branding. After much work with focus groups and help from Bord Bia, we decided to put "Margaret's Eggs" on our packaging.'

Margaret and Leo Farrelly's business started out initially as a way to supplement their small farm income. Today, through their willingness to work hard, their relentless focus on innovation, and commitment to continuously reinvest in the business, they have become the largest producer of free-range eggs in the country. At no point, however, during that time have they lost sight of the welfare of the hens they look after, nor the importance of the quality of the eggs they produce. With three of their four children now working full-time in the business, it looks like the journey for O'Egg is set to continue well into the future.

Margaret and Leo's Advice for Other Businesses

Embrace failure

There is no failure, only feedback. When you try something new and it doesn't work out, accept the lessons learned and use these to do better next time. You will never succeed in business without experiencing failures. Learn to embrace rather than fear them.

Build on basic values

There are few short cuts in business. The foundations of success are often basic traditional values: a willingness to work hard, commitment to your business, staff and customers, and developing a reputation for being honest and honourable in your business dealings.

Focus on your USP

To start a business, you have to identify a product or a service that customers need. To excel, you have to identify your own USP – that something special about you and your company that enables you to stand out from competitors.

CHAPTER 44

SEEING THE WHOLE PICTURE
– The Story of 3D4Medical

www.3d4medical.com

Most successful entrepreneurs endeavour to set up businesses in markets where opportunities are significant and where there exists the possibility of disrupting the status quo. John Moore, whose company 3D4Medical develops revolutionary medical software applications, has succeeded in accomplishing both of these objectives.

Set up in 2004, the company already has twelve million users worldwide, including leading education and clinical organisations. And with 110 people employed between their offices in Dublin, the US, Poland and Russia, the company is on track to achieve annual revenues this year of more than €10 million. John's is a story of vision, talent and innovation.

'For the last 100 years, medicine has been taught using standard text books with flat 2D images,' explains John. 'My vision was to transform the teaching of medicine and anatomy by using technology where learners could interact with a virtual human body. Using our applications, users are now able to zoom in from any angle, remove layers and structures and cut through or dissect skin, muscle and bone. They can even edit these 3D models to simulate specific injuries and disease states.'

The company's target market includes both the medical education sector, where their ground-breaking technology is being used by medical students and professors across the world, as well as professionals such as doctors, surgeons, nurses, paramedics, physiotherapists and chiropractors, who use it to give patients a better understanding of their particular conditions.

'99.9% of our sales are exports, with the US being our largest market, followed by the UK, Germany, Japan and Australia,' explains John. 'Our Essential Anatomy app is the best-selling anatomical atlas in the world, while our Complete Anatomy app is the top grossing application in the App Store medical category in 131 countries.'

Not bad for a young man from Mount Merrion who never finished college. John's parents were academics: his father a professor of engineering in University College Dublin and his mother a doctor of psychology, but John realised from an early age that his career path would be as an entrepreneur.

'I remember the moment I made the decision,' explains John. 'I was eighteen and working in the US. I had a job at a Christmas tree lot where I would take a tree, saw off the lower branches, lift it into the customer's car and secure it. I was paid $3.25 an hour. After the hard day of work, I got paid $32.50. I did the math in my head: there were four other people working on the lot; each tree sold for an average of $50 and we each processed about four trees an hour, which meant the boss was making $6,500 a day – and I was making $32.50. I decided right there that in future, I wanted to be on the other side of the deal. I even worked out how the process could be streamlined to ensure that each person working did ten trees an hour. I explained this to my boss and asked for a raise. He fired me,' laughs John.

Back home, John spent the next year and a half in Trinity College Dublin, where he studied pure mathematics. However, so intense was his desire to start his own business that he left the course early. The next few years were spent in a mix of eLearning and software development companies. Then, in 2014, he set up 3D4Medical in his attic.

'I went on to create the largest library of stock medical images in the world, including over 18,000 made entirely from 3D digital models, and then distributed these through Getty Images and others,' he explains. 'Our images were so popular that they appeared on the front cover of *Time* magazine, *National Geographic*, *Newsweek*, *Scientific America* and *Discover*. But when the recession hit in 2009 I realised that I needed to reinvent the company. I did an evaluation, not just of the business but also of myself. I came to the conclusion that what defined me was being an innovator – coming up with new ideas, designs, markets and solutions was what I was good at. Coming from a family of scientists and engineers, I was always fascinated with how things worked and how they could be improved. I promised myself that the future of 3D4Medical would be based on innovation.'

John decided to focus exclusively on developing 3D medical training applications for the new iPhone App Store. Putting everything on the line, he even remortgaged his family's home.

'I worked hard to forge a relationship with Apple and within a short time 3D4Medical's apps had hit the number one spot across most Apple App Stores around the world,' says John. 'As our success grew, we hired the best developers we could find to push the boundaries of what could be done on new mobile devices.'

Support from Enterprise Ireland, together with an investment of $16.4 million from Malin plc in 2015, also helped underpin the company's growth rate. Today their anatomy software, encompassing their innovative Lecture Builder software for teachers, is being used in 125 of the top 150 medical colleges around the world.

What's next?

'We are in the middle of launching two new clinical products for surgeons and patients in the areas of orthopaedics and cardiovascular-related diseases, and after that we plan to release a further three products for COPD [Chronic Obstructive Pulmonary Disease], Diabetes and Ophthalmology. We also expect to be employing over 200 people by then and have new offices already planned for Romania and India.'

'My real goal is to transform medical education, not only in the developed world but also by making it more accessible in the developing world. We are moving into the age of individualisation in technology and one of our more exciting projects is to replace our current models with living ones. Imagine a digital model rendered as a living, breathing model with a beating heart and blood flow that can be dissected and even made to simulate disease states on command. Eventually this human model will have the flexibility to morph and match the specifics of the patient's body, using information from, for example, their own MRI scans.'

John Moore is a talented and inspiring entrepreneur. He understands that to win you have to disrupt your industry. To achieve this he has put innovation at the heart of his company's culture. He also partnered with a giant in innovation, Apple, and has won every major Apple award for innovation including their Design and Innovation 2016 award, beating over 2 million other apps on Apple's App Store. That same year he also made it into the finals of the Ernest & Young Entrepreneur of the Year programme.

Should John ever again meet the man who fired him from his job selling Christmas trees, he might have a word of thanks for the inspiration that set him on his current path.

John's Advice for Other Businesses

Speed to market

I believe that thoughts travel. If you have a good idea, you can be sure that someone else is having the same good idea. So you need to get to market as quickly as possible to secure first mover advantage. It helps focus you to realise that if you delay, someone else might get there before you.

Innovate or die

Innovation is essential to remain continuously relevant. Simply put, if your company is not innovating, your company is going to die. To survive in business, you have to be continuously looking for new and better ways of doing things. You can be sure that's what your competitors are doing.

Talent is key

Try to surround yourself with talented, driven people. They will be key to growing your business. Evaluate your own abilities, including your strengths and weaknesses, then hire people whose talents and capabilities complement yours.

CHAPTER 45

PUTTING THE WHEELS IN MOTION

– The Story of Agrigear

www.agrigear.ie

According to former American baseball player Sam Ewing, 'Hard work spotlights the character of people: some turn up their sleeves, some turn up their noses, and some don't turn up at all.'

Fred Clarke, founder of Agrigear, one of the largest wholesale suppliers of tyres and wheels in Ireland, is one man who has never been afraid to roll up his sleeves. Set up in 1983 and located in Bailieborough, County Cavan, Agrigear employs sixty-two staff. Fred's is an inspiring story that demonstrates what can be achieved through hard work, resilience and an enterprising mindset.

The volume of tyres and wheels that fill the warehouse and expansive concrete yards surrounding the Bailieborough facility is remarkable. A man-made mountain of black rubber, there are tyres to suit every type of car and truck as well as for every sort of farm, construction and grass-cutting machine imaginable. But Fred never intended to start a tyre business. In fact, his first love was machinery.

'Even when I was at school, I was always more interested in making or fixing things than doing homework,' he says.

Fred went straight into farming after school and, in order to expand, began to rent additional land. At one point he had more than 1,000 acres rented on which he grew barley and wheat. On top of this he milled grain for himself and others. While continuing to farm full-time, he also set up a contract building company erecting silage pits and grain stores for other farmers.

By the mid-1970s Fred was employing over thirty staff. He decided to diversify even further and, along with two other business partners, built a 600-unit piggery. However, during the period 1978–80, economic conditions deteriorated. Diesel prices rose dramatically and interest rates soared to a staggering twenty-three per cent. Bad weather further compounded the situation, leading to a poor yield from his crops during those years, culminating in serious financial losses. This could have spelled disaster for Fred. But he was not one for giving up easily.

'I had my fingers in too many pies,' he admits readily. 'There were just too many things to control. I had to close the piggery, sell off most of my farm, including 100 acres I had received from my father. That hit me the hardest.'

In the summer of 1980 Fred went to Holland to visit a business contact who shared his love of machinery. While there, the two men visited a local car-dismantling business and Fred left a few hours later having bought 1,200 good-quality second-hand wheels and tyres. At a price tag of only £1.50 each, he thought he couldn't go wrong. His Dutch friend even loaned him the money to buy the stock – an act of kindness he never forgot.

Fred's hunch proved correct. He shipped the stock to Ireland and began selling the tyres and wheels from his farm at £10 each. Word spread quickly and his stock soon sold out. Before long, Fred was travelling to Holland every month to buy more. He was now officially in the tyre business.

However, some of the tyres he imported did not readily fit standard European-sized wheels and so Fred began to manufacture new wheels to suit them. 'That was the start of the manufacturing end of our business,' he says. 'Today, we make, modify and refurbish all manner of wheels.'

Fred began to learn that opportunities often come disguised as problems. During the mid-1980s the weather was so bad that turf contractors were struggling to get their cutting machines to travel on waterlogged bogs. Thinking about how to address the situation, Fred discovered that if he bolted an extra wheel on each side of these machines, to create double wheels, this would spread the weight and make it less likely to sink in the wet ground. This proved such a success that Fred patented his new invention. Today, these quick-fit dual wheel systems are used by many farmers to harvest valuable grass and tillage crops where the land is too wet to allow standard machinery to do the job.

In 1999 Agrigear was appointed the main distributor in Ireland for tyre manufacturer Nokian and in 2001 they became the main distributor for Indian-based manufacturer BKT. To expand his reach and increase sales, Fred developed relationships with a national network of fifty agents throughout the country, most of whom owned their own garages or machinery stores. These agents became a strong distribution channel for the company and became an important element of the company's ongoing success.

In 2007 the company built a new 20,000 square-foot facility to support their continued growth. It also began manufacturing wheels for third-party manufacturers of grassland and farm machinery, who were themselves experiencing huge growth in export sales to such places as South Africa, New Zealand, Norway, Sweden and Holland. In turn, Agrigear began exporting their own wheels to places such as Saudi Arabia and Russia.

'Wheel manufacturing now represents about one-third of our business and is central to our company's overall vision and business tagline, which is "Solutions in Motion",' says Fred.

By 2015 space had again become a constraint and so Fred and his team embarked on a €3 million expansion to extend the existing factory buildings, as well as installing state-of-the-art CNC plasma drills, shot-blasting facilities and a new powder-coating paint plant. They also built a new 23,000 square-foot dedicated dispatch and logistics hub.

Today the business continues to go from strength to strength. 'We have experienced, on average, between ten and fifteen per cent increases in sales each year over the last ten years,' Fred says.

He is keen to stress the role that John McGauren, the company's general manager, and all the staff have played in the success of the company to date.

'You can't build a strong and successful company without good staff and good management,' insists Fred.

Fred's wife, Joyce, also plays an active role in the business. In addition, when the couple lost their dairy herd some years back through disease, she decided to buy six young Friesian heifers and, over the intervening years, has grown the herd to more than sixty cows, which she milks herself every day. Fred and Joyce's son, Allister, and his wife, Rose, also have key roles in the company.

Family is important to Fred and it is easy to see that he is proud of both his business and his family. He is wiser now than when he started out but he is no less committed and no less afraid to work hard. With business growing steadily there seems to be only one direction in which Fred and Agrigear are going and that is forward. The wheels are definitely in motion.

Fred's Advice for Other Businesses

Trust your own instincts

Learn to trust your own instincts and your intuition. It will serve you well. But ensure that you also have a good financial and business plan in place to guide you. Make sure to develop a good working relationship with your bank or funders, it helps too.

Stick to your core principles

Do not get distracted or diverted by opportunities that are not in line with your core business. Stick to what you know, what you are good at and what you have experience of.

Don't be a busy fool

Make sure you get paid for the work you do and for the products you sell. You do not have to be everything to everybody. Focus on those that matter most in your business.

CHAPTER 46

AIM HIGH, DREAM BIG

– The Story of Voxpro

www.voxprogroup.com

Voxpro is one of Ireland's most impressive companies, and its founders, Dan and Linda Kiely, are among the country's most inspiring entrepreneurs. Set up in 2000, the company now employs over 2,000 staff and has an annual turnover of more than €60 million. Their growth continues to increase at a phenomenal pace, with three offices in Cork, one in Dublin, two in the US – in Folsom, California and Athens, Georgia – and one in Bucharest, Romania. In addition, they are soon to open additional offices in Manila in the Philippines, as well as in the US and Latin America. This will bring employment numbers to well over 3,000 globally, with annual revenues in excess of €100 million.

'Voxpro are Ireland's largest international provider of multilingual customer experience, technical support and sales operations solutions,' says Dan. 'We work with some of the world's best-known brands, including Google, Airbnb, Stripe, Nest, Travelzoo, It Works! and Neways. We also work with a growing list of great Irish firms such as Pinergy, Core HR, Magnet and Inhance Technology. If a Google customer has a problem accessing their Gmail account, for example, and they contact the Google technical support helpline, that email or telephone call comes to our dedicated Google team here in

Ireland and we deal with it on behalf of Google,' he explains. 'If a customer who is booking accommodation through Airbnb encounters a challenge completing their booking and contacts Airbnb's customer service support, that mail or call also comes to our dedicated Airbnb team members.'

Such outsourcing models have become very popular in recent years as global companies continue to grow and scale. Many are challenged to recruit the right staff quickly with the right combination of languages, or to put in place the necessary infrastructure to support the pace of their growth. As a result they partner with outsource firms such as Voxpro, who act as a third-party provider of such services.

'At Voxpro, we have team members from thirty countries and we conduct business in fifteen different languages,' explains Linda. 'Such multilingual capability has been key to our success,' she adds.

Staff are organised into teams, each one looking after a particular company and that company's customers. Each team has their own allocated space, fitted out in the style and colours of the company they are representing, and each team adopts that customer's distinct culture and vibe. Environment is important here. For example, in one area of the office is an American Hollywood section with a sign in bright lights that says 'Dream Big'. In another Asia-Pacific-themed area, every room has colourful Asian artwork hanging on the walls and low furniture similar to what you expect to find in that region.

'We understand the importance of aligning our vision and culture with that of the companies we work with. These organisations don't just want a service provider – they want a partner,' explains Dan. 'So we immerse ourselves in our clients and their customers, in everything from training and development of team members, to the physical environment in which they work. In essence, we become our clients.'

Dan and Linda Kiely both grew up in Cork city: Dan in Turner's Cross and Linda in Douglas. Dan spent his teenage years working part-time in a local supermarket and then in a bar. It was this experience, he believes, that first honed his entrepreneurial drive. Later, he graduated from the Cork Institute of Technology with a degree in business studies and began working in advertising sales for *The Cork Examiner* newspaper (now the *Irish Examiner*). It was there he met Linda.

Linda, who had her children early in life, had returned to employment running a number of bars around Cork city. She joined the *Irish Examiner* as sales and marketing manager for their new glossy magazine. However, when the magazine became an early casualty of the economic downturn in the 1990s, both Dan and Linda found themselves out of work. Linda got a job in administration with the local office of the Department of Foreign Affairs, while Dan went to work for an electronic paging company called Pageboy.

'At that time, there were no mobile phones. Pagers and beepers were what was being used by doctors and those who needed to be contacted in emergencies. At the time, it was seen as cutting-edge technology,' laughs Dan.

By now a couple, Dan and Linda decided they wanted to run their own business and so bought the paging company.

'What attracted us was the opportunity to build on what was already there. We realised that more companies were beginning to use this type of technology to contact staff outside of normal office hours,' explains Dan.

But the couple had one major challenge; they had no money.

In a courageous move, Linda remortgaged her house to raise the investment they needed.

'It was definitely scary,' recalls Linda. 'But once committed, failure was no longer an option for us.'

Later they bought a similar business, Eirpage, which gave them access to a much larger customer base. Then, in 2000, they rebranded as Voxpro. As their customers became more sophisticated and began to demand additional services, the pair decided that they would have to innovate. That's when they moved to the fully outsourced support solution that they currently provide. The response was overwhelmingly positive and business began to really take off – at least until 2008, when the economy went into free-fall.

'Many of our customers were small at that point,' says Linda, 'and they had to cut back their spending on our services. It forced us to change tack and as a result, we began to focus deliberately on larger multinational-type customers who we felt were more recession-proof.'

Their strategy proved so successful that business began to pour in. However, this also presented challenges. They quickly realised that they needed to invest further in both staff and technology in order to keep up with demand. But the banks were not lending at the time. Dan and Linda can remember one occasion when, two days before getting a massive cheque from a major customer, they had to face the possibility of their payroll cheques bouncing. Family and friends rallied around and the pair cashed in what monies they had built up in their own retirement pensions to fund the business through what turned out to be an important developmental period.

As their customers' businesses began to take off, they turned to Voxpro to provide a rapid but high-quality outsourced model. As a result, Dan and Linda's business exploded. To ensure a sound footing, both understood the need to put in place a strong and clear company culture that could support such ongoing expansion.

'It's impossible to reduce our culture into a few sentences without it sounding like a corporate soundbite,' explains Dan. 'The focus on excellence that we have here comes from gathering hundreds of people together from the four corners of the world to work, as one, towards our shared goal. It comes from the team themselves who we continually encourage to be entrepreneurial and seek to make a difference. Our people really are the business.'

'Voxpro has always been a start-up. Every time we got a new client it was a case of beginning from scratch. We never followed the "we did it this way last time so let's do it that way again" line of thinking,' adds Linda.

With turnover having increased eighty per cent year-on-year in recent years, their growth has been little short of incredible – a credit to Dan and Linda's combined vision and leadership.

Linda Kiely is a strong, strategic businesswoman. She has an engaging personality matched with an astute business sense. She has a fundamental belief that customers should not only be satisfied, but delighted. Dan loves to dream big. He is ambitious, even audacious. His pursuit of excellence is contagious. He possesses a drive to do things differently and to challenge the status quo. He wants to raise the bar in their industry. And above all, he wants the company to become known, not for the ordinary, but for the extraordinary.

In August 2017 Dan and Linda's vision and hard work came to fruition when Voxpro's majority ownership was acquired by

Canadian company TELUS International, in a deal reported to be worth in the region of €150 million. As part of the transaction, Dan remains as Voxpro's CEO and joins the TELUS International senior leadership team, while Linda has now become a non-executive director with the company. Their story just goes to show that it pays to dream big.

Dan and Linda's Advice for Other Businesses

Dream big!

Have a clear grasp of who you are, what you stand for and where you are going. Set aggressive but realistic goals. These should stretch you beyond the comfortable. Pick goals that are significant and will make a difference. Then go after them with all your might.

Surround yourself with talent

Surround yourself with the most talented people you can find. It's also imperative that they have bought into your vision and want to share the journey with you.

Do not fear failure

Failure is the nursery of success. Everything in business, as in life, involves risks and challenges. Set your sail in the direction of your dreams and remain relentless in pursuit. If failure does pay you a visit, then dust yourself down, learn from it and keep moving forward.

CHAPTER 47

THE MOTHER OF ALL DUCKS

– The Story of Silver Hill Farm

www.silverhillfarm.ie

Founded over fifty-five years ago by Ronnie and Lyla Steele, Silver Hill Farm is located outside the picturesque village of Emyvale, in County Monaghan. Now run by the couple's son, Stuart, it has grown to become a global leader in the production and processing of duck meat and duck-related products. Today the company employs 210 staff, processes over 90,000 ducks each week for distribution to twenty-four countries around the world and has a turnover in the region of €50 million.

'We are essentially a family-owned and managed duck company,' explains Stuart. 'Everything we do here is fully integrated, owned and controlled by the business. That includes everything from initial breeding and egg production to hatching and final processing and cooking.'

Over the years the company has developed a market for every part of the duck. The meat is sold in various cuts, both raw and cooked. The livers are exported for pâté, while the feet and tongues are sold to the Asian market as a delicacy. They have even built their own feather plant where feathers and down are made into high quality pillows and duvets, and sold to the residential and hotel sectors.

'Until recently we used to say that we use every part of the duck except the quack. But recently we've even made that into a ringtone for mobile phones,' adds Stuart laughing.

The company supplies many of the large retail multiples throughout Ireland and has built up a successful trade business supplying the food service sector and many of the country's leading restaurants and hotels. They are also hugely successful in export markets including the UK, France, Germany, the Netherlands, Belgium, Sweden, Norway, Denmark, Singapore, China, South Africa and the UAE.

'Our success can largely be attributed to the quality of our Peking breed of duck, which we have developed over the years. It's our own breed and is unique to Silver Hill Farm,' Stuart explains. 'Our focus on developing our own breed has enabled us to produce duck meat which is renowned for being both succulent and tender. For us, it's all about quality and consistency.'

Among the company's innovative product range are duck wings in Chinese plum sauce, duck sausages, shredded duck in Hoi Sin sauce with spring onion and cucumber accompaniments, aromatic duck, and roasted duck in honey glaze and orange sauce.

'All spices and sauces are made by us here in the factory using only natural ingredients and are free from additives and preservatives,' insists Stuart.

The business was originally set up in 1962 by Stuart's parents, Ronnie and Lyla Steele. Ronnie had moved to the area from the UK, while Lyla grew up in nearby County Cavan. He had a background in chicken farming, while she had an interest in getting into the turkey business.

'Like all good marriages they compromised and decided to go into the duck business,' laughs Stuart.

Their initial idea was to start a hatchery where they would sell day-old duck chicks to local farmers. However, Ronnie and Lyla soon found that it was hard to get paid for their produce and decided instead to rear the ducks themselves. They then began supplying local hotels and restaurants, and quickly discovered there was a growing demand for duck that came pre-prepared for cooking. They also discovered that there were better margins if they undertook this value-added process themselves.

In a small shed in a corner of the current site, Stuart explains that this is where it all started. He recalls how his parents would rear the ducks in one half of the shed while carrying out the processing and packaging in the other. It is in stark contrast to today's modern production plant, now spanning several acres.

Stuart joined the business straight from school. Starting at the bottom, he worked his way up, learning each aspect of the business. When he joined, the business was processing about 6,000 ducks each week. Today, it produces a staggering 90,000 ducks each week, of which over eighty-five per cent are exported.

Stuart explains the various stages in the process. First, the eggs are incubated on the family's farm until they hatch, which takes about a month. Once hatched, the day-old chicks are transported to independent grower farms around the area, where they will be reared for the next seven weeks until ready for processing. During this time they are fed only on natural feedstuffs, which have been formulated by the company and consist largely of wheat and soya.

'Great care is taken of the birds both when they are on the farms and while they are being transported. We make sure that they experience as little stress as possible as this can adversely affect their growth. In addition, the wellness of the ducks is of paramount importance to us,' explains Stuart.

Once back in the plant, the final processing begins. The birds are largely plucked by hand to ensure that there are no blemishes on the skin. Once cooked, they are air-chilled and packed for dispatch.

'We do not add any water to our ducks, in order to increase weight, like some producers do. When we sell duck, we sell duck. Not water,' insists Stuart.

'Breaking into the Chinese market was a major game changer for us,' he explains. 'The Chinese have a long tradition of eating duck and prefer high quality birds that are rich in flavour. That's why we developed our own special breed, which cannot easily be replicated by our competitors. That way we can offer a premium-quality product, while at the same time insulating our need to continuously have to compete on price. In China, our duck is regularly referred to by locals as the mother of all ducks,' he adds proudly.

Although a family-run business, Stuart is quick to acknowledge the importance and contribution of the company's staff, eighty per cent of whom have been with the business for more than ten years.

'They really are the glue that holds the business together,' he insists.

In 2011 Stuart introduced a new senior management team to help grow the business following his participation in the prestigious Enterprise Ireland-supported Leadership 4 Growth management development programme in the International Institute for Management Development (Europe's foremost business school) in Lausanne, Switzerland.

'We are continuously expanding our range of products and

recently invested over €3 million developing our World Class Centre of Excellence here in Monaghan. We have also established a new product development department and a show kitchen where we work with leading chefs and retail buyers to come up with new recipes and flavour combinations. We are also continuing to expand our reach into both the retail and food service markets here in Ireland, while internationally we are continuing to break into new territories, most recently Singapore,' he explains.

Looking to the future, Stuart is focused on continued growth and expects the company to double in size over the coming year, with a very large expansion planned to cope with the growing demand particularly from Asia.

Outside of the goals for the company, Stuart and his family are committed to giving back to their local community. They recently opened a farm shop close to the factory where they stock not only their own products but also those of other local growers and producers. In addition, they provide land for use as allotments at a peppercorn rent to the local community, as well as paying for a horticulturalist to visit local schools to teach young children how to grow their own fruit and vegetables.

The story of Silver Hill Farm is an inspiring one. Begun when a newly married couple decided to start their own small farm enterprise, it has grown into a thriving international company. Through careful management and an innovative approach to maximising output and eliminating waste, they have managed to find methods and markets that use every single part of the ducks they produce. In addition, their clear and unwavering commitment to quality has enabled this Monaghan company to become global leaders in their sector.

Stuart's Advice for Other Businesses

Don't be afraid of change

Things are forever changing so make sure you know your market, your customers and your production processes. Be careful not to be distracted by the macro environment over which you have little control, and worry, instead, about the micro issues, the things over which you do have control.

Do not take quality for granted

Quality is something you have to work at every day. Similarly, every person on your team has to have the same level of commitment to producing consistent quality. This is something that can protect and insulate your business against price-only battles.

Don't be afraid to fail, but learn from it if you do

Take all the advice you can get from other entrepreneurs, experts in your field and enterprise support agencies. But believe also in your own vision of what you want to achieve and your own ability to make your vision a reality. If, for some reason, things don't work out as planned, learn the lessons and quickly move on.

CHAPTER 48

STARTING WITH ALL THE RIGHT INGREDIENTS

– The Story of Teeling Whiskey

www.teelingwhiskey.com

Whiskey takes its name from the Gaelic term *uisce beatha*, 'water of life', and has been produced in Ireland since as far back as the sixth century. The fastest-growing spirit in the world for the past twenty years, and with an average annual growth rate of twenty per cent, the demand for Irish whiskey shows no signs of slowing down. This demand has led to the expansion of several existing distilleries, as well as the construction of new ones, among them the Teeling Whiskey Company.

Set up in 2012, the new distillery, complete with visitors' centre, is located in Dublin's city centre and already employs seventy-five staff and has an annual turnover of more than €13 million.

'To be officially called Irish whiskey, it must be distilled and aged on the island of Ireland for at least three years,' explains founder and CEO Jack Teeling. And Jack should know because his family have been making whiskey since 1782, when ancestor Walter Teeling set up a craft distillery in Marrowbone Lane in the Liberties area of the city, close to where Jack's new distillery is now located.

'Back then, there were over thirty-seven different distilleries in Dublin, and this area – between the Liberties, the Coombe, Smithfield and Newmarket – became known as the "Golden Triangle" due to the many distilleries clustered within a one-mile radius.

'Our target market is typically people who already drink Irish whiskey but are looking to discover something new and unique within the category,' explains Jack. 'While we are respectful of our long history, we are confident in our ability to create something modern and contemporary, in terms of flavours, for current and future generations of whiskey drinkers.'

Jack is obviously doing something right because his independent whiskey company has won more than 100 international awards over the last five years, including four 'Best Awards' as well as the 'World's Best Whiskey Visitor Attraction' at a recent World Whiskies Awards.

As sales continue to grow in Ireland, Jack also exports to forty-five international markets, the largest of which include the US, France, Germany and Australia, as well as to a number of new regions, among them Cambodia and Bulgaria.

Visitors to the distillery enjoy seeing first-hand how whiskey is made. It is here that the four important stages in the production take place – milling, mashing, fermentation and finally, distillation.

To start, the barley grain is brought by way of a conveyor system from large silo bins at the rear of the distillery to the mill area where it is ground into a powder. Water is then added and this mixture moves on to the mashing process, which takes place in a large vessel called a 'lauter tun'. Here, a large rake moves over and back across the mix for the next four hours, separating the water and sugars into a liquid that is known in the industry as 'wort'. The spent grain left behind in the tun is captured for onward sale to farmers as animal feed.

'There is no waste in the process as everything can be recycled back into the food chain,' insists Jack.

Next it's on to fermentation where the liquid, or 'wort', from the earlier process is pumped into a combination of stainless-steel and traditional wood fermenters. Here, yeast is added to break the sugars in the mix into alcohol and CO_2, giving rise to a fermented liquid known traditionally as 'wash' – a process which usually takes two to three days.

'The "wash" is then piped into large copper kettle-like vessels known as pot stills where it is heated to between eighty-five and ninety-five degrees Celsius to separate the water from the remaining alcohol. The first distillation will yield a spirit of up to twenty-five per cent alcohol,' explains Jack. 'The second distillation involves the very same process but produces a spirit which has an alcohol content of approximately fifty-five per cent while the third or 'triple distillation' produces a spirit with eighty-two per cent alcohol content.'

For maturation, water is added to reduce the alcohol content to around sixty-seven per cent, then poured into wooden barrels or casks where it will remain for a minimum period of three years in order to officially qualify as Irish whiskey.

'At Teelings, we get our unique flavours by using a variety of different types of casks which have previously been used to store sherry, port, bourbon and rum,' he explains.

Jack Teeling grew up in Clontarf. No stranger to business or the world of whiskey-making, his father, John Teeling, a lecturer in commerce in University College Dublin (UCD), was founder of the well-known Cooley Distillery in County Louth. Jack studied commerce in UCD and completed a Master's degree in finance in the Smurfit Business School. His first job was in private banking in Dublin, before heading to Australia where he also worked for a time in financial services, until his return in 2001.

'When I got back I got a job in Cooley Distillery, where I started out really as a general dogsbody. But it was great because I actually got to make something for a change instead of just moving numbers around on a screen. I was immediately hooked,' says Jack.

He later returned to university where he completed a two-year part-time MSc in International Business run by Trinity College Dublin in partnership with Enterprise Ireland. The course was aimed at helping indigenous companies prepare for exporting – something that would later turn out to be invaluable. Over time, Jack worked his way up in Cooley to become sales and marketing manager and later, in 2010, managing director, two years before it was bought by US firm Beam Inc.

'I noticed the growing trend for craft beer and spirits as well as urban-based breweries and distilleries,' explains Jack. 'I decided then that I wanted to start my own Irish whiskey company – one that would have the look and feel of a premium craft spirit rather than a traditional Irish whiskey. More importantly, I wanted to bring whiskey distilling back to Dublin city.'

The search for a site was challenging, but when he came across the current premises in Newmarket, even though it needed considerable investment, he knew it was perfect. However, not being able to sell his produce for three years posed a challenge in terms of cash flow for the new entrepreneur.

'I sold my shares in Cooley and invested in whiskey stock

to start off,' explains Jack. 'The following year, when this had increased in value, I was able to release enough equity to fund the growth of the business without the need for external investors.'

That year his brother, Stephen, joined the business and is now the sales and marketing director as well as a co-owner.

'The Irish whiskey market is dominated by multinational players,' explains Jack. 'For us to try to compete directly against these large brands would be impossible. Instead, we differentiate ourselves by creating unique tastes and flavours. But building the new distillery is only the start of the journey,' says an upbeat Jack. 'This industry is definitely a marathon and not a sprint.'

Jack's achievement was recognised when he was awarded best emerging business at the 2017 Ernst & Young Entrepreneur of the Year Awards.

It is no small task to start a new business, let alone a distillery, where competition is intense and regulations mean you cannot take your product to the market for at least three years. However, with forecasts for Irish whiskey sales set to continue growing by high double digit figures, Teeling Whiskey looks set to have a long and successful future. Like the whiskey they make, Jack and Stephen Teeling seem to have all the ingredients necessary to make that happen.

Jack's Advice for Other Businesses

The power of a brand

It's important to focus on getting your product right but don't neglect to build a strong and recognisable brand. A good product will get you into the game but it takes a strong brand to help you succeed in the longer term.

Know your customer

Know your customer, have insights into what they are looking for and what makes them tick. This will help you shape your product, your positioning, your price and above all – your value proposition.

Action is more valuable than a business plan

Action is what really counts, particularly in the early days. It's helpful to have a good business plan but spending months trying to perfect a set of spreadsheets can be a waste of time. Things develop and evolve once you start. Get going and act quickly to seize the opportunity before someone else does.

CHAPTER 49

QUEEN OF THE TRAVEL INDUSTRY

– The Story of Tour America

TOURAMERICA.ie

www.touramerica.ie

Mary McKenna is founder and CEO of Tour America. Set up in 1995, the business has become Ireland's leading holiday specialist to the USA, Canada and Mexico, as well as offering worldwide cruises. Headquartered in Middle Abbey Street, Dublin, and with offices in Parnell Place in Cork and Orlando, Florida, the company employs fifty staff and has an annual turnover of more than €21 million.

Like most entrepreneurs, Mary's story has not been plain sailing. She has experienced challenges and setbacks but has always managed to turn challenges into opportunities and setbacks into chances to change direction.

Most entrepreneurs will tell you that, when young, they had a role model who inspired them. For Mary, that role model was her dad.

'My father, Frank McKenna, and his brother, Andy, were both in the travel business. My father was the first person to organise trips for soccer fans to places like Manchester and Liverpool in the UK.'

From the age of five, Mary helped her dad out by putting his company's stickers on travel brochures. As she got older, her school holidays were also spent in the business.

'My father instilled in me a sense of self-belief, which has proved central to my success in business,' says Mary.

One of Mary's first jobs was as duty manager with the airline Club Air, which was just starting up at the time. She was responsible for all ground operations and if a plane failed to turn up, then it was her job to hire a replacement.

'It was a lot of responsibility at a young age but the experience taught me how to make tough decisions. And it also further cemented my passion for the travel sector,' she says.

Mary later moved to Club Travel but, following her father's death, decided to join her Uncle Andy's company, Atlas Travel, which specialised in American holidays. When the company was sold in 1995, Mary used the knowledge and contacts she had built up to strike out on her own and set up Tour America.

'I had no money, so I started the business in my sitting room,' she says.

Her former boss from Club Travel had enough faith in her to invest in the business, which enabled her to move to a small office in Dublin city centre and hire her first three staff. The competition didn't take her seriously at first but, by working seven days a week, her efforts soon began to pay off. And while many of her friends advised her not to expect to make a profit until around year three, Mary had no intention of waiting that long. In her first year in business she turned over €3 million in revenue and made a profit of €69,000.

At night, she studied accountancy and business in University College Dublin. Knowing that her most important investment would be in herself, she read every book she could on everything from business and economics to emotional intelligence.

'I have always trusted my intuition, but I knew it was important to learn about the structure and strategies involved in building a successful business,' Mary explains.

Her participation in the Leadership 4 Growth programme,

run by the International Institute for Management Development and supported by Enterprise Ireland, helped her understand the difference between leadership and management. As a result of what she had learned, Mary decided to select five key objectives and focus the entire company on achieving these first.

'It had a profound effect on the business and became a strategy I have repeated many times since,' she insists.

Mary has experienced many challenges in her business career. 9/11 was one such challenge. What happened that day was not only a tragedy for people and businesses across America, but was also a commercial tragedy for businesses in the wider travel sector.

'For up to four weeks after the attacks, business literally fell off a cliff,' she says. 'We really thought the company was gone.'

At the time, she was forced to let go of ten of her thirty-five staff.

'It was the hardest thing I ever had to do. I personally had to dig very deep to let good people go. It was then that I really understood how hard being an entrepreneur can be,' she says.

But with fewer people travelling by plane, Mary spotted an opportunity to set up a business specialising in cruise holidays and immediately rehired the ten people she had laid off.

'Since then, our sister brand, Cruise Holidays, has become the top Irish seller of cruises.'

Similarly, the ash cloud catastrophe in 2010 struck the airline business badly.

'Again, no one travelled; people stopped making bookings altogether,' Mary explains. 'To make matters worse, we had customers who were stranded in the US and it cost us more than a half a million euro to look after them all.'

In January 2012, when the Costa Concordia cruise liner sank, the company also lost more than €1 million in potential sales revenue.

'But you have to work through these challenges and find new angles and new opportunities. Such as during the recent downturn in the economy, when people had less disposable income. We had to find ways to add value for the customer and so, in order to remain competitive, we began to contract directly with hotels to create exclusive offers for customers,' explains Mary. 'We had to become more innovative and more focused on the customer experience.'

Similarly, when digital and social media began to take off, Mary worked hard to ensure that her company became leaders in using this technology to communicate with current and potential customers. With repeat customers making up forty-two per cent of her turnover, Mary clearly understands the maxim that 'it is cheaper and easier to keep a customer than it is to find a new one'.

In 2016, and having had a business partner for over twenty years, Mary decided to go it alone and bought out her partner. As the 100 per cent shareholder of the business, she is more keen than ever to drive the business forward.

'About twenty per cent of our business is now coming from online and so, in line with this, we recently launched a UK website to target business there also. We might even open an office in Australia,' she says.

Mary is quick to recognise her staff and how crucial they are to her success. Committed to supporting their continuous training and development, she regularly invites guest speakers to make presentations to them on relevant topics. Mary and her team have won many awards, most noticeably the Deloitte Best

Managed Company, which they have won for the last eight years.

Challenges of a more personal nature were also visited on Mary. In 2004 she was knocked down by a jeep and, for a period, her injuries seemed life-threatening.

'The experience caused me to re-evaluate my entire life,' explains Mary. 'I don't sweat the small stuff any more, and I now cycle to work every day. I've even run marathons for charity since. It's important to give back to life when life gives to you.'

Her attitude to what life has thrown at her is testimony to her strong character and her sense of determination.

Mary is committed to giving back in business too and today mentors six female entrepreneurs through 'Going for Growth', a women's enterprise support programme.

Having learned the value of hard work at an early age, Mary McKenna possesses a strong work ethic and exudes a passion for life and for business. She is constantly on the lookout for opportunities, even those that come camouflaged as challenges. She has demonstrated a commitment to life-long learning and is equally committed to the training and development of her staff. She has learned the importance of focus and being able to prioritise key objectives in order to drive lasting success. Just like her father, Mary has now also become a great role model for others to follow.

Mary's Advice for Other Businesses

Push beyond your comfort zone

Everything you want in life that you do not already have lies on the other side of fear and comfort. To grow and develop means pushing yourself outside your comfort zone. We all experience fear doing new things, but don't allow this to hold you back. Use it to motivate yourself.

Learn from the past – but don't live there

The past can't hold you back unless you choose to live there. We all experience setbacks, but we have to learn from them and move forward. Don't allow yourself get stuck in ways of thinking that no longer serve you.

Set goals and find an experienced mentor

Always be learning. One of the best ways to motivate yourself is to write down your goals and share them with others. That way, you are more likely to achieve them. Find an experienced mentor, too, who can help guide you on your journey.

CHAPTER 50

FROM POTATO FARMER TO THE KING OF CRISPS

– The Story of Tayto and Tayto Park

www.taytopark.ie

People who leave Ireland to live abroad often remark that one of the things they miss most about home, apart from friends and family, is a packet of Tayto crisps.

The man who set up Largo Foods, the company that owns Tayto and built it into what it is today, is Raymond Coyle. His is an interesting story of the power of ambition matched with a can-do attitude.

Raymond comes originally from Ashbourne, County Meath. In fact he grew up just 200 metres from where his famous Tayto Park is now located. His family were farmers who reared cattle and grew barley. For a time, too, they ran the local pub.

In his early twenties Raymond set up his own small farming enterprise: twelve acres of potatoes and four acres of vegetables. From here he sold his produce in the Dublin fruit and veg market. By the 1970s, and still only in his mid-twenties, he was making over £1 million a year. Encouraged by his early success, he bought 800 acres of land and began to grow potatoes on an even larger scale. By 1980 he was supplying potatoes to the company that was then making the Tayto brand of crisps.

'I never could have imagined back then that one day I would actually end up owning the brand,' he says modestly.

In 1981, however, things went terribly wrong for Raymond. Along with many other farmers, he lost his contract to supply Tayto. As a result, he lost almost everything he had worked so hard to build.

'I actually owed the bank £1.2 million and had absolutely no way of paying it. The market was so bad at the time that I couldn't even sell the farm to pay it off,' admits Raymond.

In what can only be described as a stroke of genius, Raymond decided instead to raffle his farm. He had been travelling back from the south of the country and had spotted a boat on a village green which was being raffled to raise money for the community. A light bulb went on in Raymond's head.

'Why not raffle the farm?' he thought. And that's exactly what he did.

He proceeded to sell 4,000 tickets at £300 each – on the basis that the winner would get the entire farm. It was so novel and drew so much publicity at the time that he quickly succeeded in raising the £1.2 million he needed to pay off his debts.

Researching the market to see what he might do next, Raymond realised that Tayto had ninety per cent of the Irish crisp market at the time and he felt that there had to be an opening for a new entrant into the Irish snack-food market. So in 1983 he set up Largo Foods and began manufacturing his own brand of crisps. A year later he purchased the Perry brand and then, in 1996, acquired the Sam Spudz brand, having bought out Donegal-based Irish Snack Foods. That same year, in a move to enter the UK market, he came up with the now-infamous Hunky Dory's brand, a move that cemented his position as a significant player in the sector.

In 2005 Tayto, then owned by C&C, closed its own crisp factory and outsourced production to Largo Foods. The following year, in a brave and courageous move, Raymond Coyle bought the Tayto and King brands in a deal valued at over €68 million. The wheel had now come full circle.

In 2008, by which time he was employing over 600 staff between his Irish and European operations, he entered a partnership deal with German snack food company, Intersnack Group, to whom he would eventually sell his shares in Largo Foods in 2016. The move left him free to concentrate on his newest project, Tayto Park – a unique mix of theme park, recreational activity centre, zoo and educational facility.

Opened in 2010, the park is primarily aimed at those aged between three and eighteen. In its first year of business the park attracted 240,000 visitors, with that number rising to 800,000 by 2017. The park is packed with all types of fun attractions, from the 20-metre high tubular slide known as the Tayto Twister, to large climbing walls and the high ropes of the park's famous Sky Walk, the 212-metre zip line and the twisting Vortex Tunnel, as well as the replica cave bears of the Ice Age Ice Valley.

Over 100 species of birds and animals can be found throughout the park, among them a herd of powerful American bison with their burly shoulder humps and distinctively large heads. There are tigers and other wild cats, who stroll calmly through their secure compounds. The incredible speed and power of these animals is evident when one of the staff arrives to feed them. Putting a piece of meat on a long metal rod, he slowly pokes it through the wire mesh fence. In an instant, and as if from nowhere, a large female tiger pounces forward and snatches the meat, then retreats to enjoy her spoils.

There are also pens of smaller farm animals, ranging from pygmy goats to highland cattle. And like something from high up in the Rocky Mountains, the timber lodge, with its shops, restaurant and imposing structure, is the centrepiece of the park.

It's easy to see why teachers and parents bring their children here. What better way to learn about nature and wildlife than to experience it first-hand?

So where did the idea for the park come from?

'I came across a number of similar types of parks in the US, such as Hershey Park in Pennsylvania, built by Milton Hershey, owner of the world's first chocolate factory. I decided I wanted to build a similar theme park based around the Tayto brand. By locating it beside our factory, visitors could also visit the factory and see how Tayto crisps were made,' explains Raymond. 'Our professional market research studies concluded that it was high risk, but I felt it would work. It really was a case of build it and they will come,' he adds.

While it was never going to be an easy project to execute, things were made even worse when, well into the €16 million build, the bank withdrew their support. Raymond, however, was not for stopping. More determined than ever to finish the project, he decided to sell a factory he had built fourteen years earlier in the Czech Republic. The money from the sale allowed him to finish the work and in early 2011 the park opened.

'When 25,000 visitors arrived during the first Easter period, I knew it was going to work,' explains Raymond.

The newest addition to the park was opened in the summer of 2017, a €5.5 million Viking Village, complete with five replica Viking ships. More recently, an application for planning was lodged that will see a 250-room family hotel built on the grounds of the park. Seven floors high and projected to cost almost €50 million, the hotel will be capable of accommodating up to 1,000 guests. When complete, it will create a further 300 jobs, to add to the 550 jobs that the park already generates during the summer season.

'Our plan is to reach 1.2 million visitors per year by 2021 and we are well on our way to achieving that,' says Raymond.

He is pleased too that his wife, Roz, works in the business and his son, Charles, has become the park's general manager.

Raymond Coyle is a remarkable man. He has shown incredible ambition and extraordinary drive throughout his life. When, at an early age, he lost almost everything, he found a way to get out of debt and start again. When he spotted an opportunity to enter the crisp business, he showed little fear in taking on larger competitors. Similarly, he was unafraid of the challenges of acquiring other firms in order to grow and scale his own business, even buying the Tayto company that he had once supplied as a potato farmer. But perhaps the biggest risk he took and the greatest challenge he has faced during his distinguished career was to build Tayto Park.

Raymond Coyle has created a great legacy through the businesses he has built and the jobs he has created. But perhaps his most abiding legacy will be the example he sets – an example that inspires the rest of us to see opportunities and to go after them with determination, self-belief and imagination.

Raymond's Advice for Other Businesses

Consider plans carefully, but go for it

It's important to consider plans carefully and weigh up all the risks involved in a project. However, sometimes you have to trust your own judgement, and simply go for it.

Have finance fully in place

Projects can run into difficulty, not because they are not great projects but because they run out of money before they are completed or before they can become profitable. Therefore, where possible, have sufficient finance in place to avoid running out of cash.

Don't expect miracles – be patient

Projects and businesses often take time to develop and become successful. While it's important to push ahead, sometimes you also have to learn to pace yourself and to be patient.

PART III

CHAPTER 51

NOW, OVER TO YOU

If you don't go after what you want, you'll never have it. If you don't ask, the answer is always no. If you don't step forward, you'll always be in the same place.

Nora Robert, American author

I hope that you have enjoyed reading these stories. More than that, I hope you have connected with them at a deep level and that they have inspired you to take action.

FOR THOSE ALREADY IN BUSINESS

Which of the many lessons shared by these successful entrepreneurs most resonated with you? And which can you now begin to implement, to help take your business to the next level?

Do you have a **clear and articulate vision** of what you want to achieve in your business, as was the case with Fred Karlsson of DoneDeal or David Walsh of Netwatch? Have you articulated this to your team so they too are clear about what is expected of them in helping deliver your vision for the company?

What can you learn from Paddy Matthews' story, where he used staff leadership boards and incentives to align his drivers' behaviour with the fuel efficiency agenda his company wanted to implement? Are there ways in which you can link your staff's behaviour with the outcomes you want?

Given the importance of hiring the right talent with the right skills and expertise, have you invested time and resources in **finding or attracting the very best talent** you possibly can, such as in the case of 3D4Medical, Brite:Bill and Blueface, to help grow your business?

Once recruited, are you now making the effort to **inspire your staff** with your vision, passion and energy? Do you **treat them with respect and thoughtfulness**, the way you would like them to treat your customers, as Simon Pratt in Avoca does? Do you **invest time and resources in training** them, as Mary McKenna in Tour America does, so they can grow and develop further? Are you investing in **developing a positive culture** in the workplace, as in the case of Dan and Linda Kiely of Voxpro, where staff feel supported, engaged and empowered? In that way they will enjoy coming to work, will perform better and, as a result, so will your overall business.

Are you investing in **building your own management and leadership capability**, as in the case of Jim Barry of the Barry Group or Colm Lyon of Realex Payments and Fire? Are you making room in your business to take **customer service** out from its own department and make it an integral part of your company's overall agenda, as Deirdre McGlone from Harvey's Point and Bill Kelly of Kelly's Resort have done, remembering too that your success will not be measured by a single order from a customer but from the lifetime value that customer generates?

Have you started to 'hug' your customer, as Louis Copeland and his staff do, to ensure that your customers not only stay with you but become ambassadors for your business?

Can you learn from how others have turned their **company's brand** into a household name, such as in the case of Tayto, Glenilen Farm, Flahavan's or Clonakilty Black Pudding? Do you need to reassess the impact of your existing brand and consider breathing new life and vibrancy into this, as John Tuohy and Dave Field did in the case of Nightline? And can you position or reposition your brand's reputation around quality, as in the case of Stuart Steele from Silver Hill Farm, thereby achieving higher margins in return?

Given, too, that so many business leaders stress the need for a strong focus on **innovation and new product development** as a way of remaining relevant, are you innovating enough in your business to ensure you continue to meet the changing needs of your customers? If you don't, your competitors will.

What about technology? What can you learn from Edmond Harty's experience of developing cutting-edge technology solutions for the dairy industry globally, or from Eamon Moore, who now helps his clients move their information securely to the Cloud?

How about how Simon Pratt from Avoca and Rachel Doyle from Arboretum completely pivoted their businesses by introducing food to create that Saturday feeling every day of the week? How can you **pivot your business** in a similar way? What can you introduce, change or do differently to grow your business?

Are there opportunities to **harness the power of technology** to streamline services for your customers such as those developed by Realex Payments, Fire, Brite:Bill or Oneview Healthcare?

Can you begin to **think globally** if you are not already doing so? And how can companies such as Dairymaster, Horseware, No-H2O and Kent Stainless encourage and inspire you to compete in new markets that you have, until now, shied away from?

Or, if faced with the need to totally **reinvent your**

business, can you learn from what David Bobbet did when he courageously repositioned H&K International from only supplying new restaurants to offering a complete supply chain model, thereby cementing his position and reputation as a one-stop-shop solution provider to fast food restaurant chains around the world?

In times of **adversity and challenge**, can you draw on the example and inspiration of people like Michael Dawson of The Gift Voucher Shop and One4all, and Henry and Shirley O'Kelly, when they had to dig deep and reinvent their business model in order to keep their company alive?

You will also have heard advice from these successful entrepreneurs about the **importance of networking** and surrounding yourself with other entrepreneurs from whom you can learn and with whom you can collaborate. What new networks can you join that could help you extend your reach while building additional support for yourself and your company?

Are there **experienced board members, non-executive directors or advisors** you could look to bring on board who have already travelled the road you are now on and whose expertise, sector know-how or industry contacts could help fast-track your success?

Have you tried or are you open to seeking the assistance of a proven **business coach or mentor**, who could help you focus on key steps and strategies to help your business grow?

You may find you get just one simple idea from this book that makes the reading of it worthwhile. I encourage you to pick at least one, if not a few ideas and commit to action by incorporating these into your business in the near future. I hope they bring you closer to the success you desire.

THINKING OF STARTING YOUR OWN BUSINESS?

Success often comes from risking more than others think is safe and dreaming more than others think is practical.

Howard Schultz, CEO Starbucks

If you are thinking of setting up your own business or working for yourself, the task ahead may seem very daunting. But on reflection, isn't every new activity difficult at first, until we have mastered it?

Perhaps you might be thinking that your business idea is on a much smaller scale than many of those you have read about in this book. Businesses come in all sizes and what matters most is that your business provides you with the level of success you desire, regardless of the expectations of others.

The truth is that most entrepreneurs wrestle with the same fears and apprehensions: Will this work? Am I good enough? What will I do if it doesn't work out?

The best piece of advice I got when starting my first business was from an entrepreneur who at the time employed more than 10,000 people around the world. When I told him how much in awe I was of his achievements and the size of his business compared to ours, his response was simple yet profound. '**Nobody ever starts a big business**.' Even his business had once started out with only a handful of employees.

The most any of us can hope to do is prepare ourselves as best we can for our new venture. Think about why you want to run your own business. **What's your motivation and what do you hope to achieve**? Consider, too, the sacrifices you are willing to make to get there.

In searching for an idea for your new business, start by asking yourself **what you are passionate about**. This often includes activities that you enjoy, that you naturally excel at, that others say you are good at and that you would do even if you were not getting paid. These could include anything from cooking, artwork, writing code and developing apps, to the welfare of animals, sports, teaching or taking care of others.

It's important to remember that almost all businesses are focused on **being of service to others** and improving the lives of those around us in one way or another. **What skills or experience do you have** that could benefit others? How can you build your business around meeting the needs of others profitably?

The greatest success in business is if you can identify something you are passionate about, that fulfils you and that positively impacts the lives of others, and then find a way to get paid for doing it.

Next, can you **visualise** what it might look like to run your own business? What would you be doing? How would you be feeling? This vision will help ground your dream and ambition and make it feel more achievable. Spending time defining and shaping your vision will also help when it comes to articulating this to others, whether enrolling staff, customers or potential investors.

Invest time to **research your idea**, the potential market for your product or service, the size and characteristics of that market and how best to access your target customers. Directly? Through wholesalers? Distributors? Online? **How much money will you need** to get started and can you access additional sources if necessary from friends, family, banks or investors?

Do you need staff? Permits to make or sell? Will you need help in coming up with a **brand**, company name and logo? Do you have access to affordable **premises**? Can you bootstrap your business until such time as you are generating sufficient profits to buy or rent a more suitable facility?

It is also a good idea to **write your plans down** and attach **financial projections** to them, including potential sale revenues, costs and cash-flow shortfalls. This not only allows you to look for external investment, but gives you clear goals and targets on which to focus and against which to measure your ongoing performance.

Irrespective of all the preparation you undertake, the secret to success is often down to having the courage to simply begin. Zig Ziglar puts it very succinctly when he says, 'You don't have to be great to start but you do have to start if you want to be great.'

Becoming an entrepreneur is and always will be a giant leap of faith. In the final analysis, that decision – to step away from the security of paid employment, to invest yourself and your finances in a dream – cannot be fully rationalised. When you have done all the research you can, when you have examined the market and completed your projections and forecasts, in the end what pushes you to take the final step isn't a rational decision, it is courage.

Courage is important for all of us, but particularly for entrepreneurs. But if you have a desire to be more, have more and achieve more, then you have to be willing to do more and risk more. A quote often attributed to Christopher Columbus puts it well too: 'You can never cross the ocean until you have the courage to lose sight of the shore.'

Looking back to the earlier chapter in this book on the top ten traits of successful entrepreneurs, ask yourself how can you develop the right skill set and mindset for your entrepreneurial journey. Perhaps start by plugging out your TV, pack away the pile of novels you were intending to read and start, instead, to **read books on business** and about those who are further along the journey on which you are now embarking. **Success really does leave clues**. So **study the lives of these successful business leaders** and the actions they have taken to achieve their success.

Begin by **building or extending your network of contacts**. Choose to surround yourself with those who will support you personally and professionally. Avoid naysayers – those who only see problems and never opportunities. These will drain both your energy and your optimism, if you allow them to.

Your critics may come from within your own business, family or community. With the recent explosion in social media in particular, you may even find yourself being challenged by nameless, faceless keyboard critics, whose comments may vary from the constructive to the plain nasty. Take on board the comments that are helpful and discard, without hesitation, those that are not.

On the day I launched my campaign to become president of Ireland, my campaign director, Cathal Lee, arrived to my office with a gift – a framed excerpt from a speech called 'Citizenship in a Republic' given by former President of the United States Theodore Roosevelt at the Sorbonne in Paris, France, on 23 April 1910. This passage is commonly known as 'The Man in the Arena'. During times when I was the subject of such critics, I drew great strength and confidence from it. I hope you will too.

The Man in the Arena

It is not the critic who counts; not the man who points out how the strong man stumbles, or where the doer of deeds could have done them

> *better. The credit belongs to the man who is actually in the arena, whose face is marred by dust and sweat and blood; who strives valiantly; who errs, who comes short again and again, because there is no effort without error and shortcoming; but who does actually strive to do the deeds; who knows great enthusiasms, the great devotions; who spends himself in a worthy cause; who at the best knows in the end the triumph of high achievement, and who at the worst, if he fails, at least fails while daring greatly, so that his place shall never be with those cold and timid souls who neither know victory nor defeat.*

Remember, too, the **second law of thermodynamics** – that when you put something cold beside something hot, the cold object will extract the heat or energy from the hotter object. This is what critics and pessimists do.

Kaleel Jamison, the first American female management consultant, wrote about this in her small but powerful book, *The Nibble Theory and The Kernel of Power*. In it she describes people as circles, and explores the idea that circles naturally come together with circles of their own size – a sense of needing to belong. But when one circle decides it wants to grow, develop or expand, the other circles instantly begin to nibble at it, asking 'Who do you think you are?' 'Why do you think you are better than us?' 'Are we not good enough for you any more?' 'What makes you think you're so special?' and on and on. At which point, the ambitious circle faces a tough decision, a crossroads of sorts. It must choose to either shrink back down in size to fit in and be accepted by the group, thereby sacrificing its ability to reach its own true potential, or it can decide to grow, thereby leaving these smaller circles behind while it goes in search of larger circles.

Choose, therefore, to **surround yourself with those who**

will encourage you to raise your game, rather than those whose agenda is to see you play small.

Sadly, many of us can also collude in nibbling ourselves through our own negative self-talk. Begin to **believe more in yourself, your intuition and your judgement**. Practise changing your thinking and your language. Eliminate 'can't' from your vocabulary, as well as all forms of criticism, such as complaining about your circumstances or creating excuses as to why things are not the way you want them to be. Instead, resolve to make them so.

Each of us has our own unique contribution to make. Starting and running a business is not for everyone. But if it is something to which you are drawn, do not allow fear or self-doubt to hold you back. None of us is able to see the full stretch of road in front of us when starting out on a journey. But as we go from one bend to the next, the route makes itself visible and bit by bit we make our way to our final destination.

Launching a new business is similar.

Be willing to **embrace change and uncertainty** along the way. Recognise that **failure and setbacks are a natural part of your entrepreneurial journey**. Recognise too that there are few shortcuts to success, and that achievement usually only comes after much **effort, hard work and perseverance**.

And do not be afraid to **ask for help**. Most people, especially experienced business owners and entrepreneurs, will be only too willing to offer advice or support, knowing that they too were once where you are now. Often we are afraid to ask for help because we feel it makes us appear either weak, forward or pushy. Many of us are also afraid of rejection and so decide it is better not to ask than have to deal with the embarrassment of our request being turned down. But the possibility of getting what you need should far outweigh your fear of rejection. The more you practise asking – starting first with less important items – the more proficient and confident you become. The more confident you are, the more likely you are to get a positive response.

Above all else, **enjoy the journey**. After all, you are following your dreams. Many people never do. In later life you do not want to look back and have regrets, or wish you had been braver.

Well-known author Wayne Dyer put it so succinctly in *10 Secrets for Success and Inner Peace*, when he tells us: 'don't die with your music still in you'.

My wish for you is that you do not die with your music still in you but that you get to follow your dreams wherever they take you. And, when you finally get there, as with many of the successful entrepreneurs featured in this book, I hope you will do well for yourself and do good for others.

Now, it's over to you.

SEND ME YOUR STORY

I hope that you enjoyed reading these stories as much as I enjoyed writing them.

I would love to hear your reactions to these stories: which stories most connected with you, for example, or if they have helped inspire you to action in any way.

I invite you to send me in the story of your own business or another business you would like to see published in future editions of this book series.

To find out more about how to submit a story, please visit our website: www.seangallagher.com/secretstosuccess

I am sure that future readers will benefit from your story, just as I hope you benefited from those in this book.